ELEMENTS OF
NEWSPAPER DESIGN

ELEMENTS OF NEWSPAPER DESIGN

STEVEN E. AMES

With a Foreword by
Edmund C. Arnold

PRAEGER

New York
Westport, Connecticut
London

Copyright Acknowledgments

The author and publisher are grateful to the following for allowing the use of excerpts from:

"Newspapers Are Benefitting from the Power of PCs." Report from the American Newspaper Publishers Association Technical Exposition, Las Vegas, Nev., 1987. *presstime* 9, 7 (July 1987): 31. Reprinted by permission from *presstime*®, the journal of the American Newspaper Publishers Association.

"Some Editors Feel 'Abused' by Pagination." Report from the American Newspaper Publishers Association Technical Exposition, Las Vegas, Nev., 1987. *presstime* 9, 7 (July 1987): 32. Reprinted by permission from *presstime*®, the journal of the American Newspaper Publishers Association.

Tobin, Nancy. "Understanding Changes in the Growth and Shape of Newspaper Art Departments." Results of a survey prepared for the Society of Newspaper Design, October 1985. Reprinted with permission of the Society of Newspaper Design.

Library of Congress Cataloging-in-Publication Data

Ames, Steven E.
    Elements of newspaper design / Steven E. Ames ; with a foreword by
  Edmund C. Arnold.
      p.   cm.
    Bibliography: p.
    Includes index.
    ISBN 0–275–92330–4
    ISBN 0–275–92464–5 (pbk.)
    1. Newspaper layout and typography.   I. Title.
  Z253.5.A48   1989
  686.2'52—dc19   88–31892

Library of Congress Catalog Card Number: 88–31892
ISBN: 0–275–92330–4
     0–275–92464–5 (pbk.)

First published in 1989

Praeger Publishers, One Madison Avenue, New York, NY 10010
A division of Greenwood Press, Inc.

Printed in the United States of America

The paper used in this book complies with the
Permanent Paper Standard issued by the National
Information Standards Organization (Z39.48–1984).

P

Contents

Foreword

To lay areas of printers' ink on a sheet of newsprint is just as much a work of art as to arrange areas of pigment on a piece of canvas and call it an oil painting. Newspaper people are reluctant to call themselves "artists," thinking it would be pretentious. But at least in newspaper design, they *are* artists; and they can—and ought to—learn from other graphic artists.

While you cannot paint a Mona Lisa by numbers, there are basic principles that must be mastered by a da Vinci, a Rembrandt or a Rockwell. Blue and yellow make green; cool colors recede; perspective is based on mathematics. These basics every painter must know. So with newspaper design. While the final results are essentially a matter of innate skill—talent—there are basic principles that must be mastered. These principles are based on immutable standards. The Latin alphabet, for instance, sets in stone that the reader must proceed from left to right and top to bottom. This progression is not going to change come hell, high water or new typographic vagaries.

The unique complex of reading eye and translating cortex will never change. A human can never learn to digest sawdust; the alimentary canal is not subject to fads and fashion. The human eye cannot learn to read sans serif type easily and efficiently; the neuro-optical system will not be changed by the whim of designers.

This book lays down a foundation of principles that every newspaper person should have. The editor who lays out pages certainly must be steeped in these principles to do the design job. But the managing editor, the publisher and everyone concerned with the overall quality of the paper must know enough of the principles to be able to evaluate the work of other staffers.

Artists face another requirement: They must master the mechanics of their medium. They have to know how to apply pigment with brush, palette knife or wiping rag. They must know how to apply acid to etch a mezzotint plate. They must know how to strike a chisel so it will remove unwanted marble but leave the sculpture unmarred.

Newspaper designers must know the mechanics of transforming their creations from their minds to dummies to video tubes to, finally, the images that the reader holds in his or her hand. The sheer physical processes of setting type, taking photographs, making plates and contacting them with paper all affect the look of a newspaper as well as the techniques for achieving that look. Form not only follows function; form follows the tool.

Again, this book handles the technical aspect of the newspaper designer's responsibilities. It makes interesting what some people—erroneously, let's emphasize—consider a humdrum part of the job.

A creative person must feed the computer between his or her ears with all the hard, tangible data available. That leaves the mind free, then, to soar to new creative heights. Herein lie some vital data that will allow mental images to be reproduced exactly onto sheets of newsprint.

These principles are discovered, defined and articulated in this book. Excellent guidelines for building on the elements of newspaper design are set forth.

> Edmund C. Arnold
> Distinguished Professor of Journalism (emeritus)
> Virginia Commonwealth University

Preface and Acknowledgments

The elements of design—a page's graphic building blocks—initially attract readers to a newspaper, but news content is the necessary complement for a successful product.

The Total Page Concept (TPC) lifts the graphic journalist to a greater understanding of newspaper design. For the TPC page to serve the reader, all of its elements must mesh: Typography, photography and illustrative art are as important to the page as are thorough writing and careful editing.

It is a difficult task to bring meaning to every standard broadsheet or tabloid newspaper page. However, through the recognition of TPC principles, simple design steps can be applied to give a more satisfying result. Sensing the balance in a page, realizing the focus of stories, seeing how white space directs the eye: These serve to make reading a rewarding experience.

If there was ever a time when the designer's tools and language were mysterious to the person beginning to read this book, they should quickly cease to be so. Those wishing to become graphic journalists will discover how it is done by reading about people who work in design on a regular basis. Design terminology is explained throughout the book.

Elements of Newspaper Design has 16 chapters which are divided into six parts:

I   Basics of the Total Page Concept
II   Principles of Design
III Building Blocks of Typography
IV Design Creativity
V   Finishing Touches
VI Putting It All Together

All too frequently, graphic designers become so involved in the design process that they place an overemphasis on the importance of graphics; text content becomes a distant second consideration—an attitude that fails to serve the newspaper readers' needs. Our ordering of the chapters within the six parts of this book is intended to show how graphics and text must complement one another on a TPC page.

Just as designing and writing for a newspaper is a team effort, so has been the writing of this book. *Elements of Newspaper Design* is now a reality because of the valued assistance of many.

Special appreciation must be extended to these people for their various perspectives on the contribution of graphic journalism to newspapers: John Bodette, St. Cloud (Minn.) *Times;* Ken Bruns, Don Clement, Michael Hall, Patrick Lynch, Matt Moody, Terry Schwadron, Brian Steffens, and Tom Trapnell, Los Angeles *Times;* Rob Covey, *U.S. News & World Report;* George Delmerico, Santa Barbara (Calif.) *Independent;* Joseph Dill, Fargo, N. D. *Forum;* John Ferguson, Thousand Oaks, Calif. *News Chronicle;* Michael Gordon, Los Angeles *Herald Examiner;* Tom Hardin, *Courier-Journal* & Louisville (Ky.) *Times;* Craig Harrington, Burney, Calif. *InterMountain News;* Ernest E. Hines, Walnut Creek, Calif. *Contra Costa Times;* Bill Hodge, Long Beach, Calif. *Press-Telegram;* Nigel Holmes, *Time* magazine; Harvey C. Jacobs, Indianapolis *News;* William W. Lemmer, United Press International; Robert Lockwood, News-Graphics; Sam Matthews, Tracy (Calif.) *Press;* Tom Maurer, Bakersfield *Californian;* Merrill Oliver, Providence, R.I. *Journal;* Ron Patel, Philadelphia *Inquirer;* Darell Phillips, Manteca (Calif.) *Bulletin;* Ron Poppenhagen, Green Bay (Wis.) *News Chronicle;* Peter Romano, American Newspaper Publishers Association; Reid Sams, Manteca (Calif.) *Bulletin;* Don Sevrens, San Diego *Union;* Louis Silverstein, New York *Times;* Randy Stano, Miami *Herald;* Pegie Stark, University of Florida, Gainesville; Lisa Vanco, free-lance designer/copywriter, Westlake Village, Calif.; Wayne Welch, Tulare, Calif. *Advance-Register;* Robert L. Wilson, Memphis, Tenn. *Commercial Appeal* and William L. Winter, American Press Institute.

These quote sources and several others provided many excellent page examples. Their interest in this book is greatly appreciated, as is the permission of these newspaper representatives for use of their design style guides: Richard C. D'Agostino and Michael Dresser, the *Baltimore Sun Typographic Design Stylebook;* William Dunn for Mark A. Williams, editor, *Design Guide: Design and Layout Rules for the Orlando Sentinel;* Alan Jacobson, the *Virginian-Pilot and Ledger-Star Design Stylebook;* and Ron Patel, the *Philadelphia Inquirer Typographical Manual.*

Edmund C. Arnold graciously agreed to write the foreword for this book; J (John) Archer designed the illustrative examples; Keith Sloane provided editorial assistance; Larry Holden and Associates of Westlake Village, Calif. skillfully turned my collection of full-size newspaper pages into readable miniatures and several staffers of the Long Beach, Calif. *Press-Telegram* and the Pasadena, Calif. *Star-News* demonstrated parts of the computer pagination process, which were photographed by Troy Maben, a photographer at the Idaho *Statesman* in Boise.

Thanks are also due to Nanette Bisher, Santa Ana, Calif. *Orange County Register;* Ray Chattman, Society of Newspaper Design; J. Nicholas DeBonis, Texas A&M University, College Station, Texas; Frank Thompson, Merced (Calif.) *Sun-Star* and Stewart Hudson and Juanie Walker, Pepperdine University, Malibu, Calif.

I am indebted to the book's reviewers for many valuable suggestions: Gordon Cheesewright, Fort Lewis College, Durango, Colo.; Marvin Sosna, Thousand Oaks, Calif. *News Chronicle* and Joseph Webb, Milligan College, Johnson City, Tenn.

My salutations to those who provided direction at Praeger Publishers: Ron Chambers, editor in chief; Alison Bricken, editor; Catherine Woods Cunningham, former editor; Lauren Pera, project editor and Patricia Merrill, copy editor.

Special tribute must be paid to my parents, Ed and Eleanor Ames, for their support throughout this project and to my daughters, Krista and Karen, for their patience during my many hours of writing and sifting through newspapers for examples.

Finally, this book would not have become a reality without the selfless giving of Carol, my wife and editorial assistant par excellence.

I BASICS OF THE TOTAL PAGE CONCEPT

The approach called Total Page Concept (TPC) provides more than an entry into a newspaper page and is more than a guideline saying that each page should have a dominant focus. With the Total Page Concept as the foundation of design, every aspect of the page is immediately seen as belonging on that page; the staff of the newspaper recognizes this as the elements of design are placed on the page. Because the Total Page Concept is based on study of readers' needs, the group for whom a particular TPC publication is printed also senses the relationship of the elements, even if the tie is made subliminally. In the first two chapters, and throughout this book, methods of designing the TPC page will be delineated, keeping in mind the reader—the reason the newspaper exists.

Chapter 1   Putting Newspaper Design into Perspective
Chapter 2   The Newspapers' Public

The St. Petersburg (Fla.) *Times* takes into account the purposes of newspaper design and the reader. Reprinted by permission.

1   Putting Newspaper Design into Perspective

Content is still the carrying point. Readers want to be able to look at
the paper very quickly and know what the news of the day is and they
don't want to be scared away.

Randy Stano
director, editorial art and design
Miami *Herald*

"SHUTTLE EXPLODES" and a photo of a contrail clearly announced to readers of
the Syracuse (N.Y.) *Herald-Journal* on Jan. 28, 1986, that the Challenger space
shuttle crash had occurred that day. People in Escondido, Calif. saw the *Times-Advocate* "SHUTTLE DISASTER" headline the same day. Both heads were in all
capital letters. Every newspaper's approach to telling and showing the news of
the shuttle tragedy was different on that day and on the day after. Traditional
design was altered—though each paper followed its established guidelines of
style—because of the unusual news story being told. While all showed a photo
or photos of the explosion along with a news story, how photography and text
were meshed was unique to each paper.

Sometimes news breaks as a paper is going to press, as it did for many newspapers that January day. Sometimes it takes place much earlier and is almost
routine. No matter how or when news breaks, or how big a story is, the weekly
or daily paper serves as a major source of news in a community and the nation.
How the design editor places elements on the pages guides the reader as to what
is the most important news, and what is not.

In 1983, U.S. daily newspaper editors' attitudes about graphics and design on
the front page were explored by Steve Pasternack, now associate professor in
the department of journalism at New Mexico State University, and Sandra H.
Utt, now assistant professor in the department of journalism at Memphis State
University. At the time of the study, both authors were faculty members at

Texas A&M University. They reported their 1983 findings to a Visual Communication Division session of the Association for Education in Journalism and Mass Communication (AEJMC) annual convention at Oregon State University. The study was also reported in *Journalism Quarterly* (1984). Pasternack and Utt found that editors of the 1980s had become more aware of graphics, that many newspapers had hired graphics specialists and that their surveys of readers now frequently included questions on appearance as well as on content. They also reported, "When results dictate changes, publishers are becoming increasingly willing to accept the importance of appearance and allocate resources to improve it."

As editors experiment with and test the use of graphics, design will improve. Most editors will not put graphics on a page—especially a news page—randomly or for the sake of decoration. Tony Majeri, creative director of the Chicago *Tribune,* takes the position that graphics must be purposeful. Speaking to a Feb. 3–6, 1985 Southern Newspaper Publishers Association (SNPA) Foundation seminar, "Layout, Design and Graphics," that was held at the University of Oklahoma in Norman, Majeri underscored this point with reference to a phrase that virtually all designers in nearly every field use as a guideline: Form follows function. "Have a reason for every design element you use," he said.

Because newspaper stylebooks establish guidelines—not rules—graphic journalists are quick to recognize that the standards of one editor or designer do not necessarily agree with those of another. For instance, while Majeri is correct in his stand, Brian Steffens, graphics editor of the Los Angeles *Times* Orange County Edition, has an equally defensible argument.

"Form follows function is something that has been popular in newspapers," but "some of the best designs in automobiles traditionally have not been functional. Think of the fins on the '58 Caddy and the old DeSoto, and some people think that's great design of sorts. Fashion lately has gone to some glitzy stuff," Steffens said. He widened the common reference to "form follows function" for news pages with the statement, "Function does not always have to inform; when you take these big reverse letters that feature pages use to kick off chapter headings—as it were—the big T doesn't inform anything. But it does provide contrast or points of interest or a little salesmanship." With reference to fashion sections, where an attempt is sometimes made for a breakthrough in design, the pages sometimes "have weird little borders, or angled bars." Of these, Steffens said, "They don't contribute to the information or understanding," but they do serve the purpose of "salesmanship."

Although Majeri and Steffens may appear to be taking diverse positions, they are not. Both know the design style of the newspaper that they represent, and work to maintain a constant design style throughout the paper. This allows for straight news to be told with clarity, with art placed to provide greater understanding. Then, keeping with established design that complements the news pages, specialty pages are created for business, sports and lighter news subjects, titled "Life Style" at many papers.

The design editor is faced daily with the paradox of packaging content simply but also thoroughly and even elegantly. Many decisions are predictable calls; some are not. In their 1983 study of editors' attitudes, Pasternack and Utt said, "One West Coast design editor complained: 'Our top management simply does not have the commitment that is necessary to produce a well-designed newspaper every day.'" They also reported that "another editor said his newspaper rarely plans ahead on appearance as it does on content."

Every day the design editor is faced with these circumstances: Reporters have written their stories; photographers have completed their assignments, and the best pictures, maps and charts have been selected for printing by the page and section editors. After reporters, photographers and artists have created content, then designers are free to work. The question then arises: How is the news to be presented best?

In answering that question, editors use design principles to decide what size a photo needs to be to display it most effectively with a story. Another story may need a different graphic element—such as a bar graph or locator map—for clarification. Still another may require two or three subheads because of its complexity; another may require special headline treatment because of where it is placed on the page. The daily task of making these decisions doesn't change much. Even when a major news break occurs, design style is not thrown away; it is stretched to accommodate the unusual dimension of the news.

No matter what the news of the day has been, the reader anticipates an appropriate mix of local, national and international news plus news features—each presented accurately, clearly and fairly. This expectation should be complemented by design that effectively organizes the display of news so the reader will be easily guided through the paper.

Whether design is achieved extraordinarily—by an editor making decisions about momentous news—or ordinarily—by the operation of routine design decisions—newspapers achieve consistency and flexibility through a complex network of design principles. In this book, the foundation for the graphic journalist is built on guidelines set forth in the Total Page Concept.

WHAT THE TOTAL PAGE CONCEPT IS AND HOW IT WORKS

Through the Total Page Concept (TPC), editors organize a page so that the reader can easily identify the importance of the news. The Total Page Concept encompasses the relationship of all the parts or elements needed to create a page in a publication, such as captions for photos, headlines for news stories, the type and even the thin borders used to outline pictures or place a box around stories and advertising. In this book, a newspaper page will be used to exemplify the concept. However, the principles may be applied equally well for the pages of magazines, newsletters, and organization publications. The Total Page Concept articulates the fullest concept of design, on the assumption that design supports verbal content.

The Total Page Concept is design strategy without dogma; it is revolutionary because, although rules guide the design, communication of content is of overriding importance. To implement the Total Page Concept is to design each page as an integral unit, but with a similar design style from page to page and issue to issue. Where the Total Page Concept is understood and implemented, there are lots of rules, but their application is not dogmatic. Creativity is established in a structured environment, but the TPC publication has its own integral unity without imposing a rigid, cookie-cutter design structure. The Total Page Concept begins with page one—the publication's "picture window" —and continues throughout all the pages, except those devoted to classified advertisements.

Let's take a look at the front page of two newspapers on the day of the Challenger disaster. The papers' design principles are so well understood by the

On the day of a major event, newspapers with a strong design framework easily respond to the occasion and tell the story, as the Syracuse (N.Y.) *Herald-Journal*

editors that they are able to create a well-designed page for a spectacular news day with the same consistency and simplicity as usual, quickly directing readers to the news content and its relative importance. The front page provides a display of what's important of the day's or week's events, with larger headlines relating to the news that affects or may be of interest to the greatest number of people. Newspaper readers are initially attracted to the product whose type and words are easiest to read and whose pictures and other graphics most effectively portray the news.

From the front page, the audience is then lured to a story on an inside page by a short headline referral—a "reference note." Elements in the referral include a statement about a story and sometimes a small photo or other illustrative graphic enclosed in a box. In effect, the referral sells the news; it makes the

and the Escondido, Calif. *Times-Advocate* were able to do on the day of the Challenger shuttle explosion. Reprinted by permission.

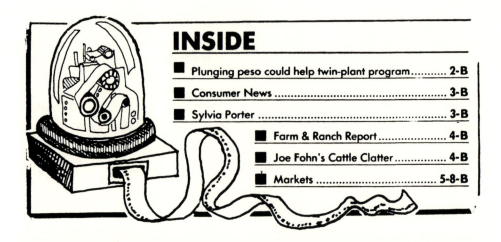

INSIDE

Monday

INSIDE TODAY'S ...

Business Monday

| Homeowners rush to refinance loans | Magazine editor likes a challenge |

Kansas, Duke in Final Four — Sports

Milkman keeps tradition alive — Page C3

Fossils are found in Antarctica — Page A5

Today's weather-A8

CHANCE OF PRECIPITATION

0%

Partly cloudy — 59°

LEXINGTON HERALD-LEADER

Vol. 4. No. 81   Metro Final   Lexington, Kentucky, March 24, 1986   44 pages   35 cents

Maroons *at home*

Military *export*

INSIDE

E2 **BOXING:** Television sports personalities believe Sugar Ray Leonard is a big underdog in his April 6th dream fight against Marvelous Marvin Hagler.

E4 **BASKETBALL:** The New York Knicks are still looking for their first win of the season . . . . .

Newspapers must get the reader quickly and easily from the front page into other parts of the newspaper, as done on page one of the Colorado Springs, Col. *Gazette Telegraph,* the Lexington (Ky.) *Herald-Leader,* and the White Plains, N.Y. *Reporter Dispatch.* Reprinted by permission.

inside pages appear useful enough for the reader to make a time commitment to them. The need for this "selling" function is clear: If the consumer stays only momentarily with the front or inside pages of a newspaper, then it is less likely that the advertising—which pays the salaries of all who are employed at the newspaper plant—will be read.

TPC design must help the reader not only through display, but also through the use of graphic elements. These elements become a part of design in the way they are treated. A partial list would include photos, drawings, charts or quotes and phrases taken from a story and set in headline type. Increasingly in modern design, white space is used with purpose as a graphic element to provide visual relief in relation to a page's heavier elements. A page with large photos and other forms of art to illustrate the news along with headline and story type can be a large mass of gray and black; white space, used in appropriate measures and carefully placed, helps make the page more inviting to the reader.

■ 4 indicted in bank collapse/3A   ■ Wesleyan takes on Wright State/1B

OWENSBORO

Messenger-Inquirer

VOL 111 NO 348   SATURDAY DECEMBER 14 1985   25¢

Plane that crashed had earlier problems

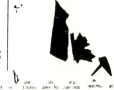

Fort Campbell offers 'shoulder' to survivors

By Bill Peterson
© 1985 The Washington Post
FORT CAMPBELL   In the Army chaplains are supposed to apply the right words the words of sympathy...

Associated Press
LOUISVILLE   Federal aviation officials and maintenance workers...

See **RAIDS/BACK PAGE**

SATURDAY MORNING

Arson ruled

Philadelphia Mayor W. Wilson Goode said Friday that arson caused a fire that damaged a vacant house occupied briefly by a black family in a southwest Philadelphia neighborhood. The fire means exactly what it says, blacks and whites can't live together and probably never will be able to live together," said Charles Williams, who moved with his family out of the house after 400 white neighbors demonstrated last month, demanding they leave. **Story, Page 6A.**

A top 'Topper

James McNary s confidence is explosive now that he s earned his way into Western Kentucky s lineup. As starting point guard for the Hilltoppers, the former Owensboro Catholic star is averaging eight points and 7.5 assists per game. **Story, Page 1B.**

Road work

City crews are removing the roads from Chautauqua Park in a move Owensboro officials hope will restore some of the setting the park once had. The work is expected to be done in time for baseball season at the home of the city s most used baseball diamonds. **Story, Page 1C.**

Common cold

Today will be mostly sunny and very cold with a high temperature of 20 **Page 2A.**

INDEX

Agriculture **7B**	Records **2C**
Astrology **8D**	Region **1-3C**
Classified **1-8D**	Religion **6C**
Comics **8B**	Sports **1-6B**
Movies **6B**	Television **7-8C**
Opinions **4A**	

40 pages, four sections
Super X supplement

The Owensboro, Ky. *Messenger Inquirer* takes the reader's referral a step further with story teasers at the top and bottom of page one.

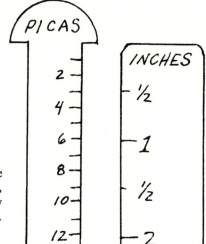

Whereas a ruler divides an inch into 16 parts, the pica pole separates an inch into six divisions, making the pica pole an easier tool for use by graphic journalists. Illustration by J Archer. Reprinted by permission.

HOW THE TOTAL PAGE CONCEPT AFFECTS STANDARD BROADSHEET AND TABLOID FORMATS

The Total Page Concept works for both the standard broadsheet newspaper and its half-size relative, the tabloid. The broadsheet usually measures about 78 to 84 picas wide (approximately 13 to 14 inches, with six picas equal to one inch) by 20 to 22 inches deep. The tabloid is the broadsheet folded and turned sideways with pages that are approximately 40 1/2 picas wide (9 3/4 inches) by 13 inches deep.

The philosophy of page design for each of these two formats is slightly different. Both formats—if designed effectively—will have a dominant feature on each page. The broadsheet page will have several other stories and photos on the page; usually the tabloid will be designed with a single story or photo and a larger headline used to catch the reader's attention.

Broadsheet and tabloid formats have different photo and headline sizes as well as different story lengths, each adjusted for the particular format. The broadsheet is more likely to have longer stories that are continued to other pages; the tabloid is more likely to have shorter stories that fit in its smaller space and fewer stories that are continued to other pages. Because the tabloid's back page can be used as a second front page in its design, a story may begin on the back page and continue inside. But even though the formats create many differences, the effective design principles and the Total Page Concept remain consistent.

In different ways, the three most important designs—informal, or contrast and balance; brace or focused; and modular or quadrant—manifest TPC principles. In each, design is strong and consistent, with the total page integrated to allow form to serve function. Whether broadsheet or tabloid, newspapers are designed according to one of a half-dozen concepts, with these three—alone or in combination—applied by the majority of newspapers. Looking at these designs more closely, they may be defined as follows:

• **Informal, or Contrast and Balance**—Elements in an informal design are displayed according to their importance or reader interest, beginning at the top right (where the right-handed majority of readers look first), then top left, back to and down the right-hand side, across the bottom to bottom left, and then to the center of the page. This arrangement follows the order that most readers will use to look at the page, before exiting at bottom right. The goal is to balance the text and graphics away from the page's center in varying distances. While an attractive informal page design is an achievable goal, the difficulty lies in not creating "walls" that would split the page in two or three sections.

• **Brace, or Focused**—The key aspect of the brace design concept is a single element used to create immediate focus on the major story. The top story is braced by the other parts of the page; elements such as headlines and photos are set much smaller than the No. 1 story. On all page designs, the No. 1 story should immediately arrest the reader's attention. Brace design does this very well, but problems arise on a routine news day when there is no story that warrants a big display. Unless justified, the top story's use as the dominant element will give it too much emphasis.

• **Modular, or Quadrant**—The modular page is broken into mostly horizontal shapes with vertical shapes to complement the design. A dominant rectangle is usually located above the page's midpoint, with large photos and illustrations adjacent. White space is used to create a breather, especially around the head-lines. Many of today's newspapers have adopted the modular design because it places the stories and graphic elements in neat rectangular shapes.

Steffens at the L.A. *Times* Orange County Edition says that the modular (quadrant) is the most frequently used design style today.

> I've never heard anybody in the newsroom in the last 10 years say "Brace," or "Contrast" or "Balance" or even "Circus" anymore. I heard them in school, and I maybe heard them from a couple of old-line copy editors, who are now retired. They are just not terms that are used in the business anymore. I don't know why. There's only one buzzword, and that's modular, and that can mean a lot of different things to a lot of different people.

While examples of modular design format are not difficult to find among suburban dailies and small-town weeklies, this style is much less prevalent among competing metropolitan dailies. However, the Dallas *Times Herald,* the Houston *Post,* and the Pittsburgh *Press* are three metro examples that were rated the best of six modular newspapers in a study of 20 papers reported by Pasternack and Utt in the *Newspaper Research Journal* (Fall 1986). Other modular design format papers in this study were the San Francisco *Examiner,* the Los Angeles *Herald-Examiner* and the now-defunct Baltimore *News American.*

The Dallas *Times Herald* displays its news by modules—rectangular packages—to aid readership. Reprinted by permission.

The 1986 Pasternack and Utt study covered 10 cities in which there were competitive and separately owned standard-size daily newspapers with a circulation of more than 100,000 according to the *1984 Editor & Publisher International Yearbook*. The newspapers were rated by 91 students at New Mexico State University and Memphis State University.

Of the 20 newspapers in the study, 12 used a "modern" design—twice as many as used modular—and two used traditional design, an informal (contrast/balance) arrangement of type and art. (In this 1986 study, there was a distinction made

The Baltimore *Sun,* the Detroit *Free Press* and the Detroit *News* present stories with a modern design. Reprinted by permission. The Detroit *News* reprinted by permission of The Detroit *News,* a division of The Evening News Association, Copyright 1986.

between modern and modular. "Modern design" meant a redesigned product incorporating techniques such as "color, large page-one photos and . . . news digests on the page's left side.") Ranked according to 15 quality dimensions including pleasant/unpleasant, neat/messy, informative/uninformative, and professional/unprofessional, the highest rated of the modern-design format papers were the Detroit *News*, the Detroit *Free Press* and the Baltimore *Sun*.

Other modern design format papers—rated in this order—were the Dallas *Morning News*, the Houston *Chronicle*, the Cincinnati *Post*, the Cincinnati *Enquirer*, the St. Louis *Globe-Democrat*, the Columbus (Ohio) *Dispatch*, the Pitts-

The Los Angeles *Times,* traditional in design, allows the size of stories and headline typefaces to break up the page. Reprinted by permission.

burgh *Post-Gazette,* the St. Louis *Post Dispatch,* and the Columbus (Ohio) *Citizen-Journal.* Of the two traditional design format papers, the highest rated was the Los Angeles *Times,* followed by the San Francisco *Chronicle.*

Modular design allows for bold and light headlines next to each other, some-times with one of the stories set in a standard-column width and one in an adjacent column set in a box. Also, modular design encourages the editor to place related stories and graphics adjacent to one another.

However, not every newspaper has rushed to adopt a modular design format. This was especially true a dozen years ago as newspapers began switching from metal type to electronic computer typesetting. As technology changed the method by which typography would be composed, editors began experimenting with new forms of layout. In 1978, the status of newspaper design in 95 cities that have jointly owned morning–evening dailies was analyzed by Gerald C. Stone, professor of journalism at Memphis State University; John C. Schweitzer, associate professor of mass communications at Texas Tech University; and David H. Weaver, professor of journalism at Indiana University. Their findings were reported in the *Journalism Quarterly.* The study was actually a secondary analysis of a 1975 survey sponsored by the American Newspaper Publishers Association. The purpose of the 1978 study was to document the use of graphic characteristics by the sample newspapers. At that time, the descriptive statistics indicated that a move toward horizontal design was under way, but that many of the more innovative elements of modern newspaper design were not being implemented.

In the modern newspaper's effort to have mass appeal while also targeting metropolitan and suburban markets with different editions, a variety of graphic elements are being utilized to make a more attractive product. These include printing special topic pages and sections, printing photos larger, a greater use of reference boxes atop page one and on inside section pages, more use of short digests of information, printing small thumbnail photos along with stories, and the use of six wider columns rather than eight narrow columns per page.

Like any other competitive product, newspapers constantly look for ways to appear similar to their competition in that they produce a vehicle to portray the news, but also dissimilar so they can attract their own committed readers. When two newspapers in the same city are produced by the same management group, the factors that usually bring readers to one paper or the other are the work schedules of the population and the delivery time of the publication. Therefore, the two newspapers may be different only in their use of headline type or caption type—but seldom text type—while designing their papers according to similar guidelines. This is a convenience for the editors and designers because it obviates having two extremely different design styles.

By 1983, suburban newspapers in most regions of the United States—in the face of competition from two or three papers in the nearest big-city market—had incorporated modular design into their page layouts. In their paper presented at the AEJMC convention in 1983, Pasternack and Utt said, "Graphically, the largest percentage of modular newspapers was in the Southeast (87.5 percent).

The least modular region was the Southwest, where 50 percent of the dailies have a modular front page" (See Table 1).

If the design style is modular, then—according to Majeri at the Chicago *Tribune*—"All makeup should be modular, whether on open pages or those with ads." Steffens says that designing in the modular format also encourages the packaging of news text with photo and illustrative art. This brings the reader into the story and makes obvious the relationship between text and art. Steffens pointed out that at most metropolitan daily newspapers a dominant package is the key to many of the pages, whether section or specialty pages or page one; but on the inside pages, the content is placed in the best possible arrangement while working around the advertisements.

When four-, five- or six-column advertisements take up the major portion of a page, the designer is left only to fill the difference. "You're just backing in the jumps," Steffens said. "You do it artfully enough, you square it off, you're modular and all that, but you can thumb eight, 10, 12 pages in a row and there's no such thing as a 'dominant.' Sometimes there's only one story on the page, period. They [people in the advertising department] have given you a well down the side, or a shelf at the top." The designer tries to create a dominant graphic element on the page, "but in practice there's a whole lot of pages where that's not a major consideration."

Table 1
Regional Percentages of Modular and Nonmodular Newspapers

	Nonmodular	Modular
Northeast[a]	29.4	70.6
Southeast[b]	12.5	87.5
South-central[c]	61.5	38.5
North-central[d]	31.6	68.4
Northwest[e]	———	100
Southwest[f]	50.0	50.0

[a]Northeast = Maine, New Hampshire, Vermont, Rhode Island, Massachusetts, Connecticut, New York, Pennsylvania, New Jersey, Delaware, Maryland and West Virginia.

[b]Southeast = Florida, Georgia, South Carolina, North Carolina, Tennessee, Virginia, Mississippi and Alabama.

[c]South-central = Missouri, Kansas, Arkansas, Oklahoma, Louisiana and Texas.

[d]North-central = Ohio, Indiana, Illinois, Kentucky, Michigan, Wisconsin, Minnesota, South Dakota, North Dakota, Iowa and Nebraska.

[e]Northwest = Washington, Oregon, Idaho, Montana, Wyoming and Alaska.

[f]Southwest = California, Nevada, Arizona, New Mexico, Colorado, Utah and Hawaii.

Source: Sandra H. Utt and Steve Pasternack, "Front Pages of U.S. Daily Newspapers," *Journalism Quarterly* (1984):879–84.

Most of the generally dominant large-circulation newspapers of the big cities—although they have made some changes in their design—have been less than anxious to adopt modular design. This is because they have been long established as major newspapers of record for their city and sometimes state. Their staple is news—straight news. The lighter news may find its way into the pages of these papers, but not if it will shorten or compete with a straight news story.

MAKING THE DESIGN SYSTEM WORK

Some newspapers have evolved from a weekly to a daily. Others remain a weekly, but have grown larger. On all of these changing publications, adjustments in staff and management philosophy occur. Each editor of the paper and each specialized section sets up a design identity, beginning with the familiar style of page one. Day after day, the reader is presented with an orderly package of news, features and stories in such special-interest areas as sports, business and life style. But if the paper's typography and art are to look like they have indeed been published as a single entity, a subtle but unified design philosophy should be obvious to the reader.

Marvin Sosna, editor of the Thousand Oaks, Calif. *News Chronicle,* commented, "I have taught my students—and urged the desk editors at the *News Chronicle*—that design is the deliberate arrangement of objects to achieve a predetermined effect. In graphics, that effect is the two-dimensional representation of an abstract idea." However, the newspaper fails as a vehicle of communication if the editor places the elements on any page by fitting them into a preconceived design pattern such as we saw with the brace design. It is neither creative nor responsive to the news merely to design a page with all elements laid into a rigid format, then place each day's or week's pages of text and graphics in locations where the measurements are exactly the same as the day or week before. The news should be packaged with a logical sense to the text and graphics relationships, but the packaging should be subtle.

News does change from page to page and section to section, and the design should be altered accordingly. But if the Total Page Concept is to be consistent, standards should be written to guide designers in their placement of heads, stories, photos and illustrative material. With one newspaper's editors/designers numbering as many as 50, there are too many people working too many shifts to sit down and debate how best to maintain consistent design. Consistency through flexible standards serves a twofold purpose: The staff is able to make design decisions, and the reader is likely to see the newspaper as a uniformly credible product.

Among U.S. newspapers, consistency enhances the credibility of the whole product. A chaotic collection of typefaces, differences in standing head or in page jump style, or variations in photo and illustration caption styles take away from the publication's purpose: communication. Each paper's book of guidelines need not control the way absolutely everything is done. Ideally, it will set out parameters within which editors can respond creatively to communication needs. The style book is likely to be a more valuable tool for staff members if they have input in creating or altering the standards that it sets forth.

Guidelines that assist one staff will not necessarily assist another. However, many aspects of building a Total Page Concept will be helpful to all who face the design challenge (see Chapter 16).

To help the reader in a hurry, an efficient and imaginative newspaper package is vital. Elements must be placed on each page with a conscious awareness that the newspaper is published to convey the news to the reader: local news in the community weekly; and local, national and international news in the daily. The amount of space allotted for national and international news will vary for the daily newspaper, depending quite simply on the number of pages available. Readers look to their newspapers for information and education: to see how their tax dollars are being spent or what their city council or school board is doing, to follow a sports team, or to read about an event or a celebrity in another state or another country. Designers/editors who comprehend the reasons behind a reader's need for putting time aside to read the newspaper and who implement the Total Page Concept to serve that need are more likely to encourage the reader to buy the product regularly, and its advertised goods and services as well.

The keys to success in any business enterprise are to identify the consumer and the competition, to develop and market the product, and to provide a system for evaluating all of the above. Because the newspaper publication business is indeed a business, publishers—whose job it is to create a sound investment— work to balance the news editorial needs and the profit–loss balance sheet. A publisher's interest is to attract and keep the reader while at the same time not spending more on production and front-office support than can be earned by the sale of advertising-column inches and subscriptions. Publishers who are successful quickly learn that changing text or headline typefaces or column widths, adding a syndicated columnist or buying a comic strip does not guarantee reader loyalty or reader interest. The characters of Harold Hill in *The Music Man* and Willie Loman in *Death of a Salesman* demonstrated fully the commandment that all in the newspaper business must comprehend: Know your territory.

The territory of each newspaper is ascertained by looking to see precisely who its readers are. The effective application of demographics and psychographics can assist editors in presenting news that its readership wants and needs. The Total Page Concept will maximize the effort, especially as modern design strategies are implemented for ease of reading. The Total Page Concept is detailed in many ways over the remaining 15 chapters of this textbook. Understanding and applying TPC to every page decision means that the publication's design will be free of clutter and have an orderly display of content—a clear communication, which makes it easy for readers to comprehend the day's events and find the advertising helpful in making important buying decisions.

2   The Newspapers' Public

We are giving readers much more in areas of interest to them. We appeal to a broader range of interests through the new sections. We provide much more information and service. We modernized the look of the paper. We became a graphic as well as a textual and photo medium. We became more youthful and vital in appearance. We established a base for broad promotion and marketing in many desired areas.

Louis Silverstein
former assistant managing editor, corporate art director, and
presently consultant to the New York Times Company

Each newspaper is different. The staffs for news editorial, advertising, clerical and pressroom are unlike any other paper, regardless of the size of the community. Even if the community has the same population as another, it may have more or fewer newspaper subscribers. Employment opportunities are different, as well as the ages and education of the people, the weather and the leisure activities available. All that the newspaper facility has to offer in personnel and equipment and all that the circulation area itself offers mix together as the newspaper aims to serve its readership.

The balance of news content and presentation must complement the readers' needs. According to George Tuck (professor of photojournalism and typography in the College of Journalism at the University of Nebraska) in the *APME* (Associated Press Managing Editors) *News* (1985), Broc Sears, art director of the Dallas *Times Herald,* said that editors have "realized through marketing studies and the improvement of all media systems that people are demanding better products for their money." Newspapers are a consumer product. Sears underscored this point when he said, "Looking at our papers as a product or package has opened many editors' eyes to the fact that appearance and content must go hand in hand to compete for consumer attention and money."

Newspaper management's goal is to reach the largest number of households; to effect this, management needs to meet the community's expectations and to be consistent in a time of tight economy. The successful newspaper uses the most sophisticated market methods in monitoring its readership.

A reader purchases a particular newspaper for a variety of reasons, mostly related to a sensed information need or a sense of identity with the community that the paper serves. The purchase may be one of convenience—the time of day that the paper is available—or perhaps this is the only newspaper that covers community news in depth. In addition, the delivery or newsstand price might be less than that of the competition, or the reader may like the paper's use of color, the stories' lengths or the amount or quality of photos.

James K. Batten, president of Knight-Ridder Newspapers, says that newspapers must serve the reading public if they are to continue to publish.

> Over the years, some newspapers have had a reputation in the trade of being "a reporters' paper," or "an editors' paper." Those newspapers whose futures will be most secure in the next 10 years will be neither "reporters' papers" nor "editors' papers," but in the best sense of the word, *readers' papers.* (emphasis in original)

DEMOGRAPHICS/PSYCHOGRAPHICS

The key to an organized newspaper design is the Total Page Concept. Before discussing the Total Page Concept specifically, it is appropriate to examine how a newspaper should measure its potential readership. Many important, specific decisions about TPC must be based on a statistical, sociological/psychological and researched assessment of the audience.

Speaking during a panel session at the Inland Daily Press Association convention in 1985, Joel H. Walker, publisher and editor of the Troy (Ohio) *Daily News,* stated that a newspaper's survival is directly related to its seeing the value of a strong product and making a correct measurement of the product's recipients.

> If you're going to try to survive with undereducated writers and correspondents, with low quality photos, with sloppy graphics, design and poor press work, you're kidding yourself. You won't make it with ad people who are merely pickup clerks rather than aggressive, innovative salesmen. And survival will be difficult with editors and reporters who aren't tuned in—tuned in not only to your community, but to your area, your state, the U.S. and the world.

Unless the editorial staff has a working knowledge of its particular newspaper's circulation area, it is operating in a vacuum. The market should be thoroughly analyzed for reader interest before newspaper editors allot standard "hard news" pages and sections for local or metropolitan, regional, national and international coverage and special interest areas such as business, life style and sports. Gerald L. Grotta, associate professor of journalism at Texas Christian University, told a seminar audience at the University of Oklahoma that editors should use facts in order to make decisions about design. Grotta was speaking at the "Layout, Design and Graphics" seminar sponsored by the Southern Newspaper Publishers Association (SNPA) Foundation. He said, "Editors often make assumptions about readers that have no basis in fact. Therefore, research is necessary to establish what readers want in a paper's particular market." Grotta suggested that the research be "specially prepared, because many surveys deal heavily with the paper's content rather than appearance." Three important factors should be established from design research:

- the nature of the market and the lifestyles and attitudes of the people in it;
- the nature of the newspaper; and
- the nature of the competition.

Availing themselves of recent research in the areas of demographics and psychographics, the Chicago *Tribune* and the Minneapolis *Star and Tribune* tie themselves into the metropolitan community. Reprinted by permission.

"The results of this research," Grotta said, "should be used to supplement the ideas of editors about design changes. Changes should be promoted aggressively and always geared toward giving readers what they asked for."

Readers' needs are found through demographic and psychographic critiques. Demographics are the statistics kept about populations related to records of births, deaths, marriages and diseases. Psychographics are the quantitative data about the activities, interests and opinions of a population that describe segments by the individual and collective lifestyles of their respective members. However, these critiques must be done carefully. A scientific procedure with full analysis must be established so the demographic and psychographic data accurately measures the public that a newspaper serves. People's needs and attitudes change; the kinds of jobs that they have and where they live change. The city's or region's civic life reflects these changes. The newspaper that pays attention to how its news stories are written and how they can be most effectively displayed will do a better job in its attempt to mirror the people and their lives in the community.

In a paper's review of its subscriber area, it must investigate economic status, income and types of occupations, partisan political party activity, racial and social backgrounds, the education of the people and community resources. Monitoring why readers purchase a particular newspaper is the best way to gauge the void that the paper fills for its readership.

USA Today, from its very first issue on Sept. 15, 1982, has proven the value of presenting the news in a tightly packaged format. John C. Quinn, the paper's editor, is abundantly aware of the void that his newspaper fills. Quinn spoke to a February 1987 Arkansas Press Association Awards Banquet.

> The press, too, must cover the news in a way the reader can grasp, edit the news in a way that fits its audience, [and] deliver the news in a cool, consistent manner that will win confidence, not Oscars, or even Pulitzers, although those of course are great capstones for good work. The public must be encouraged to do its job, too. It must demand and treasure comprehensive coverage of the news it sees, even the news it may not enjoy hearing. It must applaud the full and fair exercise of the free press in principle, even when its practice may turn up news it would rather not know.

Ken Bruns, design director of the Los Angeles *Times,* knows that design depends a great deal on how audience and demographics are viewed by the designer and the newspaper. As Bruns commented, "Our paper, for instance, would never go in the direction of *USA Today,* yet *USA Today* is very successful" because it does what appeals to its own audience. When redesigning a newspaper, probably the first thing to recognize is its audience: how the paper is sold and its geographical area. Bruns added, "Our paper is about 90 percent home delivered, so we don't need flashy headlines, skylines or ears for newsstand recognition. This is one example of what should be taken into account."

Each weekday, *USA Today* provides the entire nation with comprehensive coverage, starting from page one and throughout the newspaper. Reprinted by permission.

The paper should reflect in content what the readership wants to read, and in design whatever is appropriate to the specific audience's interests.

The reading audience is selective. A paper is received into the home for solid information and education along with its more entertaining features. For the purposes of this book, "news" means information that mirrors the readers' immediate needs and interests and—in the best sense—reflects the unusual rather than routine depiction of the local and global community's events and personalities.

Part of the enticement to read is embodied in the content of the news: the subjects and stories that are written about, and how well they are written. But the news department must contend with much more than that. To keep the reader engaged, an attractive design utilizing the Total Page Concept must be presented. This is why it is crucial that editors know their audience, know how to make realistic decisions on what is run, and plan how stories and graphics will be displayed in the precious space available.

UNDERSTANDING WHAT NEWS IS

John Bodette, managing editor of the St. Cloud (Minn.) *Times,* believes that the news is best presented by reporters and editors if they "understand news." This may seem obvious enough, but sometimes, in an effort to fit the news into a space, incorrect decisions are made that cheat the reader out of vital information. "Oftentimes," Bodette said, "you see the news twisted and butchered and chopped and rearranged to some desired design concept, rather than taking the news and using the tools of design to make that come alive for the reader. That's what's very unfortunate."

If news is the paper's central purpose and the reason readers purchase the paper, the news staff should do its best to serve that purpose with well-written and tightly edited stories and the use of strong, purposeful graphics. Tuck in the *APME News* quoted R. D. Engle, executive editor of the San Jose (Calif.) *Mercury News,* on the subject of "trimming text vs. trimming graphics." Engle said that "a paper's most lucid writing will be ignored by the many readers if it's not presented in an appealing fashion and augmented by graphic reporting as well."

When a market review is conducted, news policy must be carefully considered so that changes are not made arbitrarily. People who read the newspaper frequently take it as their own personal possession, an extension of the community's personality. Readers make jokes about the paper—about its name, or the time some (local or outside) personality's name was misspelled or a wrong photo identification was made. However, the local paper is also the first place that people take their wedding announcement, or look for a "write up" about a family member elected to office in a community organization, or a story about a high school or college team's outcome in a sports event.

Walker of the Troy (Ohio) *Daily News* sees the newspaper as having a responsibility to the community far beyond the most basic delivering of news. "Local news coverage, no matter how you define it, must not be shortchanged," he told the Inland Daily Press Association audience. "Local news needs strong writing and capable people to report it. It can't be left to clerks and stringers. Good reporters and good editors are essential. Readers are becoming more sophisticated every day. They know when a story is covered and written correctly or when it is just left to a non-professional." Walker said that news is not "a catch-all phrase, a cure for all of our ills." He suggested that the scope must be broader. "Local news is more than covering council and school board meetings.

It's more than running the photo of the homecoming queen. It's more than covering Friday night football games."

As the community market and the newspaper's policy are simultaneously reviewed, much consideration must be given to why the public purchases the paper. Usually, the reason given is: "I can't get along without knowing what is going on in the community." In addition to reading about social activities, the community's citizens want to read stories about:

- how their tax dollars are being spent;
- new developments in the education of their children;
- voter options for elections;
- meetings of governmental bodies;
- the effects of community growth; and
- implications of the local crime rate.

If readers are to make better sense of their lives with the aid of newspapers, then the papers need to effectively direct readers to the relative importance of stories. Thus, the serious reader's expectations will be served, along with those of the browser. The reader who sets aside less than half an hour to read the whole newspaper will depend on design with direction to see and read the day's key stories. Grotta at the SNPA Foundation seminar, "Layout, Design and Graphics," said that, in the 15–20 minutes the average reader spends with the paper, only 10 percent to 12 percent of the news is read. Research indicates that readers classify information in the paper into two areas:

- information that is interesting and/or useful; and
- information that is not interesting and/or useful.

"Therefore," Grotta said, "all sections must adopt a consumer approach."

Randy Stano, graphics design director of the Miami *Herald,* agrees with Grotta's reference to serving readers' tight schedules which seldom allow extended periods of reading. "A typical reader spends 17 minutes on it [newspaper reading], at best. We in the industry look at the paper and spend more time than the average reader does; we've got to make it easy for the readers," Stano said. While no newspaper satisfies everyone, most readers "want news quickly, easily and they want a lot of it," he said. "Yes, you get people who want the New York *Times,* the Washington *Post,* the Los Angeles *Times*—even the Miami *Herald*—type stories, but you've got to be able to break these stories up." Stano suggested breaking up the 100- and 200-inch stories into packages and subpackages by using subheads, pulling out quotes to be set in headline type as graphic elements, and making a portion of the story into a sidebar. "The reader needs as many points of entry into a package [windows into the story] as are feasible.

The St. Cloud (Minn.) *Times* ties a national story into one that is local on the day the stock market dropped dramatically. Reprinted by permission.

This approach captures the attention of both the casual scanner and the in-depth reader." Newspaper readers feel that their purchase of the paper involves an unspoken contract: The newspaper is the vehicle they have chosen for discovering news content, but finding it should not be a matter of chance.

Pegie Stark, associate professor of journalism at the University of Florida in Gainesville and visiting professor for 1989 at the Poynter Institute in St. Petersburg, Fla., has also directed graphics at the Detroit *News*, the Detroit *Free Press* and the St. Petersburg (Fla.) *Times*. According to Stark, part of serving readers is to complement their expectations. "I think readers start expecting

The day after a raging fire burned out, graphic reporting tells the story to readers of the San José (Calif.) *Mercury News*. Reprinted by permission.

certain things," because they have gotten used to them. She said that the environment is largely responsible for these expectations. For example, many readers in St. Petersburg are senior citizens, who "want a different kind of feel to their paper" than the mixed age group in Detroit. Because Detroit "is not a retirement community," the people there have less time to read. Stark went on to say that, to a large extent, content is a major factor in the newspaper's look. Readers in St. Petersburg want more international, global news—"a more literary feel to their pages"—whereas readers in Detroit appear to be interested "in more active, local daily information. But," she added, "I frankly don't think

Many stories are displayed on this Miami *Herald* page one, with
capsules of several others to tell the news quickly and eliminate
clutter. Reprinted by permission.

readers are really too aware of those things that, to us, seem so obvious"—like
one paper looking different from another—"because I don't know if readers
would really pick up on that."

Interesting, pertinent information, especially "hard news" stories—the stories
that readers should know about to be informed citizens—must be carefully
written and creatively displayed.

Design purpose must make sense to the reader even if only subliminally.

Excellence in writing is no less crucial, but this too can be helped by design. If the story's important points are made in the lead paragraph and several that follow, and if subheads are printed boldly enough with sufficient white space around them to provide direction, then the reader should correctly perceive the story's importance, catch its main points and be satisfied. Using boxed news stories, quote and statement boxes, graphics, and subheads, TPC can be employed to direct the reader through the timeless human interest story as well.

Whether presenting "hard" or "soft" news, it is vital that reporters, editors and graphic designers realize the importance of telling the story completely. This is because publication is a one-way medium. The reader who does not understand the story is not likely to pick up a telephone and get into a two-way conversation with the writer to have the story clarified—but is likely to buy another newspaper, if it happens too often. The Total Page Concept—or any other term used to identify a design method—is irrelevant to the reader who finds it difficult to read and understand the news.

NEWS STAFF DECISIONS

Lloyd G. Schermer, president and chief executive officer of Lee Enterprises in Davenport, Iowa, spoke as a panelist on the future of U.S. newspapers during the Inland Daily Press Association convention in 1985. In regard to readability, Schermer suggested that editors take very seriously their task of presenting the news in a form quickly grasped by the busy reader. "Perhaps we should think about each story that appears in our newspapers as though we would have to sell each one individually at a profit, rather than assume people want them because they are part of the entire package," he said.

Newspapers have tried many experiments on their inside pages, on section fronts and on their softer features; but, with few exceptions, radical changes have not been tried on the news pages themselves. This is because most news editors believe that treating hard news lightly might take away from the paper's news integrity. Nevertheless, the news pages set the tone for a TPC-designed newspaper. Since news pages must clearly signal story importance, they should have no less vitality to them than the rest of the paper.

Creative and effective design is indeed possible on news pages without making a mockery of the news and its serious nature. According to Harvey C. Jacobs, editor of the Indianapolis *News,* an awareness of the need for useful graphics purposely placed in the newspaper has been very slow to develop. "For many years," he said, "newspapers gave too little attention to graphic display of the material in the news hole. Now, the pendulum has swung the other direction." Jacobs believes that television and a "few faddish publications" have hyped color and graphics too much. "The danger," he said, "is that editors will tend to lean too much on display as a marketing tool, downgrading content and coverage. We are first *news* papers, not visual showcases." Jacobs sees this as a problem of "diminishing returns—when more resources and personnel should be allocated to the editorial product rather than to graphic arts. There is, of course, middle ground, and that is what we should be striving for."

On all of its pages the newspaper must be recognized by editors and readers as a visual medium. The mosaic of shapes and sizes in a particular paper will be chosen by the harried reader only if there is an immediately understood organization of graphics and words. Organization makes the news accessible, and it clarifies the paper's sensitivity to readers' needs.

According to Robert Lockwood, president of NewsGraphics in New Tripoli, Pa., it is not unusual to find a lack of direction when it comes to the linking of written content and design. Lockwood was formerly art director at the *Morning Call* in Allentown, Pa., and worked with the *Christian Science Monitor* editors on design. For the most part, in his opinion, "there's little attention given to having the visual and verbal parts of the paper relate and support each other." Lockwood said that the visual is usually handmaiden to the verbal; an editor often assigns a story and then waits until it comes back before saying, " 'Oh, let's get art for the story.' Then, after that, somebody's going to lay it out. But it won't be laid out organically, that is, having had a designer read the story and suggest how it should be displayed." The result? "What we get," Lockwood said, "is a narrative approach where we have a story and a picture; story, picture or story and a graphic; then add a headline. That's how many people lay out a page, but there's little thought to integrating all the elements: text, photos and graphics."

TPC page design—in and of itself—does not compromise the seriousness of the news, or turn hard news into soft news. Most readers will be able to determine immediately the difference between hard and soft news by reading the story's headline, or—if not by that—then by reading the first paragraph or two.

A newspaper's philosophy regarding its news sections can be determined by examining how thoroughly its stories are edited, how its photos and illustrative art are displayed, and the role that the art department has played in making decisions.

Integration is achieved when the art and news departments have both given careful thought to the final product from its conception to completion. According to Lockwood, the important point is the beginning. "It's just a matter of when you begin the design process," he said. "If you wait until all the elements are in—the photos, stories—it's too late. The process of design should begin at the inception of the story." Lockwood illustrates what he calls the "structural approach" with an example about obtaining information for a local story on the gasoline shortage.

> If, from the inception of the story, the designer is involved in the process, he might say, "While you're out getting the story on the gasoline shortage and the car lines at service stations, perhaps you'd want to get which gas stations are open and which ones think they'll

Page one of the daily national tabloid newspaper *Christian Science Monitor* provides verbal and visual direction to ease the reader into the inside pages. Reprinted by permission from *The Christian Science Monitor,* © 1986 The Christian Science Publishing Society. All rights reserved.

have gas for the week and a map of the area—we might decide not to do the traditional story, but make a list of the stations with a map of where they are and which are open so the reader would get the kind of information he needs in his daily life from the story—rather than writing a story and simply showing a picture of cars in a line." It's an entirely different approach. It's a structural approach that helps complement the narrative one.

In setting up guidelines for the Total Page Concept, the art department is considered a partner with the news department. The art and news staffs may have been only like distant relatives at one time, but now they are working hand in hand on many newspapers. The news department has its own special graphics needs. Papers are now hiring illustrators who can create drawings and make charts to help tell the news stories, just as photographers are employed to portray the news in pictures.

Among the graphic design questions that dynamic, growing newspaper staffs must address, the most basic include:

- Does the newspaper's art department actually serve as an advertising support department, or are some art people being integrated into the news department?
- Is there a plan for training news editors in the use of graphics and in working with or as art department people?
- Does the newspaper have a graphics editor or editorial designer; and, if so, is this individual part of the news team, or news trained enough to provide input when the paper is on deadline?

For a publication to be successful in the computer age, its editorial staff members need to understand the function of art. Likewise, the art department that truly complements the news department has a department head and staffers who participate in news meetings with the news editors and reporters; this kind of arrangement also serves well the purpose of the newspaper: to provide the full story, in written and graphic terms.

Brian Steffens of the Los Angeles *Times* Orange County Edition, agrees that bringing together personnel of the art and news departments will better serve the news effort of the paper and, in turn, the needs of the reader.

> Even in production areas, I suggest artists spend some time in the back shop learning how platemaking, the color lab and stripping work. Reporters ought to ride with photographers; photographers ought to ride with reporters. The copy desk ought to get out. Reporters or photographers ought to sit on the copy desk for a couple of days or nights and wrestle with some of those caption-writing [problems].

Art people may seem threatening to news people; but, if trained as graphic journalists, the art they create can make the news easier to tell. Informational or illustrative art can enhance a story in the same way that the work of photojournalists has done for many years. A news, art, photo and production team should schedule adequate time—varied according to the "breaking" nature of the news—to plan, gather and prepare written and graphic materials, make various drafts, edit one another's work, package stories clearly, meet deadlines and evaluate the outcome of their Total Page Concept.

II PRINCIPLES OF DESIGN

News space design—while its framework should be consistent throughout the newspaper—will be different on an open page than on one that includes advertising, and different in standard broadsheet format than in a tabloid section or tabloid newspaper. All the structural elements of the TPC design must have the same relationship within each page of a particular newspaper. The key is unity. In the next three chapters, basic principles of designing news space will be exemplified, showing how the various elements can be positioned on the available space and coordinated to achieve a unity of presentation.

New York Newsday EDITION

THURSDAY, JULY 10, 1986 • 25 CENTS

War on Porn

Federal Report:

- Links Hard-Core Porn to Sex Crimes

- Calls Women And Children Victims

- Says Porn Industry Provides Income For Organized Crime

- Calls for Grass Roots Pickets, Legal Action

Attorney General Edwin Meese stands before 'Spirit of Justice' statue during press briefing on report yesterday.

Stories on Page 5

PART II	**CRACK TEAM**	**INTERVIEW**	**TRADE SCHOOLS**
Israel's Ultra Orthodox	D'Amato, Giuliani: Big Buy *Page 4*	He Chases Wall St.'s Wicked *Page 77*	Regan Gets Tough *Page 3*
PULLOUT SECTION			

Newsday, the daily tabloid published in Melville, N.Y. for readers in Long Island and New York City, begins its packaging of the news on the page-one cover. Copyright 1986, Newsday, Inc. Reprinted by permission.

3   Designing News Space

The public's appetite for news and information is never fulfilled. The USA public wants all the news, the bad and the sad along with the good and the glad. It wants to enjoy the best of the news and learn how to cope with the rest of it. It wants to look beyond the color to the content, beyond the cosmetics to the consistency, beyond the promotion to the product, beyond the immediate emotions to the logical conclusions. It wants its media to keep up with its needs and adapt to its lifestyle and it does not buy the old way-we've-always-done-it views of editors and publishers who do not think anything should be tried for the first time.

> John C. Quinn
> editor, *USA Today*
> (Quoted from a speech at the February 1987
> Arkansas Press Association Awards Banquet)

Pages are not just brought together by magic—even by a design editor. Sequence, or the placing of elements on the page in a prescribed order, is essential to designing news space. When advertisements are included on a page, they are placed first, by the advertising department. Then the news department takes over, placing photos and illustrated art next, and headline and text type last. This placement order is the rule because:

- advertising sizes must be exactly as they have been sold to clients;
- photos and headlines can be sized somewhat smaller or larger, but they cannot be cut or enlarged drastically to fit a space; and
- text type can be set to fit a space, or the story can be tightened or continued on another page.

Comprehending the orderly relationship of advertising, art, headline and text materials—while creating the greatest possible impact on every page—will greatly aid the designer of a Total Page Concept (TPC) newspaper.

Brian Steffens of the Los Angeles *Times* Orange County Edition says that on larger metropolitan newspapers many editors must assign both length of text and the accompanying art for stories. At the main downtown office where departments are on several floors or around the county and beyond, the process of melding the news and art departments is complex and cumbersome. By contrast, working at an edition office is simpler because the news and art departments are physically closer. With reference to working at a downtown metropolitan newspaper office, Steffens said that at the San Diego *Union,* where he worked in editorial art prior to accepting the *Times* position, the news budget is prepared by as many as 12 different people.

> The news editor assembles the budget for national and foreign; the politics editor handles the CNS [Copley News Service] and his politics writers; the photo desk does the photo budget; the county desk does a budget; the city desk does it—they do four separate budgets: courts and politics, general assignment, special reporters and countywide. The Currents Department does one. The copy clerks assemble it and put it in this big package and send one to everybody so all the rest of us know what everyone else is doing.

While every newspaper does it differently, some system of organizing assignments for the news budget is vital. Otherwise there may be unnecessary duplication of stories due to a lack of communication between editors of the various sections.

NEWS PAGE DESIGN STRATEGIES

News pages particularly need a special design strategy to convey each story effectively, which will necessarily be related to news judgment. The best story of the day may not have or need art to accompany it; the best art may not have sufficient importance to be on page one or anywhere else among the straight news pages. An insignificant news item or photo should never receive undue play or be slanted or edited without consideration for the integrity of the news.

One of the main difficulties with elevating the importance of design has been the ever-present pressure of the deadline. There may be a story partially written with its art yet to come, and the page is on deadline. A beautiful page that impels people to read it because of its content and design is one thing, but every news editor—even despite the pleas of the strongest graphics editor—has to go with the graphics that are present at deadline. In such a situation, the page design should allow for a "chaser" or update story—one that will be published in the next edition, easily replacing the original story with a minimal amount of page redesign. This ability to drop in one story in exchange for another is one of the beauties of using horizontal and vertical modules in page design. While modular design is a valuable assist for the daily newspaper, it may also be used for the weekly where the publication staff has more time to produce the paper.

Whether perusing a news page, lifestyle section or the sports, the reader of any newspaper should have a sense that all these parts are in the same paper because the design is consistent throughout. Design style standards should be established on page one and carried through the whole paper. "Page one is very important to readers," says Gerald Grotta of Texas Christian University. Speaking to the Southern Newspaper Publishers Association (SNPA) Foundation seminar, "Layout, Design and Graphics," Grotta said, "Studies in the early 1970s show that the front page format established a newspaper's personality in readers' eyes. Readers prefer modern—that is, modular—design." (Remember, however, that—as noted in Chapter 1—Steve Pasternack and Sandra Utt made a distinction between modern and modular design in their 1986 study.) Mark Fitzgerald, writing in *Editor & Publisher* (1985), said that, whether designing in modular style or any other artistic influence on newspaper graphics, "graphic artists have transformed the look of today's newspapers in nearly every aspect but one: the front page."

Page one is the page by which the remainder of the newspaper is measured in terms of stories and design. It is where the reader initially becomes acquainted with the paper, and—while it changes with every edition and every day—its look is the product's instant identity, positive or negative. The close proximity of front-page text and art can cause them to compete with one another. If the design fails to direct the reader through the page, his or her interest will be redirected to other options—including not reading the newspaper at all.

James Batten of Knight-Ridder Newspapers underscored another aspect of newspaper reading when he told an audience at a 1983 SNPA convention that "just because the editors thought a story was important enough for page one no longer means—again, if it ever did—that readers will feel any obligation to read it; they're too busy, and their attention spans are too short." Considering the need to lure readers to page one—says Fitzgerald in *Editor & Publisher*— the "failure of Art departments to gain day-to-day influence over the look of the page that sells the paper remains a source of deep frustration for graphic artists."

A reader's response to stories is encouraged or impaired by their "play" or placement on the page. Again, this is especially critical on page one because the news of the day must provide instant perspective on its relative importance to other text and art on the page, and page one must also guide the reader into the other pages. Story count—the number of stories on a page—serves to help or hinder the page's organization. In 1979, reader reactions to newspaper design were studied by Chic Bain, then a graduate student at Indiana University and

An airplane crash is big news, especially for a suburban daily. To respond, the newspaper may have to publish several editions, as the *Contra Costa Times* in Walnut Creek, Calif. did when a plane slammed into a Concord shopping center. Reprinted by permission.

now a publications design consultant and the chief executive officer of Gillis & Krebs in Austin, Texas, and David H. Weaver, professor of journalism at Indiana University in Bloomington. They reported in *Newspaper Research Journal* that "the number of stories played on the front also affects the size of pictures on that page and the size of headlines, particularly among the lower ranking stories."

In the opinion of Steffens at the L.A. *Times* Orange County Edition, story count and design are related. Modular design contributes to the page's story count and to its look as well. Steffens says that one newspaper commonly considered to be modular is not, in his mind: He was referring to *USA Today*. "*USA Today* is modular, but not in the technical sense that a lot of other people use it. I tend to treat modular as four-sided; there are a lot of six-sided packages in *USA Today*." Steffens pointed out that some papers, such as the New York *Times* and the Los Angeles *Times*, design page one and many other news pages in a vertical style. "It looks like a high story count, it looks like something is going on," he said.

InterMountain

THE News

Burney, California   July 24, 1985   Vol. XXIV   No. 30   50°

Excitement in Hat Creek and Round Mountain
See page 8

Doctors get hospital privileges

By MEG FOX
Staff Writer

FALL RIVER MILLS — Admitting privileges for the three new physicians practicing in the Intermountain area were approved by the hospital's board of directors here Monday at the request of Chief of Staff, Dr. Michael Huey.

After confirming that the physicians' state and controlled substance licenses were current, the directors of Mayers Memorial Hospital approved privileges for doctors Stephen Berthelsen, Jim Halverson and Dan Dahle.

Reappointed to the medical staff were Dr. Thomas Ruak, a surgical pathologist from Northern Laboratories in Redding, Dr. Bruce Gattie, a surgeon with Mt. Shasta Community Hospital, and Dr. Ray Nichols, a Fall River Mills dentist.

In giving his staff report, Huey told the board that at the recommendation of Dr. Berthelsen, a surgical committee and monthly death reviews had been approved.

The surgical committee, to be headed by Dr. Chris Camarata, will decide on each matters as surgical policy and equipment needs, Huey said. Appointed to the committee were Dr. Berthelsen, Pat Anderson, supervising nurse, and Kim Wheeler, certified nurse anesthesiologist.

Camarata was also appointed to oversee the death reviews which, Huey explained, "is a quality assurance mechanism done by all hospitals. It's purpose is to point out how we can be better coordinated and know where we're good and where we need improvement." All critical care patients will be discussed at these meetings, Huey said.

In other business, Everett Beck, hospital administrator, read the board a letter from Bill Krapf, a Fall River Mills chiropractor, who asked if the hospital would "set aside old-fashioned biases" and assist him with X-rays of his Medicare patients.

While the hospital did in the past provide him with X-ray services, Beck said Krapf has since purchased his own equipment.

However, Beck said, it is his understanding now that Medicare will not pay for X-rays ordered by a chiropractor.

Board member Ruth Koech suggested they table the matter while Beck looked into the matter further, including asking Krapf if he would consider paying the 20 percent difference himself or bill his patients directly in full.

"Check on it," Koech said. "We'd better be concerned about our malpractice as well as the 20 percent," she said.

Before adjourning, Mrs. Beck noted that RPS a pharmaceutical management company which runs the hospital's pharmacy had hired a Southern California pharmacist, Mark Larabee, to replace Gary MacMullen who has left the area.

Larabee, his wife Linda, and their four children are expected to arrive here in early August.

County planners: SP needs no EIR

A decision is expected Thursday on whether Sierra Pacific must file an environmental impact report (EIR) on its proposed cogeneration plant at the west end of Burney.

Shasta County planning commissioners will hear the matter at their regular meeting beginning at 1 p.m. in the board of supervisors chambers at the Redding courthouse.

The planning department has recommended the project be approved and that an EIR would not provide a better report than the department has prepared.

An EIR, prepared by a third party private consultant may go a long way to satisfy an apprehensive citizenry, the planning department noted.

Staff's biggest problem with preparing an EIR is that the best available information, which is considered by staff to be adequate to assess potential impacts, has already been analyzed, and it is our opinion that an EIR would not provide a better analysis.

The air pollution control article's report indicates that the air emissions will meet the existing standards. In staff's judgement, no other information has been presented which suggests that a significant effect will occur.

Planning commissioners are Irwin Fust, Pat Knight, Glenn Hawes, Dean Hinkle and Richard Ros.

For your eyes only

Quinn Larson, 11, of Round Mountain is lashing out with painted eyelids at the Mountain Aire Country Faire Saturday. His father, John, is the artist shown in lower photo as he paints Brenda Durst, 13, also of Round Mountain with washable tattoo for 25 cents.

—Please See Page 3

Man 'stable' following fiery crash

The California Highway Patrol is still investigating the accident which critically injured a Placerville man taking a detour through Burney Thursday.

Donald Mitchell, 31, was westbound on Highway 299, west of Tamarack Avenue in Burney, when for unknown reasons, he drifted off the road to his right and hit a tree at approximately 8:30 p.m. the CHP said. The U-Haul truck he was driving reportedly burst into flames with Mitchell trapped inside.

He was transported to the Chico

Related photo on page 3

Community Memorial Burn Center with second and third degree burns. Mitchell was listed in stable but serious condition Tuesday as the Center's intensive care unit after having had both his legs amputated above the knees.

Mitchell was reportedly traveling from Grants Pass to Placerville when he was rerouted from Interstate 5 onto Highway 89 due to a fire north of Redding. The accident was witnessed by his mother and a younger brother and friend who were traveling in vehicles behind him, the CHP said.

Wall OK for 'discipline'

BIEBER — A request for a wall to separate the bus garage from the auto shop at the high school here was granted Thursday by the directors of the Big Valley Joint Unified School District during their regular monthly meeting.

"We discussed it and agreed that if we're all going to be there at the same time, we need a wall," Hugh Mooney, Big Valley High School ag teacher and welding instructor, said referring to his associates Larry Highbarger, who was hired this summer to teach industrial arts, and Al Vigollo, also recently hired as transportation mechanic.

"We thought it'd be better to have the areas separated for discipline," he explained.

The eight-foot-high wall and a 16x35-foot welding classroom will be built from material left over from the original shop construction two years ago.

In other business, the 1985-86 sports schedule for football, volleyball and basketball received the board's unanimous approval. Joe Blevins, high school administrative assistant and coach, was thanked by board members

—Please See Page 3

Behind the cover

New fair queen
Kristy Klapases is crowned Intermountain Fair queen. See page 8

Ducks Unlimited
Tickets are available for the third annual Ducks Unlimited banquet at the Mt. Arthur fairgrounds. See page 6

Remains in custody
A McArthur teenager accused of kidnapping remains in custody in Lassen County jail awaiting a preliminary hearing. See page 3

Local fishing tips
Duane Milleman offers his weekly Intermountain area fishing tips on page 4

Forecast
Forecast for the Intermountain area calls for continued sunny days and fair nights throughout the rest of the week and the weekend. Little change in temperatures expected with highs in the low to mid 90s and lows in the upper 30s to mid 40s.

A weekly newspaper may display its news according to a modular format, such as in the Burney, Calif. *InterMountain News.* Reprinted by permission.

A PRESIDENT DIES
Mozambique's head of state dies in a plane crash in S. Africa. FOREIGN, Page 9.

WORLD SERIES 1986
BEATING THE ODDS
The Red Sox, two games up, are bucking history. SPORTS, Page 11.

FAIRBANKS
Daily News-Miner
Your Locally Owned Independent Daily Newspaper

VOL. LXXXIV No. 289   FAIRBANKS, ALASKA, MONDAY, OCTOBER 20, 1986   35¢ Per Copy   22 pages

Soviets expel U.S. diplomats

MOSCOW (AP)—The Soviet Union on Sunday expelled five U.S. diplomats for "impermissible activities," the official news agency Tass announced. The expulsions appeared to be in retaliation for the U.S. order for Soviet diplomats at the United Nations to leave New York.

A U.S. Embassy spokesman said an American diplomat was summoned to the Soviet Foreign Ministry on Sunday, but he refused to give any other information. Tass said an official protest note about the diplomats, four in Moscow and one at the U.S. Consulate in Leningrad, was given to the embassy on Sunday.

Tass said a statement was made to the

U.S. Embassy in Moscow today on the impermissability of the activities of a number of workers of American diplomatic missions in the Soviet Union. A firm protest was lodged with the U.S. Embassy in connection with the actions which are incompatible with their official status, the above mentioned workers of the embassy and the consulate general were declared to be persona non grata and were asked to leave the U.S.S.R.

The attention of the U.S. Embassy was again drawn to the fact of the continuing use of American diplomatic missions in the U.S.S.R. for illegal activities against the Soviet Union, and the

(See SOVIET, Back Page)

Forecast Cloudy

Interior forecast: Mostly cloudy this afternoon, high in mid 30s, light winds. Tonight partial clearing, lows in the teens, light winds. Tuesday mostly cloudy, high near 32.

Sunday skiing on Skarland

Vif Peterson, a University of Alaska Fairbanks foreign exchange student from Denmark, takes advantage of the light snowfall Sunday and tests the Skarland Trail along Ballaine Road. Tuesday's forecast is mostly cloudy with temperatures in the low 30s.

Parks Highway open; railroad still cut off

By JOHN CREED
Staff Writer

The George Parks Highway is open again after rivers swollen by heavy rains in southcentral Alaska wiped out bridges over Montana and Sheep creeks more than a week ago.

The floods also left numerous families homeless and prompted Gov. Bill Sheffield to declare the region a disaster area. Railroad and highway crews have been working ever since to bring the situation

back to normal.
Officials at the Department of Transportation of a Public Facilities said the Parks Highway out of Anchorage was open and had "light rain and good driving conditions with both bridges and other high way damage repaired.

Meanwhile, the Alaska Railroad which suffered serious damage to its link between the state's two largest cities, remained disabled and not operating between Anchorage

(See ROAD, Back Page)

Megaprojects called best alternative to militarism

TOKYO (AP)—Masaki Nakajima thinks big—like building a superhighway from central Europe to China or taming the Sahara green.

Better to spend huge sums on money on things like that, he says, than pouring it into guns and bombs.

What we need now is a concrete and widely acceptable alternative to the escalating arms race and

arms sales that keeps alive the threat of nuclear destruction. Nakajima told a recent luncheon here in his home

He is the director of the Mitsubishi Research Institute, a think tank. He also is a moving force behind the Global Infrastructure Fund (GIF), which promotes his ideas.

GIF's purpose is to get world

leaders and large corporations to fund 11 or so megaprojects like the Europe-China highway—a modern version of the ancient Silk Road—with the aim of eradicating world hunger, creating new energy sources and linking nations through prodigious transportation and communication networks.

Other megaprojects include a bridge tunnel across the Strait of

Gibraltar, a highway running north and south in Europe and a global network of super seaports.

Another proposal is a tunnel between Japan and Korea under the Sea of Japan. Still another is for a dam on the Sanpo River between China and the Indian province of Assam. The dam would divert the river through a tunnel under the Himalayas to India, making possible a hydroelectric project that could generate 200 billion kilowatt hours of power a year.

Nakajima, a former Finance Ministry official and international banker, is the first to say megaprojects don't come cheap. GIF puts the cost of financing the proposed megaprojects at $500 billion, a figure Nakajima says roughly corresponds to total U.S. military ex-

penditures during World War II.

Nakajima says the bulk of GIF's funding would come from a gradual cutback in the world's military spending on arms, thereby allowing, he argues, would more than cover the proposed budget.

Noriyo Yamamoto, a research director at the Mitsubishi Research Institute and GIF's chairman

(See IDEAS, Back Page)

Threat forces Denali Center evacuation

A bomb threat forced more than 75 residents of the Denali Center to be evacuated from their home on Gilliam Way Sunday afternoon.

Officials at the nursing home received an anonymous phone message that there was a bomb hidden somewhere in the building at 1 p.m., according to Betsy Owens, director of business and records.

Within an hour later, most of the residents were moved to shelters in Hunter Elementary School. Fairbanks Memorial Hospital and the Alaska Native Chapel on Gilliam while nurses searched for the bomb, Owens said.

Seven of the more seriously ill patients were taken to the hospital in ambulances. Others were transported to shelters in private vehicles or pushed to safety in wheelchairs. Most patients were returned to the center by 5 p.m., Owens said.

A suspect, Franklin Clay, 36, of Anchorage, was arrested at the Fairbanks International Airport at 4 p.m. and charged with terroristic threatening.

Police suspected Clay was involved with the threat because he had been in the Denali Center earlier and had a disagreement with

ALL CLEAR—Some of the 41 patients at Denali Center who sought refuge at Hunter Elementary school are wheeled back to the center.

his father-in-law, a resident of the home.

"We knew he was going to be out there at the airport and so we thought we should go out to talk him," Miller said.

An airline employee said he heard Clay make a threat over the telephone while speaking with an employee of Denali Center, according to Doyle Ruff, director of the airport.

Back in the nursing home, employees searched for the bomb while a police officer stood in the building, Owens said. That is common procedure, according to

(See DENALI, Back Page)

Land swap, utility bills for state pass Congress

By BETTY MILLS
News-Miner Bureau

WASHINGTON—In a last minute burst of activity before adjourning Saturday for the year, Congress passed several bills important to Alaska.

Among the approved measures were a land exchange for a financially troubled Native corporation in Southeast Alaska and a new program to benefit electric consumers in the state.

Major bills that died include the 1981 legislation, providing options

in Alaska Natives to deal with their stock when it becomes publicly available and a measure to reduce the adverse impacts of defiants used by foreign fishermen. Both were killed by objections from Democratic senators in the final days of Congress. Both must be reintroduced next year.

Sen. Frank Murkowski and Rep. Don Young returned to Alaska to resume their re-election campaigns before the final adjournment. Murkowski left Friday night

(See CONGRESS, Back Page)

Afghanistan pullout by Soviets called ruse

By BARRY RENFREW
Associated Press Writer

ISLAMABAD, Pakistan—The withdrawal of six Soviet regiments

News analysis

continue fighting until all of the estimated 115,000 Soviet soldiers have left.

The fundamentalist Muslim guerrillas and the countries supporting them say the Soviet withdrawal that began last Wednesday

(See AFGHAN, Back Page)

The Fairbanks (Alaska) *Daily News-Miner* and the San Marino (Calif.) *Tribune* present the news on a page that is truly a "broadsheet," each at least

San Marino Tribune

AND THE SAN MARINO NEWS
DEVOTED TO THE PROGRESS AND PROSPERITY OF SAN MARINO

Vol. 56 No. 43   282-5707   Thursday, October 24, 1985   787-3343   30c; Copy $18 Year

Prop. H Backers, Opponents Take Part In Forum

Richelieu Begins Reign As Queen

SMHS Senior, 17, Realizes Her Dream

Aimee Richelieu reacts to the announcement that she is the new Tournament of Roses Queen. Offering congratulations are princesses Tracey Langford (left) and Shannon Guernsey (rights).

Barkheimer & Aime Photo.

Aimee Richelieu

Comunity Chest Drive Begins

Along The Drive

Forum Set

Newsmakers

Sippel Named Director

Smith To Receive Award

Q and A: Board Candidates Give Their Views

News In Brief

SMHS Holds Homecoming

PTA Meeting

See Page 4

Turn to Page 11

Turn to Page 5

43

Two of five *Journal* newspapers, comparable in design and published in Maryland and Virginia adjacent to the nation's capital, are the Montgomery *Journal* in Rockville, Md. and the Fairfax *Journal* in Springfield, Va. Reprinted by permission.

When Pasternack and Utt made their 1983 study of the front pages of the nation's newspapers (see Chapter 1), 78 editors responded to the survey, out of 161 invited. All were connected with daily newspapers that had an average daily circulation of 25,000 or more, selected from the *1982 Editor & Publisher International Yearbook*. Pasternack and Utt were researching graphic and design characteristics with respect to overall design, typographical columns, the flag or nameplate, typography, photography, color, indexes/digests and the use of rules to separate columns, as well as the relationship of circulation and design to the graphic considerations that they were studying.

On a scale of 1 ("very unnoticeable") to 5 ("very noticeable"), the editors were asked to judge how noticeable to readers they felt each of several graphics to be (see Table 2). According to the researchers,

> Generally, the most noticeable items were use of graphs and maps, placement of largest photograph and body type size. Least noticed,

Table 2
Editors' Perception of What Readers Notice on Page One

	Percentage Very Noticeable	Mean Score
Overall design	67.3	3.5
Flag size	28.6	2.88
Flag location	37.7	3.04
Number of columns	22.1	2.53
Maps	75.4	4.05
Body type size	70.2	3.82
Headline typeface	50.7	3.45
Location of top story	58.5	3.63
Location of largest photo	72.8	4.01

Source: Sandra H. Utt and Steve Pasternack, "Front Pages of U.S. Daily Newspapers," *Journalism Quarterly* (1989):879–84.

in the editors' opinions, were the number of page one columns, flag size and flag location. Using the 1-to-5 noticeability rating scale, the mean overall noticeability of the nine items was 3.46.

Pasternack and Utt also studied reader perceptions of page one, and reported their findings in *Newspaper Research Journal* (1986). For this study, they selected 20 newspapers from 10 cities that had a competing and separately owned daily, where both newspapers were standard size with an average daily circulation of more than 100,000 as listed in the *1984 Editor & Publisher International Yearbook*. Students at the researchers' universities served as the study's readership population; they were asked to rate the attractiveness of graphic devices on the front pages of January 1984 newspapers.

The students rated color photos as the most attractive element (90 percent), and placement of the flag at the top of the front page next (81 percent). Further, Pasternack and Utt reported that use of a border on page one received a 27 percent response—the largest "makes no difference" score on the survey.

Newspapers have changed over the years as editors have realized the value of incorporating a design concept that unites the whole newspaper. Corollary to this is the way in which the front-page story count has changed. Today, the front page of many broadsheet newspapers rarely report more than a half-dozen events. This is a reduction from eight a decade ago—and the number of type columns has gone from eight to six, or to five in some cases.

In their 1983 study of editors' responses, Pasternack and Utt found that the "model front page" had a modular design with six columns across, and either five or six stories. In Bain and Weaver's 1979 study of student reader responses, they found that having only a few stories on page one of the *ids* (Indiana Daily Student) proved most inviting to the reader. According to the researchers,

> These experiments imply that a high story count is self-defeating. If a newspaper is striving for the highest overall readership of its stories, it will get the best results by keeping jumps to a minimum and running pictures larger.

Regarding photos, Bain and Weaver said, "The pictures experiment shows that larger photos attract more readers to accompanying stories and keep them in those stories longer." However, some editors believe that a page one with 6–10 stories on it provides "something for everyone on page one; the implication is that it won't be seen unless it's right out front."

Reid Sams, former editor of the St. Helena (Calif.) *Star,* agrees that there should be fewer, not more, stories on page one.

> While having fewer stories sometimes gives us a harder decision on which stories we should run on the front, it also gives us a cleaner looking page and the opportunity to more visually play up some of the other potential front page stories on other news pages.

Some editors have gone to running a "read" feature—a soft-news human interest story—on page one, assuming that the story will be read because of its subject. Sams, when editor of the weekly *Star,* tried to do this. "When possible," he said, "we try to run a human interest feature on the front page to interest people who don't follow hard news and to lighten the impact of having just dry hard news stories on the page."

Don Sevrens, assistant financial editor of the San Diego *Union,* says that, to be read, a story must be seen by the reader as worth the time it takes to read it.

> The secret is to have something that is readable. It does not necessarily have to be a happy story or real soft; it might be a backgrounder, a news situationer, hopefully something diverse from a trade deficit or your summit conference—perhaps something useful to people. A hard news page often can afford to contain a story that's "readable" and some art that is fun or lively—instead of two heads of state sitting in a room talking. Be imaginative.

Whether a newspaper's front-page stories have been straight news, lighter news or extended read features, the credit for its presentation being received by even the most resistant readers in recent years has been due to tighter editing and its typographical arrangement of stories and art.

Segmenting a story—breaking it into smaller units—makes it less forbidding to the reader than the same story run as an ashen-gray mass of type, and appearing long. This is especially true for news stories and news sections. Sevrens at the San Diego *Union* pointed out that "dividing the story into segments creates a greater number of entry points to lure the reader into the story."

Segmenting can be accomplished in any one of several ways, according to Sevrens.

> It may be a photo that catches your eye or the caption that tells a little bit about it. It may be the quote or splitting the story as three different phases with a 14-point intro explaining what you are doing. Segmenting gives you more chances to catch the eye of the reader and get him interested.

The design editor is given more choices to work with when segmenting within a modular makeup is the paper's style. "The more parts you have, the more ways to arrange them, group them," says Sevrens. "With one long story, the only option might be to do an L-shape wrap around a picture."

Another value of segmenting is that it can save space. Used successfully at *USA Today,* the Tampa (Fla). *Tribune,* the San Diego *Union* and many other newspapers, segmenting has become a multidimensional method of telling the story so that the reader can clearly understand its many parts. The point was made by Sevrens with this example:

> If you are doing, say, a story on the characteristics of the average real estate broker in California, median age, education and so on could be split off into a chart and edited tightly with all kinds of statistics about your average broker. Then, the story itself might focus instead on things that are drawing people into the occupation, or what kind of satisfaction they are getting from their work.

Segmenting the text and art serves the reader's needs only so long as the design is implemented according to the Total Page Concept: All elements must be arranged in a way that will enlighten—not confuse—the reader. This does not necessarily make things easier for the designer. "Segmenting does put a burden on the page designer," Sevrens said, "not just to package the parts to fill the space, but to give the reader an idea of what you are doing." Sevrens has seen pages having three or four stories, but in which the reader's eye is drawn to the sidebar—an additional story or a piece of art that supports or explains the main story. "He starts reading the sidebar and only later discovers that there is a main story it accompanies. This out-of-sequence reading is not what the page designer intended."

The organized relationship of all the various parts or elements of a page—

One story segmented into smaller bites is displayed for readers of the San Diego *Union* and the Sioux Falls, S.D. *Argus Leader*. Reprinted by permission.

the Total Page Concept—emphasizes the value of tightly edited segmenting of stories. Segmenting provides more news in less space and, as a result, is a better news service for the reader. The underlying concern is this: When stories are segmented, layouts should be clean and functional. The relationship of story and art should be obvious to the reader; text should not be wrapped around unrelated art, or displayed in such a manner that it will be confused with an adjacent story.

Liability insurance

☐ Coverage may be reinstated at higher rates

By RICHARD BALE
Argus Leader Staff

PIERRE — The Pennsylvania company that canceled South Dakota's insurance policy two weeks ago may reinstate the same policy, but possibly at higher rates.

Colonial Penn Insurance Co. and state officials have discussed continuing coverage for the third year despite the cancellation, Susan Walker, state insurance director, said.

Colonial Penn may ask for higher payments than originally agreed to for the same protection, Clyde Saukerson, an aide to Gov. William Janklow, said.

Agreeing to reinstate the old policy depends on cost; the new premiums may cost too much, Saukerson said.

Under the original policy, the state was paying about $342,000 a year for insurance against accidents and employee theft.

Walker said the state's division of insurance will look into whether Colonial Penn Insurance Co. violated a new state law by backing out of the last year of a three-year contract.

If there were a violation, the company could be forced to reinstate the old policy at the old rates.

Company officials were unavailable for comment.

The law, enacted this year, lets companies cancel policies only for specific reasons, none of which the company cited.

Saukerson said it is unclear wheth-

er the law, enacted this year, applies to the insurance contract that was signed two years ago. The contract allowed either party to cancel upon 60 days' notice, Saukerson said.

The investigation was started by Janklow after the state was notified that Colonial Penn wanted to stop insuring the state, Walker said.

Attorney General Mark Meierhenry asked Walker Monday to rule on whether the cancellation was legal. He criticized the bureau of administration's handling of the case, saying the bureau has not been aggressive enough. "I have gotten no cooperation from the bureau of administration in this whole insurance issue," he said.

☐ Lawmaker says state should insure itself

By DAVE JURGENS
Argus Leader Staff

Rep. Jerome Lammers, R-Madison, said Tuesday that he plans to propose a law for the state to insure itself.

A controversy concerning the state's insurance has arisen since Colonial Penn Insurance Co. canceled the state's liability policies Dec. 1.

"It's absurd, preposterous that any victims of an accident involving state vehicles have no remedy," Lammers said. "It's the very reason we got around to the state carrying insurance in the first place. We're going to have to do something."

With self insurance, the state would keep money normally spent on premiums and would use that money to handle claims for which the state

would be liable.

Susan Walker, director of insurance for South Dakota, said she thinks there will be many proposals on the liability issue.

"There are a lot of aspects to look at," she said. "Basically, self insurance is no insurance. The state would be taking the entire risk. I think the thing to look at is to outline the types of coverage the state is willing to pay on."

Lammers, a lawyer, said an integral part of any plan is a tort-claims act, where claims against the state are presented to a hearings officer who decides the case.

Rep. John Timmer, R-Sioux Falls, said the state should consider liability insurance only. He agrees that some form of tort law revision would be

needed if the state gets into the insurance business. He sees limits of liability and elimination of punitive damages among possible problems.

In self insurance, Timmer, an insurance salesman, sees more desire to control costs and emphasis on prevention as strong points. Cost for insurance buildings, commissions and premium taxes are avoided.

On the negative side, he asked whether the state should be involved in running an insurance company, whether the state could buy insurance to limit its liability, whether the state could implement necessary controls and supervision and whether the state should be able to use its own lawyers in defending cases brought against itself.

S.D. lawmakers are split

News pages can also include subheads, quote and statement "pullouts" set in larger-than-text type, or informational graphics to break up a sea of gray type. Design elements enhance news stories, attracting readers to the product.

Though the newspaper is a messenger of both good and bad tidings, the consistency of its design will improve its chances of being received favorably, especially if its contents are well organized and therefore easily read, right from the start on page one.

This Orlando (Fla.) *Sentinel* page one is a window that brings the reader into the paper. Reprinted by permission.

FRONT PAGE AND NEWS SECTION SPECIFICS

Page one is the entryway through which the reader approaches the entire newspaper. William B. Dunn, managing editor of the Orlando (Fla.) *Sentinel*, sees page one as being especially significant. As quoted by Mark Fitzgerald in *Editor & Publisher* (1985), Dunn said, "The front page, in effect, (is) our corporate identity, it is—as we say in Florida—the prime real estate in journalism."

In order to be worthwhile to the reader, page one must provide direct access to its own content as well as to the remainder of the newspaper. Prime content and attractive graphics are a good beginning; but, going beyond that, the ex-

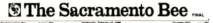

The Sacramento Bee
FINAL

Flood fears keep rising

Sacramento under siege | Dam breaks, homes awash

Many aren't waiting to pack bags

Duke declares re-election bid

Bradley forces call televised speech unfair, lodge protest

Reagan starts big push for more aid to contras

The Modesto Bee
TURLOCK/SOUTH EDITION

'85 tax forms in mail
Packet comes with an apology

Mount Etna eruption — one death

A young woman watches as Mount Etna spews lava and smoke early Christmas morning.

Record valley fog is showing no signs of leaving

MD suggests doctors attend patients' funerals

Workers gather signatures for insurance crisis initiative

Insurance CRISIS

The Fresno Bee
VALLEY EDITION

FRESNO, CALIFORNIA, Friday Morning, April 19, 1985

Nicaraguan rebels' aid passes test

Yocum witness called a sly liar
Cox murder trial gets under way

Turner will try CBS grab
Bid wins support from Sen. Helms faction

He almost gave up

Panel OKs rules for lottery ticket sales

Seat-belt bill defeated in state Senate

Saving farmland possible, Sierra Club director says

These three newspapers published by McClatchy in California offer a well-organized story presentation for readers of the Sacramento *Bee*, the Modesto *Bee* and the Fresno *Bee*. Reprinted by permission.

Inside

More fog

Fog and low clouds tonight with light northeast wind. Chance of morning drizzle, partial afternoon clearing. Lows 30 to 35; highs 40 to 45. Details on Page 4B.

Index

Classified
Phones

Our phones
Information
Circulation

- *Shuttle's holiday flight aborted on brink of liftoff. Page 3A.*

- *Boy dies two days after rescue from icy pond. Page 3A.*

- *M-I-C (see you in Paris) K-E-Y . . . (Why? Because France wins bid for Disney park.) Page 3A.*

- *Minnesota woman gets smaller version of plastic heart. Page 12A.*

TODAY'S GAZETTE

THE WEATHER
Cloudy Saturday with a chance of morning showers, highs 75 to 80. Clear and cool Saturday night, lows 50 to 55. Sunny and cool on Sunday, in the 70s.

DAILY THOUGHT
A single sunbeam is enough to drive away many shadows.
— St. Francis of Assisi

A quick index on page one organizes the reader; designs for the index vary, as seen in these from the Everett, Wash. *Herald* and the Northampton, Mass. *Daily Hampshire Gazette*. Reprinted by permission.

istence or lack of an easy-to-read index and related typographical elements will either guide the reader into or steer the reader away from the inside pages. A quick index should be provided on page one even if a more complete index— call it news summary, briefs, capsules or "What's Inside"—appears on page two or three. Readers will often first take notice of a summary referring to more details on an inside page; then they read through the whole newspaper, and check back with the summary to make certain that nothing of interest has been missed.

Gerald Stone, John Schweitzer and David Weaver in their 1978 study (cited in Chapter 1) and Pasternack and Utt in their 1983 study found little or no attempt to provide a page-one news digest, while Pasternack and Utt also noted in 1983 that the majority of front pages in their study contained an index, usually in the lower left-hand corner with a box around it.

Schweitzer also sampled 376 households of adults who read the Dayton (Ohio) *Journal Herald* to find out their reactions to the look of three randomly selected pages. His results were reported in the *Newspaper Research Journal* (1980). Readers in the survey were asked whether a front page with a news summary referring to inside pages and with index boxes over the flag would be favorably or unfavorably received. The kind of news summary that was favored by at least a plurality of those responding was the vertically placed style; next came the kind that is printed horizontally across the bottom of the page. Boxes above the flag were also favored by readers.

"Editors who choose to use news summary columns and boxes may have the best of both worlds," Schweitzer reported. "They may increase the reader appeal of the front page and keep the story count high at the same time." A corollary factor, he said, was that summaries increase story count and enhance a modern

NEWSLINE

THE WEST

Teacher workshop offered

TAYLORSVILLE — Registration will be accepted at the door for the Give Your Students the World workshop Saturday at the College Center, Utah Technical College, 4600 S. Redwood Road.

GIVE YOUR STUDENTS THE WORLD

W O R K S H O P

At the day-long workshop, which begins at 8:30 a.m., teachers will explore ways newspapers can be used to teach language arts, math, science, health and social studies.

The $25 registration fee covers lunch, curriculum materials, including the Deseret News weekly teaching aid for the remainder of the 1985-86 school year, and 150 newspapers.

Quick capsules make it easy to organize the page and to give it a sense of action, as seen in this "roundup" example from the Salt Lake City, Utah *Desert News*. Small photos and other graphic elements lure readers into the summaries. Reprinted by permission.

tabloid format—which is not to be confused with the sensational tabloid newspapers.

News summary items may be published on page two or three or on page one as a two-column "chimney." Some items refer readers to full stories on other pages, and others can be complete in themselves. On the day of an important breaking story, it may be worthwhile to scrap the traditional page-one summaries, and to use the entire page for full story and art coverage of the big event. However, breaking away from routine-day design does not mean throwing out all of the everyday guidelines. The foundation of the Total Page Concept rests on design consistency. The special-day newspaper should look like it is published by the same staff that edits the paper every other day.

Utility panel lawyer gets commission nod

By SARALEE TIEDE
Star-Telegram Austin Bureau

AUSTIN — Assistant Attorney General Jo Campbell, who has been defending the Public Utility Commission in court, today was named the third member of the commission.

Campbell, 54, immediately pledged to take a hard look at utility company costs to ensure that they were reasonable and prudent.

"I would not say I am anti-industry, but I do expect them to meet that burden," she said.

Jo Campbell

Gov. Mark White acknowleged that Campbell was indeed a graduate of Baylor University, White's alma mater, as are many of White's other top appointees.

"But I want to make it clear that she has never been a roommate of

nouncement at his weekly news conference, said he named Campbell because of her knowlege of utility law.

"She will see that consumers do not spend one penny more than necessary for utility bills," he said.

One of her first duties will be to join other commissioners at hearings in Beaumont and Conroe, where customers of Gulf States Utilities have been outraged at paying rates 40 percent higher than customers across the state line in Louisiana.

White said he requested the hearings so commissioners could discover if Texans were subsidizing Louisiana's low rates and if Gulf States mismanaged the construction of the costly River Bend nuclear plant.

River Bend and other nuclear plants soon to come on line may spell spiraling rates for Texas consumers unless the commission can devise ways of holding the line

Campbell said she wanted to explore the idea of phased-in rates that would ease the "rate shock" of the

Even a face alone can provide a story reference. Rather than printing a full-column photograph, the text–photo relationship can be made just as easily with a space-saving ''thumbnail'' photo, as shown here in the Fort Worth (Texas) *Star-Telegram*. Reprinted by permission.

2 B The MAIL TRIBUNE. Medford, Oregon. Friday, August 5, 1983

Shrine game will mark Spieg's 'last hurrah'

By DON HUNT
Mail Tribune Sports Writer

Fred Spiegelberg retired as Medford High's football coach nearly seven months ago, but the living legend isn't quite finished barking out instructions or drawing Xs and Os.

Spieg is in Portland this week, serving as an assistant coach for the South squad which will battle the North in the 36th annual Shrine All-Star game at Civic Stadium.

Kickoff is scheduled for 7:30 p.m. Saturday at Civic Stadium.

"This is my last hurrah and I have to admit I'm a little nostalgic about it," said Spieg, who guided the Black Tornado for 37 years. "They've treated me awfully good up here — wining and dining me, roasting me (at a dinner a week ago Wednesday) and what have you."

Saturday night's game will mark the 14th time Spieg has coached at the Shrine game with his debut coming in 1955.

"Geez, it sure doesn't seem like it's been 28 years since I came up here and coached for the first time," said Spieg, who had no trouble recalling the names of Paul Eckel, Rocky Stone and the late Mike DeVore, the Medford players who accompanied him to Portland in 1955.

Spieg admits he'll miss coaching but is quick to add he's happy to be able to pursue other interests such as golfing and traveling.

"There's been a reunion of my Army buddies in Pennsylvania for the past 10 years during September and now I can finally get back there and see those guys," says Spieg, a captain and rifle company commander who served in Germany during World War II. "These guys have been bugging me for a long time to get back there but with football I could never get away. I haven't seen them in 38 years."

Spieg hopes to bow out of football on a winning note Saturday night but says the South squad "doesn't look strong this year."

Fred Spiegelberg
A bit nostalgic

Head South coach Randy Wegner of Lebanon concurs, but says the down-state boys aren't about to concede.

"Last year we had exceptional speed and some good, strong kids up front," says Wegner, recalling the South's easy 34-7 victory. "This year we're not very big, but we're disciplined and have come together very well as a unit."

Medford's Jerry Varner has earned a start at offensive guard and Black Tornado grad Randy Heath will open in the defensive backfield for the South.

Ashland's Ted Leybold is in a close battle for the starting center job, Wegner said.

Both teams are expected to feature strong running games. Wegner, who runs the option-oriented veer offense at Lebanon where he's led the Warriors to back-to-back runnerup finishes in the state playoffs, will plug two of his players into the starting backfield — quarterback Cliff Walker and 5-11, 195-pound halfback Mark Halstengard.

Walker, a small (5-8, 165) but fleet signal-caller with a better-than-adequate arm, rushed for 900 yards and threw for more than 1,000 for Lebanon last season while Halstengard accounted for more than 1,300 yards on the ground.

The North had expected to open with either Sunset's Matt Poorman or Canby's Blaine Polendey at quarterback, but Barlow's Bill Fellows, who originally had been penciled in for defensive duty, has taken over the leading role.

The 6-2, 180-pound Fellows led Barlow to a 9-2 record last season at quarterback but doubled as a defensive back when he gained all-state mention.

"We were primarily looking at Fellows in the secondary but we also had him working out at quarterback and he just took over right from the start," says North coach Gary Stautz, who led Gresham to the state championship last fall. "He's been aggressive in everything he's done."

Fellows is expected to run the option and hand the ball off more often than throw it, although with assistant coach Tom Smythe, the run-and-shoot advocate from Lakeridge, you can bet the North hasn't ditched the aerial game.

"My philosophy has always been to run the ball more than pass it but Tom and I are combining our thoughts," Stautz says. "We'd like to achieve some balance."

The South is working on a three-game winning streak and has tasted victory 12 of the past 17 seasons. This season the South is considered the underdog but that was also the case last year when the South embarrassed the North.

"I think one reason the South has had the edge is because they come up here trying to show the city kids some respect," Stautz says. "The North has had a tendency to pop off before the game while the South has kept its mouth shut and done its talking on the field.

"That hasn't been the case this year. The North has maintained a low profile.

"The North has been a cocky, snooty bunch in the past but this year they've been humble and pleasant to be around. Wegner says. "It's kind of scary."

SHRINE NOTES — This year's contest is expected to net at least $50,000 for the Shriners Hospital in Portland. The All-Star game has contributed more than $1.2 million to the hospital since the inaugural game in 1948. attendance is expected to be around 15,000.

A "thumbnail" column photo works well when the type is set wide measure, as in this example from the Medford, Ore. *Mail Tribune,* or when played adjacent to the headline, as in the Oklahoma City, Okla. *Journal Record.* Reprinted by permission.

Photographs of individual faces—thumbnail size—are commonly used on the front page and throughout the paper. An action photo taken during a news event—even when it shows facial expression alone—will always have more impact than a photo made of the same person at a professional portrait studio. In every case, the person should still be identifiable despite the photo reduction.

Pasternack and Utt found that, in their 1983 study, half the stories on page one continued to an inside page (see Table 3). Projecting this pattern throughout the nation's newspapers, we find a major consideration for the designer in deciding where stories should be jumped. Many newspapers today jump all stories

Table 3
Newspapers That Jumped Stories from Page One

	Percentage
Never jump	8.0
Jump less than 25%	20.0
Jump 25–50%	24.0
Jump 50.1–75%	24.0
Jump 75.1–99.9%	18.7
Jump 100%	5.3

Source: Sandra H. Utt and Steve Pasternack, "Front Pages of U.S. Daily Newspapers," *Journalism Quarterly* (1989):879–84.

to the same page, often the back page of the section in which they began. While this is a valuable assist for the reader, it can lead to graphic boredom on the page limited to continuations. This can be alleviated by:

- providing strong enough headlines so that the reader immediately knows which jumped story is which;
- running only one or two continuations, with art, on each jump page; or
- running a nonjump story, perhaps with a piece of art, on the jump page.

State may pay Mecham's recall bill

By MARK FLATTEN
Progress Staff Writer
Taxpayers may have to pick up Gov. Evan Mecham's campaign bill if he faces a recall election.
Article eight, section six of the Arizona Constitution states that when a public official is recalled, the public treasury must pay the "reasonable special election campaign expenses of such officer."

That appears to mean Arizona taxpayers would have to reimburse Mecham for campaign expenses he runs up in a recall election, said Jim Shumway, head of the elections office for the Secretary of State's office.
John Shadegg, the assistant state attorney general who handles election matters, said no one had pointed out the constitutional provision until

he was contacted by the *Scottsdale Progress.*
Shadegg said he would have to research the article before issuing an opinion whether public money would have to be spent to help keep Mecham in office.
"We'll have to see if there is an identical provision in any other state and if so, how it's been construed before I would want to say anything

about it."
Shumway said the provision has never been invoked in Arizona and never has been raised as an issue.
There was an attempt to recall former Gov. Jack Williams, but there were not enough valid petition signatures gathered to force a special election, so the issue did not come up, he said.
Though he cautioned an inter-

pretation of the constitution would have to come from the attorney general, Shumway said he understands the article to mean the Legislature must appropriate whatever sum it considers reasonable to pay for Mecham's campaign expenses.
A new law would have to be approved by the Legislature because there is no statute providing for

reimbursement, Shumway said.
Shumway added that since the article says the law shall be passed, he would interpret that to mean it is beyond the discretion of the Legislature.
Senate Majority Leader Robert Usdane, R-Scottsdale, said today he is "flabbergasted" at the provision, saying he fears it is so open-ended
See RECALL, Page 2

 *Iraqi planes attack*

It would be ideal to have no stories continue to another page; but if jumps are kept to a minimum, as seen in the Scottsdale (Ariz.) *Progress*, they do serve the useful purpose of fitting more stories on the front page. Reprinted by permission.

While most newspapers do jump stories from page one (especially) to some other page, Jonathan Marshall, editor and publisher of the Scottsdale (Ariz.) *Daily Progress,* says that his paper avoids doing so: "Several years ago we stopped jumping stories because people don't read stories if they jump."

Over the years—in spite of variations in the specifics of design—one aspect of the successful newspaper has remained constant: the news itself. However, where the Total Page Concept prevails, even the presentation of the news has changed. To a much greater degree than was previously acceptable, all elements must be placed on the page so that they complement one another attractively.

4 Designing Inside Sections and Pages with Advertising

Determining how ads are laid out on a particular page should be a cooperative venture with both the Ad and News departments working together. While the Ad Department will definitely determine the layout of the day's paper, the overall policy of layout should be a joint venture.

Darell Phillips
publisher
Manteca (Calif.) *Bulletin*

In spite of many changes in the evolution of newspaper design—with most designers now recognizing the value of pages with a dominant piece of art or text—it is unlikely that dominant design will ever be considered more important than the news itself. Most often, pages without advertising—page one and section front pages—will be the ones where a dominant design element is found. Total Page Concept (TPC) design on the remaining pages becomes a matter of making the best with what's left over after the ads are placed.

INSIDE FEATURES AND SPECIAL-INTEREST PAGES

Newspapers have changed with the times, ever striving to attract and serve the readership. The purpose of printing inside features and many special interest pages is to encourage readers to look at every page.

Brian Steffens of the Los Angeles *Times* Orange County Edition says, "The idea of a dominant story on every page is a good one, but on section pages a lot of times the element that will get you to the page is the dominant art, and the dominant art does not necessarily go with the lead story." In the case of many news stories, including the important ones, good art is lacking. "A lot of politics stuff is important, but the pictures are mug shots. A lot of the papers run the mug shot large because it goes with the important story, but I think that's a mistake."

Steffens suggested printing the strongest picture large and in a strong position on the page to attract the reader. Editors, he said, "think because it is an important story, there must be good art with it. They are two different animals. Both photo or graphics *and* the stories should have good content. But just because one exists, it doesn't mean that the other does. It's hard to make that point (emphasis in original)." As quoted by George Tuck in the *APME News* (1985), David Owens, graphics director of the Albuquerque (N.M.) *Journal,* said, "We try to think of a story as a package on the page where the quality and quantity of content to reach the reader is directly related to how we present the information."

In the case of the dullest story in the world, or even one that has intrigue— such as the city treasurer embezzling funds—it is quite possible that it can best be told through type alone, or type with only an identifying face of the source quoted in the story, or type and a simple informational graphic such as a pie chart or a bar graph. If that is all that can be pulled from the story—along with several quoteouts or readouts, perhaps—then that should satisfy the design editor. The reader does not expect a special complete art package with a story— only the text and whatever may be available to make it easily comprehendible.

For example, Steffens said, there might be a breaking story from Washington, D.C., such as a change in the trade rules. The story itself is significant, but there may be no art available to print with the text. This causes a dilemma because most editors believe that a news story must have appropriate art to accompany it. This is a typical scenario, according to Steffens:

> "That's our best story," [the editor will say.] "We have to have the art and throw it out on the cover." And when the reader or potential reader walks by the newsstands and sees another picture [of the president] it doesn't help sell the paper or sell the story. If on the other hand, you say, "I have this nice picture of something else going on in the world, maybe not even hard news—general news or something," they have trouble with that. It's not important, it's not significant. I think the paper needs important, significant and interesting art. But is breadth so inferior to depth? Why not spread the attack?

As newspapers adapt to the computer age, TPC design is being used to develop not only the timely hard-news pages and stories, but even more so the pages with soft-news feature stories. The Total Page Concept can easily meld elements together and tell a more thorough who/what news story, as well as illustrate the how/why news or feature story in more detail. Segmenting the main article with several small stories or including a drawing and a little more white space will make the story read better than one so lengthy that most readers never finish it.

Because broadsheet pages are relatively difficult to look at all in one glance, they tend to cause visual competition. The page's "news hole"—the space available for news—must be thoughtfully weighed against the number and size of text and graphic elements if its design is to even approach being a satisfactory example of the Total Page Concept.

How inside pages are designed may make the difference between whether a reader turns from one page to the next, reads or at least glances at the news editorial matter and advertising, or only turns to a single special page or section and discards the rest of the paper. While many designers do have an opportunity to make the most of the inside pages dominated by advertising, some newspaper editors quickly dispose of these pages by filling them with any text or illustrative material that fits.

Steffens confirmed this point: "On a lot of inside pages, editors back and fill," arbitrarily stuffing news into space around advertising. "If they're modular pancakes, you have all these thin strips and you end up with all these headlines as big as the story," he explained. To span five columns, for instance, it becomes almost necessary to go to a 48-point head (where 72 points equal one inch). If the story is only two inches deep and there are four stories going down a well—adjacent to an overwhelming ad—the result is that the headlines may indeed lead the reader to each story, but the design is not especially attractive. "The heads are almost too much for the story. They take up too much space and those that are tucked up against the side of the page get missed. A story that might be below the fold on an inside page won't get seen."

Steffens recommended redoing the page vertically, getting more headlines toward the top. This will bring the reader to the page, "and you're not eating up space with all those pancakes." He said that the *Times-Picayune* in New Orleans is an example of a newspaper where the stories on the inside pages are played so that the reader can easily find them.

Inside and special section pages that need design attention include—but are certainly not limited to—the headings of advice, agriculture, arcade, arts and entertainment, business, calendar, comics, fashion, finance, focus, games, lifestyle, opinions/editorials, radio–television, religion, sports, travel and weather. Special topic sections may also be run when appropriate for a particular subject of interest or for a community day or event.

While a designer may be less restrained when displaying stories and features on these inside soft-news pages and sections, design standards established in the news sections should prevail. In certain circumstances, art type or silhouettes (figures with background cut away)—if used sparingly—might have an attractive effect on special pages. When the subject of a story calls for it, the editor can encourage people to read more of the newspaper by using the publication's design concept to create a flashy, visual, vibrant and vital look on its inside pages. Pages designed according to TPC guidelines will not be left to fate.

Don Sevrens, assistant financial editor of the San Diego *Union,* is one editor

Tackling breaks down on two 49er TD plays

By JIMMY SMITH
Staff writer

It often sounded like oversimplification when deposed Saints' coach Bum Phillips would stress how important it was to block well and tackle well.

But as New Orleans' defenders grasped hopelessly at the ozone again Sunday — for the second week in a row — that folksy prattle on fundamentals really hit home.

It certainly wasn't hitting anything else.

The Saints again proved to be missed-tackle clinicians in a 31-19 loss to the playoff-hopeful San Francisco 49ers, endlessly failing to seize ball carriers and pass receivers when the opportunity presented itself.

And, unfortunately, the opportunity presented itself on two big plays that turned into San Francisco touchdowns.

"Yep," said Wade Phillips, "it hurt us some."

"That's what it amounted to today," said cornerback Johnnie Poe. "We missed a lot of tackles."

One of the biggest unsuccessful tackling attempts came with just less than two minutes gone in the third quarter.

San Francisco quarterback Joe Montana hit 6-foot-3, 215-pound wide receiver Mike Wilson on a slant pattern from the Niners' 3-yard line

Warren's TD gains him a niche in Saints' lore

Call it another great moment in Saints' history.

It happened in the Saints' 31-19 loss to San Francisco Sunday in the Superdome.

When Frank Warren blocked a Ray Wersching field-goal attempt and ran the ball back 42 yards for a touchdown, it marked the first time the Saints had ever scored a touchdown on such a play in their 19-year history.

In fact it was only the second time the Saints had ever scored a touchdown on a blocked kick. The only other time something similar happened was when Charlie Brown returned a blocked punt for a touchdown in 1968.

Warren was ecstatic when told that his name would now be indelibly imprinted in Saints' lore.

"It hasn't sunk in yet," Warren said. "It means a lot to me, because it was the first time. That means I made history. It means a lot because I don't get a lot of chances to make big plays like that."

The play happened late in the second quarter when San Francisco was attempting a 52-yard field goal. Warren broke through the line and blocked the kick. When Warren went after the ball, it bounced into his arms at the 49ers' 42 and he went untouched into the end zone.

"I thought we had a chance to block it," Warren said. "(James) Geathers told me before the play he would drag the guard down and that should make a hole for me to go through. He dragged him down, I went through the guard and tackle and the rest is history."

It certainly is.

Mario Cruz

I do. I can make a tackle. All I've got to do is put my arm around him. It was so blatant. And they score off it.

"I'm the goat for that play. I got caught out in the middle of the field where everybody could

So you get a chance to miss a guy sometime."

Nevertheless, the Saints didn't do much of anything defensively. Montana led the 49ers to 500 total yards of offense, San Francisco' most productive output of

The New Orleans *Times-Picayune* is one newspaper that places stories according to a vertical display. Reprinted by permission.

who does not believe that every page in the newspaper should look like a duplicate of every other.

> The idea of every section of the paper looking exactly like every other part, to me, seems like we are giving the reader just a homogenized type of product. The feature sections should be fun. You have so many more possibilities than with your straight news sections. So why hobble them with ball-and-chain rules appropriate to the hard news sections?

Continuity from hard news to softer news pages and sections is created by a strong commitment to the Total Page Concept. If every page were designed with a thought for what the reader must go through to read its contents, then the reader would be lured into and through each page, as well as the adjacent or following pages where a story might be continued. More direction, packaging and white space should be provided for the reader on inside pages and sections than on front pages. The route for the eye to travel should be obvious, whether reading a scoreboard on the sports page or recipes on the food page. Packaging may include the use of large photos and illustrations, stories set in reduced width, and/or boxes that begin with a large capital letter. White space should be concentrated on the outside of pages with the story and art gathered toward the center, leaving no trapped white space. Trapped white space inevitably becomes the dominant page element. To be consistent in the use of packaging and white space, pages should be put together under the guidance of a designer or graphics editor—or at least a staff member who does other tasks but whose special talent is design.

Editors for the inside pages live with the constant challenge of placing graphic elements so that the eye catches all the stories and art. This should be done whether the elements are adjacent to one another on a tight page, whether they need to be positioned so as not to bump against or compete with advertising, or whether too many items have been anticipated for the page. Designers must

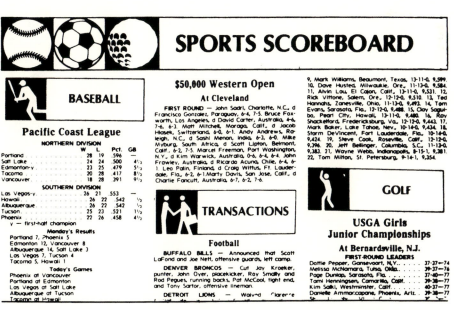

A popular feature in many newspapers is the sports-section scoreboard of capsule information about national and local athletic events and activities, arranged with graphic symbols, as in the Eugene, Ore. *Register-Guard.* Reprinted by permission.

engage in thoughtful editing and effective placement of text type, photos or illustrative art and white space within various rectangular, horizontal and vertical shapes.

Clear or open pages are relatively easy to design if there are enough stories and art to use. However, whether clear or including advertisements, the page design should have one dominant element—a piece of art or, if this is not possible, a well-displayed story—to provide a place for the eye to begin reading.

Elements that anchor the page corners where there is no advertising are also important for inside pages, especially clear pages, and may be done by a variety of methods: screening a story, running a short informational box, or printing a standing feature or column.

The Baton Rouge, La. *Morning Advocate* gives a base to an inside page with an across-the-bottom standing feature anchor. Reprinted by permission.

While the rest of the newspaper changes its content display with each issue, the opinions/editorial page should provide from day to day (or week to week) a similar design format including editorials, columns, letters and other features, so that the reader can count on at least this one page to look reassuringly predictable. The op/ed page might also contain the names of the key editors and the newspaper's mailing address, phone number and letters policy placed where they can be easily found by readers wanting to write a letter to the editor or otherwise contact someone at the newspaper office.

Robert L. Wilson, design editor at the *Commercial Appeal* in Memphis, Tenn. explained in detail how the organization process works at his paper.

> The *Commercial Appeal*'s design desk was formed in the summer of 1985 and has evolved into the nerve center of operation for the newspaper.

LETTER GUIDELINES

Today's Mail

LETTERS

Super Bureaucrat

I had a dream the other night . . .

Bud Bureaucrat was in charge of negotiating with the NFL over the use of the Rose Bowl. The NFL wanted Pasadena to waive its normal $50,000 rental fee; after all, they reasoned, "Look at all the business that will pour into Pasadena's shops, restaurants and hotels; why it could be over $100 million." But our stalwart Mr. Bureaucrat was not buying that line. Sure, Southern California may benefit from that largesse, but little old Pasadena gets only some crumbs.

Your big banquets are in Century City or downtown L.A., the teams are all headquartered in Orange County, where no doubt the biggest fans will also stay, the limo business will mostly go to the West Side boys, our better restaurants are all pretty full on Saturday night anyway, so I don't see much gain there, but then all the big spenders are being wined and dined in a special tent city (property fenced, of course, to keep ordinary folks out).

Now, efficient Bud Bureaucrat had a better idea. He said, "Tell you what I am going to do, Mr. Commissioner, we will give you the Rose Bowl rent-free, but we want to buy 1,200 tickets at face value. Then we can do something nice for the people of Pasa-

dena." And so it went. You see, Bud was going to run a little lottery with those seats and give each citizen of Pasadena a chance to see one of sport's great events live and in person. There was even some talk about using the lottery to raise a few bucks for the city.

Then I woke up and realized it was just a dream. The dream was almost true, though, the city did get 1,200 tickets but they went to the city directors and officials, who sold them to their friends, who sold them to their friends and maybe they will sell one to you, for only $500.

ROBERT DEMPSTER
Pasadena

In displaying the letters to the editor policy, it is as important to clearly tell readers how they might write as it is to choose the most advantageous placement and type point size. The three different examples here are from the Cedar Rapids (Iowa) *Gazette,* the Lincoln (Neb.) *Star* and the Pasadena, Calif. *Star-News.* The latter adds interest by printing photos of the letter writers. Reprinted by permission. Lincoln (Neb.) *Star* copyright by the Journal-Star Printing Company.

Victor H. Hanson II/Publisher

James E. Jacobson/Editor   Thomas E. Bailey/Managing Editor   James R. McAdory Jr./Editorial Page Editor
Victor Hanson/Publisher 1910-1945   Clarence B. Hanson Jr./Publisher 1945-1983

Thursday · May 29, 1986

For State Senate

In the only Democratic primary contest for the state Senate in Jefferson or Shelby County, Birmingham City Councilwoman Bettye Fine Collins is seeking to unseat Sen. John Amari in District 15

Amari's tenure in the Senate has been controversial, at least in part because it is so difficult to categorize or pigeonhole his voting record. He votes independently, not following the lead of any special interest group...

Sen. Soaper
By Doug Larson

After you become a senior citizen you wonder what happened to the freshman sophomore and junior years.

Roanoke Times & World-News

BARTON W. MORRIS   GENE A. OWENS   WALTER RUGABER
Chairman of the Board   Editorial Page Editor   President and Publisher

FORREST M. LANDON   ROBERT N. FISHBURN   WILLIAM K. WARREN JR.
Executive Editor   Commentary Page Editor   Managing Editor

EDITORIAL

Duane K. McCallister President and Publisher
Frank Sutherland Managing Editor
Ben Lee Editorial Page Editor
A GANNETT NEWSPAPER
Leonard Lowrey (1921-1982). American reporter and editor 1938-1982.

The Associated Press is entitled exclusively to the use for publication of all local news printed in this newspaper as well as all AP news dispatches.

The desk was conceived as a method to lend consistency and organization to the appearance of the newspaper. It was felt that centralizing this portion of the daily operation would smooth copy flow and allow an added area of specialization, thereby sharpening another aspect of the product.

This is how it works, Wilson said:

Design desk personnel assemble every page in the paper, except the sports section and the editorial and op–ed pages.

On any given day, one person is handed the responsibility for the design of one section of the newspaper. The *Commercial Appeal* has four live news sections each day, not counting sports. One designer handles page one and the rest of Section A, which consists mainly of jumps from page one and a few inside wire stories.

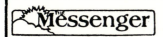

▲The Messenger	Fort Dodge, Iowa L. Jay Smith Walter B. Stevens	131st Year General Manager Editor

Statesman ✦ Journal

John H. McMillan Publisher	**Edward P. Bassett** Editor
Van Eisenhut Managing Editor	**John Ericksen** Associate Editor
Daniel W. Davies City Editor	**J. Wesley Sullivan** Chairman Editorial Board
Don Scarborough News Editor	**Lance W. Dickie** Editorial Page Editor
Wilma Bonsanti Regional Editor	**Don Black** Features Editor
Larry Roby Community Affairs Editor	**Steven K. Bagwell** Government Editor
Mike Williams Photo Editor	**Marc Faulconer** Sports Editor

The editorial policies of the Statesman-Journal are established by an editorial board. Its members are J. Wesley Sullivan, chairman; John H. McMillan, publisher; Edward P. Bassett, editor; Van Eisenhut, managing editor; John Ericksen, associate editor; Steven K. Bagwell, government editor; and Lance W. Dickie, editorial page editor.

The Statesman-Journal is the successor to The Oregon Statesman, founded March 28, 1851, and the Capital Journal, founded March 1, 1888.

The staff box on the editorial page may be presented in at least three types of display: (1) across the full top of the page, as done at the Birmingham (Ala.) *News;* (2) in a box at the top left, usually above the editorials, as found in the Roanoke (Va.) *Times & World News* and the Hattiesburg (Miss.) *American;* and (3) as the lower left page anchor, as at the Fort Dodge, Iowa *Messenger* and the Salem, Ore. *Statesman-Journal.* Reprinted by permission.

The front of Section B and the first couple of inside pages are designated for regional coverage and metropolitan news. The pages are, as a matter of course, changed with each of our six editions nightly, though they are not always redesigned wholesale. One designer is responsible for these pages for the course of an evening.

The *Commercial Appeal* gets double duty from Section B for news fronts, giving the newspaper five wide open fronts in four sections. The back page of the section serves as our business front, and any stories on that page that jump into the inside business pages actually jump to pages with a lower number. This arrangement, though it sounds strange on the surface, actually gives our readers an added menu of departmentalized material from which to choose and allows almost daily use of color on an additional section front. One designer is assigned to assemble these pages, along with placing the stock market agate. Changes are fewer in later editions in this section, so

A section page like this one in the Memphis, Tenn. *Commercial Appeal* should come early in the paper's production process and be given adequate time for planning and execution, especially if it has a color feature display. Reprinted by permission. Copyright by the *Commercial Appeal.*

the business designer has the added responsibility of helping out on late changes on the regional and metro pages.

Section C is the Appeal section, our lifestyle coverage. Though the preponderance of the copy in this section is of less timely nature and can be termed "soft news," the *Commercial Appeal* prefers to make its assembly a day-by-day operation. This tends to give it a more immediate feel and allows flexibility for last-minute changes and coverages. One designer is responsible for this section, which runs from six to 12 pages, depending on the day of the week. The Appeal designer also gets an earlier start than the others.

The other five designers on the desk are involved in the assembly of Sunday off-sections and special projects. One of these design desk employees is the makeup editor, whose responsibility it is to see that artwork is distributed to the appropriate pages and that corrections in type coding are expedited rapidly. He serves as a troubleshooter in the composing room, anticipating problems and heading them off. His main function is to do whatever is necessary to get the edition in on time.

Wilson went on to say,

Copy is fed to the design desk from the various originating departments—the wire desk, business news department, Appeal department, regional news desk and the metropolitan desk. They give the designer a list of story slugs that includes a recommended length, notation of cutability and an indication of the story's priority in relation to other material on the list.

Photographs, whether they accompany copy from any of these departments or stand alone, are furnished by the picture desk. Their responsibility is to decide how the photographs should best be displayed in terms of size and cropping.

The designer takes recommendations from both the copy originating desk and the picture desk and assembles them into pages that reflect the design goals set forth for the *Commercial Appeal*. It should be noted, though, that these goals evolve constantly, so that the newspaper does not develop a stagnant appearance. This effort is tempered by those areas of the newspaper that should be predictable, such as the wire news brief column which is anchored on the same page every day.

All copy that is handled by the design desk is coded for length and forwarded to the copy desk with headline instructions attached. Our universal copy desk edits all the copy and writes headlines and sets the copy into type. At this point, designers usually go to the composing room to oversee the composition of their individual pages.

Every individual and department in the copy chain has its own deadlines to meet, with the preset composing room closing time being the final one.

And in summary, Wilson said,

We feel this operational chain offers the production of the *Commercial Appeal* strength that is also flexible.

The design desk is but one link in that chain, but it continues to get stronger while it assumes an evermore vital role in the daily operation of the *Commercial Appeal.*

DESIGNING NEWS/ADVERTISING COMPLEMENTS

Inside pages are seldom open display pages. Story lengths and graphic elements must compete for the balance of space available; the designer receives pages after the advertising has been placed on them. Pages with advertising—especially with many ads or a few very large ones—need to be designed so the reader will miss neither the stories nor the advertising. This does not make the task of being creative any easier, but it does make application of the Total Page Concept challenging. It follows, then, that a basic understanding of advertising is needed in order to design news space.

Facing the formidable competition of television's color and movement, newspaper advertising departments have had to change their old ways to attract readers. Advertisers who once exclusively used newspapers to sell their products no longer do so. Today, newspaper advertisements must lure the reader immediately to the ad through design. The reader must notice something in the ad worth purchasing, usually seen in black and white amid fierce competition from every other ad on the page and in the newspaper—and in a world that abounds with color. It is not an easy task to design a memorable advertisement using only black, white and shades of gray.

While some pages—such as the front page, the opinion/editorial page, a photo section or a special section page—may be ad free, most pages will have one or more advertisements. Size and design are the keys to advertising readership, not position on the page. According to John Ferguson, business manager of the *News Chronicle* in Thousand Oaks, Calif., "Ads should always be designed with the idea that advertising is news, too. A poorly designed ad will not only have poor readership, but will also detract the reader from the entire page."

Based on the ad sizes that have been sold, advertisements may be placed horizontally across the bottom of the page, vertically stacked as a chimney of same-size ads on the left- or right-hand side, in a vertical pyramid or stair-step manner (also on either the left or right side) or some combination of these. Darell Phillips, publisher of the Manteca (Calif.) *Bulletin,* commented that some might say "it is up to the Ad Department to determine if a well or pyramid right layout should be used. But a News Department layout policy which, for instance, has a briefs column down the left side of each page must be considered."

Horizontal advertising provides the best page-design possibilities because jagged edges around the ads are avoided. However, horizontal ad pages require the most cooperation from the advertising department since all ads or combi-

A news briefs column is published down the left-hand side of the
page with advertisements stacked down the right-hand side in this
Manteca (Calif.) *Bulletin* example. Reprinted by permission.

nations of ads do not necessarily fit into a perfectly level horizontal line. Ferguson
agrees that news editors prefer horizontal ad lines because they provide the best
page design. "However," he said, "it is virtually impossible for a daily newspaper
to accommodate every page in this manner." With reference to the *News Chronicle*, Ferguson explained that its policy of pyramiding from the left makes the
advertising consistent in design "as well as having the layout editors not having
to worry about which page is a right-hand page and which is a left-hand page
since all pages are dummied the same."

This horizontal advertisement across the bottom of the Thousand Oaks, Calif. *News Chronicle* anchors the page and—as the only ad—receives the reader's immediate attention. Reprinted by permission.

Phillips (at the *Bulletin*) said that what brings people to an ad is not its placement on the page, but the content of the ad itself. He said that creating horizontal ad lines may result in "burying" an ad—placing it in such a way that no part of any news story touches it—which is generally considered undesirable.

This would happen if you had three two-by-four ads [two columns wide by four inches deep] and two two-by-two ads across the bottom of a page. The two-by-two at the bottom would be "buried." This is somewhat of an old fashioned idea, and no longer seems to be the sign it once was. After all, the idea assumed that readers only read ads accidentally as they finished news stories. Now it is recognized that a good ad can stand alone and draw as much if not more readership than a news story. Then too, the industry has been "burying" theatre advertisements for years with no ill effects.

One idea for the newspaper staff desiring to create horizontal ad lines is to "float" some ads in a field of open white space with a straight horizontal border. True, the advertiser might receive slightly more space than was paid for in this arrangement. Alternatively, the newspaper could have several prearranged ad sizes that fit the space, or it could run free public service ads in the unpaid ad portion of the pages. While not generally advocated since it's a bit tricky and costs the newspaper money, this design solution can make up for the sacrifice involved by resulting in advertising space that complements the news display.

Inside pages with ads on them do sometimes present awkard challenges. For instance, advertisements set right up next to photos will compete for the eye's attention. And more generally, if ads are straight type, most publications will use a different typeface than they use for news matter. Many typefaces can be used for ads; the key is to complement the typefaces in the ads with those in the news columns. Some serif typefaces—those with ornamentation—look well with one another, and some do not; some sans serif typefaces—those that are straight strokes of type—look well with one another, and again others do not. Whether all serif, all sans serif or some of both, the use of too many combinations of typefaces takes away from the message of the advertisement.

Ferguson said that the *News Chronicle* clearly separates news and advertising by not using the same typefaces on both. "This allows the reader's mind to shift gears," he said. "When the advertiser wishes his ad to be designed like a news story, we insist on three things:

- border around the ad;
- the word 'Advertisement' above the ad and inside the border;
- different type styles than our News Department uses."

Two other areas that the news and art departments should be at least mindful of are the consistency of the ad column widths and the look of the advertising itself. Maintaining consistent column widths in the news editorial and advertising copy keeps the newspaper looking professional. Therefore, in 1984, the Expanded Standard Advertising Unit (SAU) System was adopted to assist publications in achieving this ad-size consistency (see Table 4).

As a result of the SAU, stories are no longer dummied into news column widths that leave irregular pockets of white space adjacent to the ads. According to Ferguson, "this [the SAU] was also done, in part, because of 'pressure' from major and national advertisers that had to prepare their advertisements in various

The placement of advertisements and story text on this Manteca (Calif.) *Bulletin* page is done so that the ads are separated from the story art. Reprinted by permission.

sizes to accommodate the requirements of the various newspapers." Once newspaper ad department personnel were convinced that the SAU measurements were advantageous to themselves and the advertisers, it was not difficult to convince publishers of their valuable assistance.

Advertisements must not only conform to space limitations; they must be written accurately and clearly if their message is to reach the reader and sell the product or idea. Poorly designed ads or those with language errors in them or illustrations of poor quality, take away from news editorial presentation. Just

An advertisement is placed next to a photograph in the Thousand Oaks, Calif. *News Chronicle;* for this to work, the photo must be strong enough to compete favorably with the ad. Reprinted by permission.

as when "stories are inaccurate, or contain language errors"—Ferguson said—unattractive advertisements "detract from the credibility of the advertiser as well as the newspaper itself."

Advertisements are built on the message that the typography sends to readers. As a complement to the type, illustrations, logos, drawings and photos of the product may be used in ads. To effectively handle these graphics, some newspapers employ a staff artist; others use art clipbooks, or they combine artists and books.

Table 4

The Expanded SAU™ Standard Advertising Unit System

Depth in Inches	1 COL. 2-1/16"	2 COL. 4-1/4"	3 COL. 6-7/16"	4 COL. 8-5/8"	5 COL. 10-13/16"	6 COL. 13"
FD*	1xFD*	2xFD*	3xFD*	4xFD*	5xFD*	6xFD*
18"	1x18	2x18	3x18	4x18	5x18	6x18
15.75"	1x15.75	2x15.75	3x15.75	4x15.75	5x15.75	
14"	1x14	2x14	3x14	4x14	5x14	6x14
13"	1x13	2x13	3x13	4x13	5x13	
10.5"	1x10.5	2x10.5	3x10.5	4x10.5	5x10.5	6x10.5
7"	1x7	2x7	3x7	4x7	5x7	6x7
5.25"	1x5.25	2x5.25	3x5.25	4x5.25		
3.5"	1x3.5	2x3.5				
3"	1x3	2x3				
2"	1x2	2x2				
1.5"	1x1.5					
1"	1x1					

N

1 Column 2-1/16"	4 Columns 8⅝"	Double Truck 26¾"	13xFD*	13x18
2 Columns 4¼"	5 Columns 10-13/16"	There are four suggested	13x14	13x10.5
3 Columns 6-7/16"	6 Columns 13"	double truck sizes:		

A newspaper with one or more staff artists who specialize in advertising art is likely to have some latitude when it comes to how an advertisement will be created. The artist works directly with the advertising sales department, receives information from the salespeople, goes to the location of the product to make sketches, or combines advertiser-supplied and original art with type available at the newspaper. However, a newspaper with a very small advertising staff and a part-time or only one full-time artist must work to use effectively the resources of the artist along with clipbooks and the materials supplied by the advertiser.

Purists might say that editorial workers don't need to be aware of what ads are on a page, but Phillips at the Manteca (Calif.) *Bulletin* believes that they should know.

> Let's say you're editing a community newspaper and you're running a wire story telling that GMC was forced to recall a million cars with faulty brakes. The story naturally deserves coverage, but there are better places to run that story than directly on top of your local Chevrolet dealer's biggest ad of the year. This is not favoritism, nor is it sacrificing of journalistic ethics. It is merely good common sense.

Regardless of the TPC newspaper's size, the news and advertising department staffs see themselves as working toward a single common goal: providing the best possible source of information for the readership. In an ideal complement, the advertising department alerts the news department about special advertising needs, and delivers to the newsroom—on time—dummied and proofed final pages that are of a size indicated on the dummies and that have attractive art and type. This requires coordinated effort from editors and managers of the two departments, who must communicate frequently and make occasional compromises.

5   Designing Tabloid News Space

It's a mistake to treat a tabloid page simply as a miniature broadsheet page. While you can't fit as much material on it, you should create the impression that just as much is happening as on a full-sized page.

Michael Gordon
graphics editor
Los Angeles *Herald Examiner*

Some newspapers have gone to a tabloid or pullout magazine for their entertainment stories, the television listings or special community day celebrations. Therefore, in discussing tabloid newspaper design, it is primary to have a clear understanding that a tabloid is not simply a miniature or half-size standard broadsheet newspaper turned sideways. Indeed, the tabloid demands its own special Total Page Concept (TPC) design considerations, no less important than the broadsheet main part of the newspaper.

Many things that have been said about standard broadsheet-size papers—for instance, in terms of the size of art and headlines, and story count—are not true of the tabloid. The small page size demands a rethinking of design. In fact, regarding design, it can sometimes be easier to devote a full tabloid page to each department—such as business—rather than work the same material onto half a broadsheet page.

In the TPC newspaper, tabloid sections—from cover to cover—are seen by the reader as belonging to the rest of the newspaper. This means that, while column measurements might be different in the paper's tabloid and broadsheet sections, the design style and typefaces must be uniform throughout.

One selling feature for the tabloid newspaper is that single-page containment can be accomplished easily, as done on this page from the San Jose (Calif.) *Metro*. Reprinted by permission.

The tabloid pullout magazine can be published with a regular tabloid newspaper, as in this issue of the Philadelphia *Daily News*, or as part of a standard broadsheet newspaper when creation of a separate distinct section is desired. Reprinted by permission.

The Miami *Herald,* along with many other standard broadsheet and tabloid newspapers, uses the tabloid format to provide its readers with a weekly presentation of business news. Reprinted by permission.

TABLOID FORMAT COMPARISONS

Newspapers printed as tabloids are not plentiful among the nation's dailies and weeklies. The leading nationally published example is the *Christian Science Monitor.* Tabloid newspapers are also found in Chicago, Denver, New York City, Green Bay, Wis., Melville, N.Y., Jasper, Ind., Santa Barbara, Calif., and at many colleges and universities.

Michael Gordon, graphics editor of the Los Angeles *Herald Examiner,* said that there is a confusion surrounding newspapers that publish in the tabloid format; many people mistakenly classify all tabloids as being like the sensational papers available at the supermarket checkout stands.

> Mention "tabloid" and a lot of people seem to think you're talking about giant headlines in red ink and stories about Elvis [Presley] speaking from beyond the grave. It's a bum rap, as readers of perfectly respectable tabloids like *Newsday* or the *Christian Science Monitor* can tell you.

The Green Bay (Wis.) *News Chronicle* sees itself as not being a "tabloid" in the traditional sense, according to its editor Ron Poppenhagen. His paper is not filled with sensationalistic news—lots of crime news, sex and such—but "rather, we are a traditional community daily newspaper which happens to be published in a tabloid format."

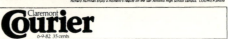

This Claremont (Calif.) *Courier's* cover page shows how a dominant photograph accompanied by a story that starts on page one can quickly direct the reader into the rest of the tabloid pages. Reprinted by permission.

Daniel van Benthuysen, senior art director of *Newsday* in Melville on Long Island in New York, is also aware of the "sensationalistic" image that the tabloid newspaper carries with it.

> While many weekly publications use the tabloid format intelligently, most notably, the *Village Voice* and a number of trade journals, for most journalists the word "tabloid," when applied to dailies, has long been a pejorative label.

Poppenhagen said he believes that it is easier to read a tabloid-size publication.

> As a morning paper, the *News Chronicle* is read at thousands of breakfast tables and in dozens of restaurants. A tabloid paper is easier to handle, easier to spread out on the table, easier to hold up with one hand.

Gordon says that another factor about the tabloid newspaper speaks to its special audience.

> It has something of the feel of a magazine, which is why many broadsheet papers publish some of their feature sections in tabloid format.

Four tabloid newspapers—each with a different readership—show how a variety of page designs can be used to attract readers into the paper: the New York *Post*, with large type and dramatic art; the Chicago *Sun-Times*, with large type, a large photo and a portion of a story; the Denver *Rocky Mountain News*, with large type and photo; and the *Christian Science Monitor*, more subdued, and almost like a miniature standard-size page. Reprinted by permission. Chicago *Sun-Times* © with permission of Chicago Sun-Times, Inc., 1987.

George Delmerico, now creative director of the Santa Barbara (Calif.) *Independent* (a tabloid), was design director at the *Village Voice* in New York from 1976–85 and had worked at the New York *Times* from 1974–76. According to Delmerico,

> A tabloid is smaller and easier to handle than the larger format; whether on a subway or at the breakfast table, it simply consumes less space without having to be folded in halves or quarters to be read.

The small feel of the tabloid format creates another design possibility, a feature not seen in the broadsheet: A story or a section such as sports may be started on the back page and jumped inside. The back page then becomes the beginning page for a story, or a second cover page with its own teasers to attract the reader's attention to the inside.

Newspapers publishing in the tabloid format started in that size for a variety of reasons that set them apart from the design of standard-size newspapers. The Green Bay (Wis.) *News Chronicle*—for instance—began in 1972 as the offspring of two publications, according to Poppenhagen. A broadsheet daily had sprung up as a strike paper published by composition and pressroom employees striking the *Press-Gazette* in Green Bay and the Brown County *Chronicle,* a weekly tabloid shopper. The owner of the *Chronicle* bought out the strikers and transferred the tabloid format to the daily.

According to van Benthuysen, *Newsday* began as a tabloid less than 50 years ago. Its format was considered easier to handle than broadsheets by the 35 percent of the adult work force who traveled by train from Long Island to work in New York City.

John Rumbach, managing editor of the *Herald* in Jasper, Ind., is also committed to print in the tabloid format. His paper publishes as a tabloid because "our readers wouldn't have it any other way." Rumbach said that the paper went to daily publication at a time when its circulation did not really warrant the change. As a weekly, the *Herald* had been a broadsheet, he said, "but the publisher knew that on many days, the advertising would not support the minimum 4-page broadsheet. Therefore, he decided to go tabloid so that he could run four tabloid pages on slow days. The tabloid format stuck."

Speaking about the Santa Barbara (Calif.) *Independent*, Delmerico said that, "like many alternative weekly newspapers," it is published as a tabloid for many reasons, but the main consideration is "probably the fact that no one involved in its creation ever considered a broadsheet format in the first place." The *Independent* is a descendant "of the so-called 'underground press' movement of the late '60s," and "alternative weeklies, as a rule, have chosen the tabloid format for its many virtues."

Tabloid formats have a long history, says Delmerico.

DR. KOd

BAD DAY FOR GOODEN: It was a rough one for Dwight Gooden and the Mets against the Reds yesterday at Shea. Gooden was shelled for four runs in the first inning and was yanked after the fourth as the Mets were crushed, 11-1, and swept for the first time this year.   **Brown, Lang, Lupica — Pages 62, 64, 65.**

Cops: Richardson using crack
Fred Kerber, Page 67

The back page of the tabloid newspaper can also act as a "second front page," in which case news and photos can be displayed on that page with stories jumped to the inside, as shown in this New York *Daily News* example. Copyright © 1986 by New York News, Inc. Reprinted by permission.

Bishop of Memphis
Story by Brian Blair   Photos by Steve Mellon

The Most Rev. Daniel Buechlein finds himself caught between farewells and welcomes as he leaves the monastery for a role in the Catholic hierarchy.

The Saturday **Herald**
Dubois County, Ind., March 7, 1987

The Jasper (Ind.) *Herald* provides its readers with a dramatic presentation of the news, with large photos as the dominant element. Reprinted by permission.

[Tabloids] have their antecedents in the large urban dailies created early in this century, with their eye-catching big photos and their emphasis on a single story to sell the edition—a form perhaps ideally suited to present the more thoughtful, magazine-style stories today's weeklies often publish.

The *Independent,* as an alternative weekly, is so unlike the traditional tabloid dailies that its real competition in the market comes from a broadsheet daily. To stand apart, it was necessary to give the *Independent* a different look and feel. However, for many alternative tabloids "economics and the logistics of printing may be the most important factors," according to Delmerico.

Large dailies are designed to print broadsheets; very few would willingly sell downtime on their presses [hours not used to print the daily] to these upstart weeklies, competing as they do in the ever-shrinking newspaper market. But many smaller printers print advertising tabloids also; it's a small jump to a big client for these printers when they sign up a weekly publication with a circulation in the tens of thousands.

While most editors of alternative tabloids do face the challenges that Delmerico described, they all understand the value of a front page done in traditional newspaper format—with photos, headlines, stories and a dominant element to grab the attention of the reader.

DISADVANTAGES/ADVANTAGES

According to Poppenhagen of the Green Bay *News Chronicle,* "The limited story count on a page, particularly on the front page, is one of the disadvantages of the tabloid format." But, he added, "to keep the number of elements on the page up, we run a refer [reference] package across the top of page one, incorporating an index, weather-at-a-glance graphic and teasers for two or three inside stories. That package, plus the flag, leaves us with our 45 inches of space on page one." This means that the *News Chronicle* has a page one with one photo and two or three stories, with one or two continued inside. "We'd like not to jump, but it becomes imperative if we are to get three stories started on page one," Poppenhagen said.

The way around tabloid design problems—says Gordon at the Los Angeles *Herald Examiner*—is simply to "write tight." The purpose of writing tight is to keep the reader with the story. "To avoid a drab look, you've got to run more than one story per tabloid page, unless you have a lot of terrific art to go with that single story," Gordon said. "Go for two or, better, three stories per page—plus art, of course. This means editors must restrain reporters' natural tendency to write too much." Editors must realize that "a 20-inch story may be routine

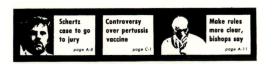

The Green Bay (Wis.) *News Chronicle* brings its stories on page one, jumps two or three inside and places referral boxes on the page to tell readers that there is more news inside. Reprinted by permission.

in a broadsheet, but it's long in a tabloid." Furthermore, "jumping stories isn't the answer, either; the grayness it prevents on one page simply gets shoved onto another." The whole story should be on one page because "readers hate jumps." Gordon said that limiting stories to a single page serves the reader of a broadsheet paper also, "but because tab pages fill up more quickly, it's doubly important to edit stories as tightly as possible."

While there are distinct advantages to using a tabloid format—such as the single-page containment of stories and the availability of full pages for advertisers—some headline size restrictions are inevitable. Sizes as large as 72- and 60-point (where 72 points equal one inch) type should be used sparingly. The headline should serve as a complement to the text. It must be large enough to carry or support the story's length, but not so large that it is bigger than the story it heads. On the other hand, a tabloid newspaper will often print its largest headline at 30- or 24-point. When the point sizes begin this small, there is not much farther to go down. This does not provide much page design variety and does little to focus readers' interest on the relative importance of the news stories.

Poppenhagen shared his thoughts on the ease of tab layout:

> Tabloid pages, I believe, can be laid out more rapidly than broadsheet pages, given equal amounts of space. My experience with both formats is that the broadsheet is much more of a jigsaw puzzle to work out, while the tabloid is fast and easy to lay out, especially in a

The New York *Daily News* uses photos and a variety of headline sizes to provide page balance. Copyright © 1986 by New York News, Inc. Reprinted with permission.

modular design. Given the limited staff of a smaller, start-up publication, the tabloid design can be produced more easily.

Tabloid stories can be packaged differently than on a broadsheet because the smaller paper can be held open in both hands, and the two pages then viewed almost as one. Gordon said that "market research shows that women, in particular, often prefer the compact size." The story flow from page to page makes reading the tabloid an easy experience.

Gordon added that

> For publications with fewer pages than a major metropolitan daily—college newspapers, for example—a tabloid has the additional subliminal advantage of giving an impression of more bulk. It's twice as thick and has twice as many pages as a broadsheet section containing the same amount of space.

Editors of tabloids do commonly hold this to be a virtue of the design.

Again, the words of Poppenhagen:

> I would never give up the tabloid format for the *News Chronicle*. If I were starting a new daily, I would look very seriously at the tabloid

format. Because of people's perceptions, it would be difficult to change a broadsheet to a tabloid, but it might even be the right move for someone with a specific competitive or market situation. I've seen a lot of small town dailies that are six, eight or 10 broadsheet pages that would be better off with a tabloid format.

DESIGNING THE TABLOID

A poster-cover front page or this in combination with the beginning of a single cover story are effective design options for the tabloid page one. The poster cover using a photo or illustrative piece of art along with a headline and a cutline—or explanatory note—will permit the reader to see the TPC tabloid newspaper as something special, provided the art is worth the space given to it.

The page might also have "boxcars," or reference notes keyed to the cover story and other stories inside. A front page like this—with large headlines, inside references and large photos—is seen in several newspapers, although competition for the reader's attention can sometimes be distracting.

Unique to the *Herald* in Jasper, Ind., are its interior sections, Rumbach says. "We can print only one section. Therefore, what are normally individual sections in a broadsheet—sports, lifestyle—must be packaged inside the tabloid in a way that the reader can easily find these popular sections." As with other tabloids, the *Herald* reader sees adjacent pages as one. While those who "lay out broad-

The *Sporting News*, published weekly for a specialized readership, uses short item summaries for inside reference so page one can have two or three cover photos. Reprinted by permission.

sheet pages worry about a single page," Rumbach said, "our page designers must worry about side-by-side pages."

Gordon of the *Herald Examiner* agrees that, in every case, the designer should "think about the opposite page" when planning out a tabloid section. "Because tabloid pages are smaller," Gordon said, "each two-page spread forms a tighter unit than in a broadsheet. Every page layout should take the appearance of the facing page into account." Rather than stretch banners across facing pages, the design editor might lead off one page with a strong one- or two-column headline next to a strong photo. "If you use a horizontal photo on one page of a spread, look for a vertical photo for the other," Gordon suggested.

Articles on the inside and section pages of a tabloid newspaper also have different requirements from the equivalent sections of a broadsheet paper. Because subjects in their entirety should be contained on a single page, stories must be edited to fit. Some pages might have many short items run as news summaries for national and international news, sports, entertainment and other topic areas. To make the inside page work from a readership standpoint, says Gordon, the designer should learn to "think vertical: Calm, cool horizontal layouts are popular in broadsheets these days, but too many of them rob tabloid pages of energy." Also, horizontal layouts "make for shorter columns of type, forcing the reader's eye to jump up and down more often than is ideal. Strong vertical elements help make tabloid pages look larger and more active."

Poppenhagen, the Green Bay editor, adds that, even though "it can be more difficult to come up with a really smashing large graphic, while getting copy on the page," the *News Chronicle* will remain a tabloid.

And on Long Island, van Benthuysen said that *Newsday,* too, will continue as a tabloid.

> In recent decades Long Island has sent smaller percentages of its work force commuting to New York, and the paper's management has occasionally considered broadsheet formats, but the tabloid format has been retained because we strive for the look and feel of a daily news magazine. That means clean, squared-off, modular layouts that avoid awkward wraps and dog-leg construction.

Photos throughout should be printed large enough for the reader to discern the subject immediately. Gordon of the Los Angeles *Herald Examiner* advised that photos and headlines not be run half-size just because a tabloid page "is only half the size of a broadsheet page." In addition, Gordon said,

> Graphic elements on [the tabloid page] should be larger than half the size they'd be in a broadsheet. Three-quarters size often seems about right. Where I'd use a 60-point banner headline in a broadsheet, for example, I might use a 42- or 48-point headline in a tabloid.

Where I'd run a photo four columns wide in a broadsheet, I'd run it three columns in a tabloid.

Rumbach at the Jasper *Herald* explained how a photo on a tabloid page has a bigger impact than the same photo on a broadsheet page:

> We can dedicate a whole page to a three-picture combo so that a page will stand on its own as a unit, compared to a picture combo in a broadsheet that has to share page space with unrelated stories.

With reference to photos in relationship to each other, especially on picture pages, Rumbach said that the effective arrangement is horizontal. This relationship—also known as "double truck" because facing pages can overlap across the middle—can be very advantageous to the designer, since nothing is lost in the crack between pages. "The space of a single broadsheet page is just a little less than a double truck in our tabloid," says Rumbach. "Therefore, when we run a full picture page, we are actually running a double truck. The layout for this is horizontal rather than vertical; it is natural for a reader to view a picture story from left to right, rather than up to down."

Delmerico in Santa Barbara, who conceived many of his ideas about tabloid newspapers while at the *Village Voice*, expects the *Independent* to grow and change. The tabloid is the vehicle best suited for the market that his paper serves. Furthermore, says Delmerico,

> The tabloid form is uniquely suited to the sequential, magazine-like "flow" of weeklies such as the Santa Barbara *Independent;* what we do would not be possible in exactly the same way if we were a broadsheet. A broadsheet page demands variety—variety of headlines, photos and most important, subject matter. And while many tabloids are very dense, at the *Independent,* we're emphasizing the potential of the tabloid format to reveal the combined strengths of both newspapers and magazines.
>
> A tabloid is, after all, an uneasy hybrid of the two, and whether to look like one or the other is one of the fundamental questions that confronts every tabloid editor and art director. As a result, every tabloid tends to "tilt" in one direction. Those that are guided by a strong news bias tend to look like a "newspaper"—that is, a *daily* newspaper—while "softer" weeklies are much more magazine-like in appearance.
>
> I think there's nothing inherently logical about these tendencies, though they are understandable. After all, *Life* magazine is, or was, hard journalism; so is *Time*, which owes nothing to newspapers. It may be possible to create a more perfect union of these two parents

of tabloid journalism, and if those conditions exist anywhere, they exist at our small paper here, which is not even a full year old [in 1987].

I'm certain our formats will change as we grow, but we will never abandon certain fundamental premises that currently guide us, which include using strong photographs of journalistic nature, as well as adopting certain graphic "guideposts" that lead the reader through the maze of ads in a forward-moving, linear progression.

The tabloid newspapers cited in this chapter, and others whose purpose is to publish straight news and features, provide a special kind of TPC publication for their readers. Writers and photographers are sometimes provided with a full page or facing pages for their story's text and photos. Advertisers, too, are sometimes given space where their ad is the only one on a page, or only one of two or three on facing pages. The news tabloid is compact; it is easily read; and its readers are served with a format designed especially for their particular needs.

III   BUILDING BLOCKS OF TYPOGRAPHY

The specifics of a TPC-designed newspaper are first seen by the reader through the manner in which continuity elements, headlines, and typographical text are positioned on the page. The Total Page Concept is able to mesh if these complement one another, and it fails as a design strategy if the relationship among these elements is not understood by the designer. For a newspaper to be a successful TPC publication, the logo or flag must be clearly readable, special typefaces should only be used to give clear directions to readers, and headlines and story type should never hinder the news presentation. The next three chapters explain how to make these elements sell and tell the news through the building blocks of typography.

This page from the Charlotte (N.C.) *Observer* shows how design elements can effectively build on one another. Reprinted by permission.

6   Continuity Elements

A continuity element is the big thing. We're updating our design stylebook with the idea that we want increased continuity from section to section. The Lone Rangers are people who want to show us all the great things they can do in design, and in effect show off with design rather than to really aid the reader and aid the display. We want to squash that as much as we possibly can. It is an integrated element. . . . There has to be a continuity from section to section, page to page.

Ernest E. Hines

editor

Contra Costa *Times*

Walnut Creek, Calif.

Regardless of a newspaper's format, Total Page Concept (TPC) continuity begins with the identifying logo on page one, and flows from page to page throughout the newspaper. The relationship of the Total Page Concept to continuity includes a conscientious effort to plan the mix of all headlines, to package each story with photos and a purposeful arrangement of headlines, and then to plan stories and photos that complement one another. The designer must never take the reader for granted. Through the use of strong continuity elements, a newspaper can be designed to make reading easier. This is important since reading in the age of television is voluntary and therefore the news audience must be seduced into reading a newspaper—beginning at the top of page one with a boxed package of teasers.

Sam Fosdick, executive editor of the York (Pa.) *Daily Record,* says that

Our page one teasers come from a strong desire to market what's inside the paper not only to the newsstand buyer, but also to the home subscriber. The latter group is the bread and butter of any newspaper circulation department. And it just makes good sense to

us to sell the paper to the person who opens it over the breakfast
table as [well as] to the person who opens it over his office desk or
the doughnut counter.

The Total Page Concept sees all parts of the paper as having one goal: a subtle
simplicity that will direct the reader through the publication. We live in a time
of images created by advertising, television, and corporate logo creators. Logos
today solidify and unify people's reactions; they are the positive images that
advertisers and other groups project to foster believability. When images become
fragmented, credibility decreases. The greater the integration of images through
the effective use of a logo, the greater the acceptance enjoyed by its associated
group and its ideas.

THE FLAG

An initial indication of the importance of continuity lies in how the "flag,"
"logotype" or "nameplate" —the type that displays the name of the newspaper—
is designed and placed on page one. In addition, how this element serves to
complement the column signature boxes, headline type and inside page folios
is important. The flag should identify the newspaper so well that the reader can
easily distinguish one publication from another.

According to Fosdick, the page-one flag—how it is seen by the reader or
potential reader—is critical to sales when the environment is competitive. "We
are the second banana in the second—or third, depending upon whose numbers
you like—smallest competitive newspaper market in this country," Fosdick said.
"Because of that, and because of the required clarity of presentation in modern
American journalism, our page one flag, and appropriate teasers to inside elements, is extremely important to us."

Usually the flag is placed in the top third of the page, as found in the 1983
study of front pages done by Steve Pasternack and Sandra Utt (see Table 5).

Most often the flag is found beneath teasers, although other content
is occasionally found above the flag. While many newspapers have
moved their flags around the page, a majority [53.2 percent] have
retained the traditional text typeface. And 72.7 percent of the flags
do not have an emblem included.

When the *News Chronicle* in Thousand Oaks, Calif., introduced its redesign
on June 17, 1984, its editor Marvin Sosna announced that "we have unfurled a
new flag." Explaining that the change would be helpful to the reader, Sosna
said,

[The new flag] includes a large day-of-the-week identifier, since most
people looking for a particular back copy in a stack of newspapers

SPORTS

**HBO fight series
standing in way
of Cooney: 1D**

LIVING

**Who will be the
next Miss York County?**
Contestants in the Miss York County Scholarship Pageant honed their routines this past
Saturday, their last big rehearsal before the
show, set for 7 p.m. Saturday at the Strand-
Capitol Performing Arts Center.
1B

LOCAL

**Supervisors retain
jobs in new vote**
Two Dover Township super-
visors Monday night were appointed again to paid township
jobs, but this time they didn't
vote for themselves.
3A

York Daily Record

TUESDAY   25¢

York's first newspaper

January 28, 1986   171st Year, No. 23 • York, Pennsylvania   © 1986 York Daily Record

State of the Union will be brief, tailored to TV

By ELLEN WARREN
Knight-Ridder Newspapers

WASHINGTON — President Reagan delivers a streamlined State of the Union address to Congress today and soon afterward plans to embark on a presidential selling spree to underscore his message.

Reagan's speech is expected to emphasize growth, theme, light, parts, and

Wednesday at two federal departments and a talk Thursday to young people at a suburban Virginia high school, an ideal setting for a more personal speech on his vision for the future.

"All in all, a busy week. He decided to make news," presidential spokesman Larry Speakes said Monday.

Mindful of the public's short attention span, according to sense ministration offi

tional priorities for a separate message he will send to Congress Wednesday.

Administration officials familiar with the address — there have been four drafts and some internal disputes over their content — said the prime-time (9 p.m.) nationally televised speech will include several surprises and one or more new initiatives.

Overall, though, the speech will rely on broad in year talk con

cally and in the context of a lasting, global peace, administration officials said.

More specifically, administration officials said Reagan again will oppose a tax increase, urge tax reform, delineate his views on the budget and discuss East-West relations.

A senior official said the speech has been pared so much that there will be little time for the kind of anecdotes that have enlivened Reagan's previous State of Union addresses, which have

The front-page flag of the York (Pa.) *Daily Record* serves to distinguish this newspaper from all
other publications in the area. Reprinted by permission.

Table 5
Newspapers That Place Various Items above the Flag (in percentages)

	Regularly	Occasionally	Never
Stories	14.1	29.7	56.3
Headlines	23.5	17.2	59.4
Photos	14.1	21.9	62.5
Digest	11.0	9.4	78.2
Teasers	70.3	14.1	15.6

Source: Sandra H. Utt and Steve Pasternack, "Front Pages of U.S. Daily Newspapers," *Journalism
Quarterly* (1984):879–84.

search for a day ("Where's Wednesday's paper?"), not a date. And
a line at the top of page one tells you which edition you are reading.

The flag itself was custom-designed with a ligature (a combination
of two letters into one) at the "E" and "W" in "NEWS." Using solid
and screened type, the flag carries forth the heritage of the *News* and
the *Chronicle,* the two predecessor newspapers that now form the
News Chronicle.

Ernest E. Hines, editor of the *Contra Costa Times,* in Walnut Creek, Calif.,
explained the situation at his paper:

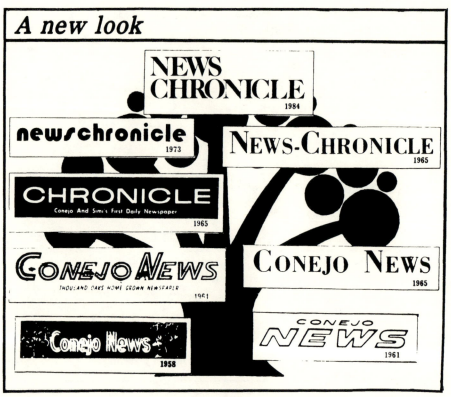

A new look

The flag, or nameplate, is a symbol by which a newspaper can be quickly identified. In the case of the *Conejo News* and the *Chronicle* in Thousand Oaks, Calif. the two papers became one in 1965; their faces changed as the publication evolved. Reprinted by permission.

Here at the *Times,* in effect, we produce three daily newspapers out of here each day, and there is some overlap in some of our areas on the flags. We're producing off of a common desk, so we can't go into several different styles. In effect, we want a compatibility of approach in the papers.

We just redesigned the flags for the *West County Times* and the *Valley Times.* They had been the traditional black on white kind of flag. We looked at what we were doing with the *Contra Costa Times,* which we thought was very successful—in a knockout [reverse] sense on the blue field with the lining. We said, "We like that look; we also want to have something distinctive, something that will set apart, say, the *Valley Times,* which has an overlap in our areas." So, we went to a different color in the flag on the background. And we were looking again for a distinctive kind of color that had a good display in the rack. . . . We think we created a far more lively paper. If you were to hold this up against what we were doing a year ago at the *Valley Times* and the *West County Times,* there's just no comparison. The life of the upper half of that page has just been greatly enhanced.

The Alexandria Gazette

America's Oldest Daily Newspaper — Established February 5, 1784

| VOL. CXCIX — NO. 154 | 1 Section, 12 Pages | Alexandria, Virginia | Saturday, August 7, 1982 | 25 CENTS |

Umps
The eyes have it

Common-law husband dead

Woman gets one year for fatal stabbing

SERVING MOAB AND SOUTHEASTERN UTAH SINCE 1896

The Times-Independent

Moab, Grand County, Utah 84532

Volume 88   Number 33   Thursday, August 19, 1982

Declining hospital use causing problems prompts request

Bangor Daily News

| VOL. 94 — NO. 47 | BANGOR, MAINE, MONDAY, JULY 26, 1982 | 30 PAGES—30 CENTS |

Arafat supports U.N. resolutions

Israeli bombing raids continue

The "Old English" typestyle flag is a familiar sight to readers of many newspapers, including the Alexandria (Va.) *Gazette* and the Bangor (Maine) *Daily News* and the Moab, Utah *Times Independent.* Reprinted by permission.

the Charleston Gazette

It'll be a little cloudier today. Highs will be in the mid-80s, lows will be in the mid-60s. Details are on Page 16A

MOSTLY CLOUDY 30%

The State Newspaper - Our 114th Year

Valley edition 25 cents
Charleston, West Virginia

Rescue teams discover bodies

Salute to ag honors students
(See Page 2)

Herd needs win vs. Davis tonight
(See Sports)

Holiday Faire Saturday

Friday   25¢

Inside

Elk Grove Citizen

82nd Year — No. 88   A Herburger Publication   Nov. 2, 1984

ARABIAN

Park district hopes for some development 'green' from state

The Elk Grove Recreation and Park District is hoping to get some ... and which are available under a regional competitive program ... The Feickert Park is located on Emerald Vista Drive near Feickert ...

These are Bear stars
See sports

CHP is watching truckers
See page eleven

Grad night at COS
See page fourteen

Mount Shasta Herald

Wednesday, June 5, 1985 Vol. 80, No. 48   Mount Shasta, Siskiyou County, California   25 cents   24 Pages

Speeding truckers nailed by CHP

By Marge Apperson
The image of a speeding truck veering into the fast lane to ...

Council balks at county charges for dump use

Mount Shastans should not be double charged for use of the Black Butte Dump the city council de ... paid by city taxpayers. 28 cents goes to the county, 6 cents to the city, and rest ... schools ... spec ...

The upper/lower case nameplate is used by a great many newspapers, including the Charleston (W.Va.) *Gazette*, the Elk Grove (Calif.) *Citizen*, the Mt. Shasta (Calif.) *Herald*, the Richmond, Ind. *Palladium-Item*, the Wilmington. Del. *Morning News* and the Ely (Nev.) *Daily Times*, the latter showing the flag floated within a ''skypiece''-displayed story. Reprinted by permission.

100

SUNDAY Palladium-Item

The forecast
Sunny, cold today
Mostly sunny Monday
Details on Page A8

Vol. 156, No. 5   A Gannett Newspaper   Richmond, Ind., Jan. 5, 1986   5 Sections   75c

Waltermann's been learning politics' lessons

By DAVID HOLTHAUS
Palladium-Item Staff Writer

What is the first part of politics? Education. The second? Education. And the third? Education.

State to submit possible sites for auto plant

Cubs rally past Phils

Two run doubles in the sixth inning by Dave Martinez and Shawon Dunston cap a four run rally that carries Chicago past the Phils 10 7   **Sports C1**

Action plan for AIDS

Delaware agencies are developing an action plan to deal more effectively with AIDS and other sexually transmitted diseases   **This morning B1**

A good rap for Delaware

Eight city teen-agers are using the rhythmic beat of rap music to get their message across. Delaware Is on the Move. And they hope the state's public officials are among those listening   **Pace D1**

Weather: pleasant

Today: Mostly sunny and pleasant high in the mid to upper 70s. Fair tonight; low in the 60s
Friday: Partly cloudy, warmer and more humid. High mid to upper 80s
Details, beach forecast, B2

Arts	D4	Editorial	A10
Business	B10	Obituaries	B8
Classified	C6	People	D3
Comics	D7	Record	B8
Crossword	D6	Sports	C1
Dear Abby	D6	Television	D2

The Morning News
METRO

A Gannett Newspaper • Thursday, June 26, 1986 • 107th year No 52 • 35 cents

Phillies' Carlton era ends

Record-setting pitcher balks, but bows out

● Players' reaction: C1
● Reaction from fans: C3

By KEVIN NOONAN

PHILADELPHIA — In the end...

On Wednesday the Phillies released Carlton, the only pitcher in baseball history to win four Cy Young Awards. But Carlton, 41, who was in his 22nd season in the major leagues and 15th with the Phillies, has been advised...

Stadium, that Carlton would no longer wear the red pinstripes.

The next time Phillies fans see Carlton's No. 32, it'll be when the number is retired. Only two other Phillies, Rich Ashburn and Robin Roberts...

County $102,000 in the hole
Spending cuts ordered by commission

By MARC PICKER
TIMES Editor

Emergency spending limits and possible cutbacks in personnel work hours were considered by the White Pine County Commission at its meeting Wednesday as the county faces a $102,000 deficit in the General Fund.

In an emergency joint meeting of the commission and Ely City Council, commission chairman Brent Eldridge asked if there is any way for the City of Ely to pay the $112,000 it owes on the 1981-82 contract for police services.

Eldridge said he doesn't blame the entire problem the county faces on the city, but having the $112,000 could have helped the county get through the financial crisis it is encountering currently.

Mayor Garey Harrison assured the commission that the city has cut wherever it can, eliminating four employee positions, but state tax revenue monies have been coming in slowly and short of expectations.

City Clerk Bob Spelberg told the commission, "We're cutting wherever we can and hope to come up with $50,000 of the $112,000 this year and then at least have it in the budget next year. We are trying to give you unbudgeted funds this year."

Spelberg said the city's shortfall was greater than the county's in the last fiscal year because some tax revenue figures were overprojected and the city then spent that money without getting it.

He said the city needed to...

curtail services, then the city offices should do the same. "I'm not painting a finger at anyone, but we have to do something."

Councilman Jack Smith told the commission he feels the city's main financial problem is the police services contract it agreed to with the White Pine County Sheriff's Office.

Smith said the contract amount equals about one-third of the city's total budget and "I think this is where the city is over its head. We're into a contract we can't fulfill."

He suggested that the county and city examine ways to cut back the sheriff's office at next week's special joint meeting between the commission and Ely City Council.

Smith said the county currently has 22 deputies, three Nevada Highway Patrolmen, two state investigators and five other state officers while a recent guideline study by White Pine Power Project consultant Dames and Moore shows a county with White Pine's population should only need 12 total police officers.

"We're in a bad contract we can't afford and we're short $112,000 from last year. And, we're heading the same direction this year," Smith said.

Councilman James Northness drew up for a new Ely Police Department but said the man-hour scheduling and expense projections could be used in the sheriff's office.

He said the plan calls for "cutting corners, but if you don't have the

money, you have to cut back."

Northness added that he felt "the city going back to its own police department should be the last resort."

Eldridge commented that although police services and related costs might be able to be cut, the city and county should be looking to cut other department expenditures as well.

Mayor Harrison agreed, "We have to make an overall cut, not just one department."

The county commission then voted

to impose a $50 spending limit on county departments with any purchase over that amount requiring a purchase order with the signature of two commissioners.

A plan to borrow money within the county budget to keep the General Fund afloat was also approved, with loans probably coming from federal revenue sharing funds.

Eldridge proposed that the commission vote all department heads and elected officials to curtail all capital outlay and overtime spending they can do without.

The commission chairman suggested a discussion of possible man-hour cutbacks be held at the commission's Sept. 1 meeting. District Attorney Robert Johnston told the commission it has the power to cut whatever expenditures and man-hours it wishes as long as it informs the county's two unions.

Eldridge said all of the county's department heads and budget administrators should attend the session.

Ely DAILY TIMES

(USPS No 174-660) Vol No 62 No 139   Thursday August 19 1982   12 Pages   25 Cents

AT&T, government agree to court-imposed rules

By NORMAN BLACK
Associated Press Writer

WASHINGTON —

EVENING EDITION

Chocolate Chip
The Ultimate Cookie/Page C-1

Scotty Bowman
A Sabre Forever/Page D-1

THE BUFFALO NEWS

DRY
Mostly sunny today. Clear tonight. Partly sunny tomorrow.
(COMPLETE DETAILS ON PAGE A-3)

Metro
North

60 Pages

TUESDAY, AUGUST 23, 1983

*Vol. CCVI—No. 135

25 Cents

Food Costs Help

WEATHER TODAY
Mostly sunny
High, 62; low, 31
Yesterday
High, 54; low, 29

THE INDIANAPOLIS STAR

Where the Spirit of the Lord is there is Liberty'—II Cor. 3:17

Section
A

VOLUME 81, No. 154   Copyright 1983 The Indianapolis Star

SUNDAY, NOVEMBER 6, 1983

☆ ☆ ☆ ☆ ☆   ·   75¢

Arafat supporters
flee from attack

FROM WIRE SERVICES

Tripoli, Lebanon — Last ditch supporters of Palestine Liberation Organization chief Yasser Arafat retreated Saturday from a refugee camp under fierce attack by combined Syrian and Palestinian forces, Lebanese security sources said.

Hospital sources reported 240 dead and 550 wounded in three days of fighting.

Meanwhile, the death toll in the range of Nahr el Bared security sources said.

Gunners acting in support of the assault fired artillery barrages at Nahr el Bared.

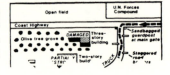

TULSA WORLD

81st Year – No. 121   *Final Edition*   Tulsa, Oklahoma, Wednesday, January 15, 1986   ENTIRE CONTENTS © 1986 WORLD PUBLISHING CO.   Single Copy 25 Cents

Analyst Says Law on Budget
To Bring Major Tax Increase

WASHINGTON (AP) — As federal officials surveyed the impact of an upcoming government-wide spending cut of nearly 5 percent, agency heads sought to make sense of a White House announcement that spending cuts of 4.3 percent in all domestic programs specifically until later in the week.

Congress, however, exempted roughly $23.6 billion in specific benefit programs administered sult in a $170 million cut in funds for the federal compensatory education program, a $224.8 million cut in student aid and a $43.6 million cut in the federal vocational.

The all-caps nameplate immediately catches the attention of readers of the Buffalo (N.Y.) *News*, the Indianapolis *Star* and the Tulsa (Okla.) *World*, the latter with outlined letters as well. Reprinted by permission.

102

Antelope
Valley Press

Including Ledger-Gazette

More Antelope Valley People Read The Valley Press Than Any Other Newspaper

Sunday, April 6, 1986   71st Year. No. 4   1986 Antelope Valley Newspapers Inc. All Rights Reserved   Price 25¢   68 Pages. Six Sections

Tears accompany Challenger tribute

By A.L. RANDOLPH
Staff Writer

There were more than a few sniffles and choked back tears at Fair Center Hall in Lancaster Friday morning when astronaut John McBride read a poem of tribute he had written to the final crew of space shuttle Challenger.

McBride making his first public appearance the Challenger ...

going to continue to do the magnificent things we've done in the past."

McBride was the guest of honor at an hour-long dedication ceremony for newly renamed "Challenger Way/10th Street East" and the rededication of Antelope Valley Fair Center Hall as Challenger Memorial Center.

All the ...

ly she was "thinking about what Mr. McBride was thinking about ... he made a very personal speech," she said.

White also said after hearing McBride that he seemed more "like a human being than a celebrity."

... board ... lyn F ... nce ...

hand, along with area students, who led the crowd in the Pledge of Allegiance.

Challenger Memorial Center was draped in red, white and blue bunting for the occasion. It was a busy place before the program got ... for ...
... evision ... ws fr ... os A ... ar ...

WEDNESDAY

Cats, Aptos win SCCAL openers/ Pg. 16

UP NORTH: Woman wins sled race /Pg. 13

Harbor-expansion plans debated /Pg. 11

■ **Cooking with frozen foods**

■ See special section in today's paper.

Register-Pajaronian

40 Pages — 25 Cents   Watsonville, Calif., Wednesday, March 20, 1985   118th Year — No. 14

Court expands
police powers

WASHINGTON (UPI) — The
Supreme Court ruled today ...
... la ... 'rigid' ... ne li ...

common sense and ordinary
human experience must govern
over ... 'rid ... ria." ... rger

Some newspapers—but not many—use a cursive style of type for their nameplate, as at the *Antelope Valley Press* in Palmdale, Calif. and the Watsonville, Calif. *Register-Pajaronian.* Reprinted by permission.

Good Morning.

It's Wednesday, March 20, 1985.

In the state: A 17-year-old girl has been added to list of victims of serial murderer. **page 9**

A high court ruling broadens the rights of public workers. **page 2**

Would you believe it's chic to drive a pickup truck these days? **page 20**

Award goes to Heal the Children

A Spokane-based charity that finds medical aid for children around the world will receive a citation for outstanding American volunteer achievement from President Reagan.

Heal the Children is one of 53 organizations and individuals in the nation to receive Volunteer Action awards or citations, the White House announced Tuesday.

The organization brings children from other countries to the United States and Canada for medical treatment they can't receive in their homelands. The medical care is donated by doctors and hospitals around the nation.

The children stay with foster families while awaiting and recovering from operations, and transportation costs are covered in part by contributions from individuals and such groups as the Rotary and Variety clubs.

The organization also sends medical teams to Asia and Central America to screen children for the program and perform some surgery in remote areas.

Heal the Children was started by three women sitting around a picnic table in Spokane in 1979 as a way to find heart treatment for children in Guatemala and South Korea.

It now has 100 children receiving free treatment in the United States, said Wes Allen, a Spokane pediatrician and board chairman for the non-profit organization.

The citation is "a very noteworthy comment" on the work of people across the country and the medical personnel who donate their time, Allen said.

♦ Dr. Wes Allen, Spokane pediatrician, examines a Korean boy.

THE SPOKESMAN-REVIEW

| 25 CENTS | SPOKANE, WASHINGTON | 102ND YEAR, NO. 313 |

Governor outlines tax stand

Looking ahead to '86:
Tax hike 'an option'

By LONNIE ROSENWALD
Staff writer

OLYMPIA — Gov. Booth Gardner renewed his no-new tax pledge today — said...

Senate hands victory to MX in 55-45 vote

WASHINGTON (AP) — The Republican-controlled Senate gave President Reagan his first big congressional victory of 1985 on Tuesday by voting 55-45 to free $1.5 billion for production of 21 nightly...

he said in a speech on the Senate floor.

But Bumpers recalled a steady drumbeat of administration argument that the MX was needed to demonstrate nations' will in G...

U.S. Helicopters To Airlift Honduran Soldiers

From Wire Reports

WASHINGTON — U.S. military helicopter crews will ferry Honduran soldiers into a remote, mountainous area along the Nicaraguan border in an attempt to trap Sandinista troops fighting Contra rebels inside Honduras, U.S. officials said yesterday.

Meanwhile, President Reagan promised $20 million in emergency military aid to Honduras to counter the push by Nicaraguan troops into that country.

The U.S. helicopters were directed to bring

Honduran troops and equipment to within "one or two kilometers of the fighting," Rep. Edward Markey, D-Mass., told reporters after a closed-door congressional briefing by Reagan administration officials yesterday afternoon.

"I can't promise you that an American boy won't be shot," Markey quoted an administration official as telling House members. Markey said the official said an effort will be made to keep U.S. servicemen away from the fighting.

Pentagon spokesman Col. Tom Hanlin said "no U.S. helicopters flew today (yesterday)" in support of Honduran forces.

U.S. troops have conducted extensive exercises in Honduras during the past two years, with the number of Americans there expected to peak at 4,600 this May, according to another Pentagon spokesman, Maj. Fred Lash. He said there are 2,000 U.S. soldiers in the country now and there are no plans to send more troops before May.

HONDURAS   **Page 16**

The Union Leader

NEW HAMPSHIRE'S DAILY NEWSPAPER
State Edition

"There is nothing so powerful as truth" - DANIEL WEBSTER

| 123rd Year, No. 308 | 64 Pages | © The Union Leader Corp. | MANCHESTER, N.H., WEDNESDAY, MARCH 26, 1986 | Tel. 668-4321 | 25 Cents |

U.S. Sinks 2 More Libyan Boats

Several newspapers reverse the nameplate, as at the Spokane, Wash. *Spokesman-Review*, which also uses all caps, and at the Manchester, N.H. *Union Leader*, where a skypiece informational graphic and boxed story are incorporated into the page top. Reprinted by permission.

The logo for some newspapers goes beyond type, also including an ornamental symbol of the area or the newspaper name, as seen in the King City, Calif. *Rustler,* the Las Vegas (Nev.) *Sun* and the Rutland (Vt.) *Herald.* Reprinted by permission.

REFERENCE PACKAGES

Complementary to the flag are the inside-reference elements, usually across the top of page one. These are sometimes called "toppers," "boxcars," "reference notes" or "skyline promo boxes." They balance the hard news of page one and tease readers to the best inside-page news and softer feature stories, often using art produced by the local staff. When reference notes are placed on page one according to TPC principles, they should be more than decorative. They should serve to sort out the major inside offerings without overwhelming the reader or taking away from the focus of page one.

Speaking at the Southern Newspaper Publishers Association (SNPA) Foundation seminar, "Layout, Design and Graphics," Gerald Grotta said that the newspaper should do all it can to guide the reader into the paper with as much clarity as possible. "Readers' images of newspapers are usually wrong with reference to what's in them," Grotta said. "Example: angry readers calling up to complain that a certain story wasn't in the paper when it really was there. So, accurate and effective promotion is necessary to let people know what's in the paper and where they can find it."

Reference notes should be arranged according to the order of the pages or sections—for instance, A–3 and then A–5. Several arrangements can be used: two- and three-column box combinations, say, with or without illustrations, line shots, cutout halftones, mug photos, reverse type and spot color. Also possible are horizontal bar listings either set by themselves or balanced against a calendar listing, daily news briefs, the index, a late breaking story, a promotional feature, the sports scoreboard, stock tables or the local weather box.

The publication's issue date should be prominently displayed on page one. Its volume and number—if not on page one—may be placed on page two or three with the masthead listing of postal and subscription information and the paper's mailing addresses—all in type large enough to be easily read.

SECTION TOPPERS

When using section flags, page headers, labels, logos and toppers as reader aids, the two most important considerations are the type selection and the placement on the page. These must be consistent throughout the newspaper so the reader will sense which paper he or she is reading—whether it be the religion page or the sports section. The whole paper should come across as a family unit with many members, all of its contents having been produced by the same staff with the same TPC design philosophy.

When the *News Chronicle* in Thousand Oaks, Calif., changed its design format, the section toppers were also revised. Its editor Sosna explained,

> The thousands of news items we carry each day—and the thousands more that we will publish as news becomes even more important and more available—call for categorizing.

So we decided to label each page of news: Local, State, Nation, World, Business, Sports, and we named one section Life Style. It used to be designated as "Living," but we figured there had been enough ribbing about the "living" editor compared to the "zombies."

While section/page designations may be used for business, food, fashion, leisure, real estate and a myriad of other possibilities, they can also become limiting when news must be left out or continued onto another page because it will not fit on the designated page. Also, regular section pages create the expectation that they will always be there; sometimes, however, there may be not enough specific material to publish a whole topic page.

As the need for new section toppers arises, a newspaper can add them to the file, as the *News Chronicle* did in 1984. Commenting about this in one of his columns, Sosna said that three new "For the Record" pages were created within the local, state, world, business, sports and life style sections.

They contain the assorted information readers want, conveniently boxed by category: the weather reports and forecasts and upcoming government meetings in the "Local" section; engagements, marriages and organizational meeting calendars in "Life Style," and the scores and standings in "Sports." And we created a new section of its own: "Food File," that will highlight one special food item.

The former "Opinion" page is now called, more appropriately, "View Point," because it presents more than opinions. And the *News Chronicle's* editorial, which formerly appeared in a different type and was therefore thought to be sufficiently identifiable, is now unmistakably labeled "Editorial."

If the "folio"—the page number, newspaper name and issue date—is not included in the section/page designation, it should be placed where it may be easily seen: top left on even-numbered pages and top right on odd-numbered pages. Even the size of the numbers themselves are an important consideration. As Sosna said in his "View Point" column, "We also made the page numbers larger, for easier identification in the larger newspaper we now publish."

SIGNATURE-COLUMN HEADLINES

As part of the packaging process, most by-line columns have a "signature" headline that runs every time the column is printed, plus a story headline to describe the theme or at least the top item when the column covers several subjects. Newspapers give these signature headlines different names: "bugs," "column titles," "logos," "sigs" or "standing sigs."

The same column-headline type style should be used throughout the paper—

Section/page toppers may be done in at least three display formats: the reference package as at the tabloid Boston *Herald,* the enlarged section nameplate as at the Casper, Wy. *Star-Tribune,* and the stand-alone folio as at the Trenton (Mo.) *Republican-Times.* Reprinted by permission.

sometimes selected from the same type family as the newspaper's flag. Also for the sake of consistency, column-headline formats should be similar throughout.

However, treatment might be somewhat different for the regular features. Tony Majeri of the Chicago *Tribune* told the SNPA Foundation seminar, "Layout, Design and Graphics" that "heads for 'furniture,' that is, standing feature or anything that's not a news story, should be in a different typeface. This tells the reader immediately that the content is different."

Often a photo of the column's writer is integrated into the head design; this photo should be kept current, and the type should be placed in a harmonizing position. In fact, however, a difference of opinion exists as to whether photos should be included in signature headlines. On the one side there is—for instance—Hines of the *Contra Costa Times,* who says, "We do have on the signature column headlines one head shot each time the column is printed, along with the story headline."

On the other side is Matt Moody, editorial artist at the Los Angeles *Times:*

ANN LANDERS

Bernice Bede Osol

ASTRO-GRAPH

'Little affair' weighs heavy on her heart

Abigail Van Buren

'Dear Abby

DEAR ABBY: I am a widow in my mid-50s. I recently became engaged to a fine gentleman I'll call Clyde. He has been an eligible widower for many years. Our wedding plans are made, but something happened a few days ago that makes me wonder if I should go through with

chat for 15 minutes, totally ignoring my obvious suffering. I finally got up the courage to tell him how sick I felt and asked him to please leave, whereupon he went into a long prayer! I could not believe the insensitivity of this man.

What gives men of the cloth the right to ignore the rules of common courtesy by dropping by unannounced and holding people captive in their homes or hospital rooms? — FORMER CHURCHGOER IN FLORIDA

DEAR FORMER CHURCHGOER: No one has that right. It's presumptuous enough to drop in unannounced at someone's home, but it's inexcusable to ignore a

LOU CANNON

The traditional standing signature head appears in many newspapers, including ones displayed with a photograph of the writer: the Columbia (Mo.) *Daily Tribune*, the Denton (Texas) *Record-Chronicle*, the Los Angeles *Herald Examiner* and the Petersburg, Va. *Progress-Index*. Reprinted by permission.

A writer is not a television personality. People are not going to walk up to you on the street and say, "You're the writer for the L.A. *Times*." You read a newspaper; you don't look at it. To have a picture up there the reader is then dealing with a personality, a person's picture and image. To know what a writer looks like maybe will change my opinion of the writer. A columnist may be 60 years old, or may be only 30 years old; there's a difference there. The *Times* likes to have the paper be known by its writers; it's a writer's paper and it's not a personality paper. There's Scott Ostler, Al Martinez or Jack Smith. They are writers; they are words, not pictures.

Laughs and tears

DAVE
NEWHOUSE

EAST RUTHERFORD, N.J. — Thrown together because the league thought two franchises would look better as one, Gary Plummer and Ray Bentley became the best of friends in six months time.

The Oakland Invaders linebackers played their hearts out last night, then cried together, tears of defeat.

"Ray and I hugged each other," said Plummer in the aftermath of Baltimore's 28-24 victory over Oakland for the USFL championship. "We told each other, 'I love you.' And we meant it. That feeling is pretty consistent on this team."

Plummer estimated that 15 to 20 Invaders shed

Some newspapers where an artist is available on staff or as a freelance illustrator have chosen to add a different form of graphic signature by way of the pen-and-ink drawing, as in the Oakland (Calif.) *Tribune* and the Santa Cruz (Calif.) *Sentinel.* Reprinted by permission.

Wally
Trabing

In the end, the quality of the TPC-designed newspaper will have given a sense of consistency—from page one with its boxed reference notes, to inside page folios that clearly mark the page number and name of the paper, to various section headers and smaller signature heads. Through the creative arrangement of these elements, the reader sees an organized presentation of the news from page to page. Furthermore, the credibility of text and art is enhanced by the subtle message provided by continuity elements. They provide the feel, the look and—indeed—the shell in which the news is presented. Skillfully displayed, the continuity elements keep the reader with the paper longer. Thoughtlessly created and improperly laid on the page, continuity elements do very little for the immediate page—and even less for the total newspaper.

It May Be Last Straw, but Reggie Has Decided to Stir Things Up Some

He came to the ballpark ready to talk, and ready to hit. So what else is new?

Isn't that the way it is every day for Reggie Jackson?

Maybe, but Sunday was differ-

SCOTT OSTLER

couldn't do it, that I couldn't hit homers, that my body wasn't any good anymore. I'm at fault. Now I

TV Tonight
Faye B. Zuckerman

LOS ANGELES -- PBS's version of George Bernard Shaw's *Heartbreak House* on *Great Performances* at 8 p.m. is another example of how good drama of any age maintains its contem- Ellie (Irving), a friend, and Shotover's daughter Lady Utterword (Ivey) appear unexpectedly. Ellie is about to marry a man (George Martin) many years her senior and inside H ri

Showing the face of the writer is not obligatory, and at the Los Angeles *Times* and the Manhattan (Kan.) *Mercury,* only the familiar styling of a writer's name designates the column. Reprinted by permission.

7　　　　　　　　　Adding Headlines

I'd love to see more declarative statements and fewer questions [in headlines]. When you have to read the story to understand the headline, there's big trouble. Designers are simply ignoring headlines and doing other things—labels for instance—and I think designers tend to be mostly at fault with that, but so are editors who let designers design pages without headlines. It's astounding.

Robert Lockwood
president
News Graphics, New Tripoli, Pa.

The headline is an integral element of the newspaper page. It directs the reader to the significant aspect of a story. As all page parts relate to one another in the Total Page Concept (TPC), the headline is not just a label on a story, an identifier or an index. Headlines are so important that even a picture story page is not complete without at least one. Designed to complement each other in size and styling, headlines give definition to the landscape of the newspaper page.

The headline is the vital link between a prospective reader and the news story. Therefore, headlines should accurately convey the story's essence—the who, what and why—while at the same time fitting into the column or columns of space available.

While advertisements and story art are the first elements that grab attention, the reader also reacts to headline typography before reading the story. Design variables include headline type families from Avant Garde to Zapf, and point sizes usually including 12, 14, 18, 24, 36, 48, 60, 72 and 84 point. Since the size of headlines makes them appear so important in a publication, the reader expects them to be in a type size that grades the story's importance. Letters may be set by a photoelectronic typesetter machine, on a computer or taken from adhesive press-on or rub-on art type pages. However, type itself is only two dimensional;

Avant Garde Extra Light (ITC)
Avant Garde Extra Light Oblique (ITC)
Avant Garde Book (ITC)
Avant Garde Book Oblique (ITC)
Avant Garde Medium (ITC)
Avant Garde Medium Oblique (ITC)
Avant Garde Demi (ITC)
Avant Garde Demi Oblique (ITC)
Avant Garde Bold (ITC)
Avant Garde Bold Oblique (ITC)

Bodoni Book
Bodoni Book Italic
Bodoni
Bodoni Italic
Bodoni Bold
Bodoni Bold Italic
Bodoni Extra Bold (Poster)
Bodoni Extra Bold Italic (Poster)

Bookman Light (ITC)
Bookman Light Italic (ITC)
Bookman Medium (ITC)
Bookman Medium Italic (ITC)
Bookman Demi (ITC)
Bookman Demi Italic (ITC)
Bookman Bold (ITC)
Bookman Bold Italic (ITC)

Cheltenham Old Style
Cheltenham Old Style Italic
Cheltenham Light (ITC)
Cheltenham Light Italic (ITC)
Cheltenham Book (ITC)
Cheltenham Book Italic (ITC)
Cheltenham Bold (ITC)
Cheltenham Bold Italic (ITC)
Cheltenham Ultra (ITC)
Cheltenham Ultra Italic (ITC)
Cheltenham Light Condensed (ITC)
Cheltenham Light Condensed Italic (ITC)
Cheltenham Book Condensed (ITC)
Cheltenham Book Condensed Italic (ITC)
Cheltenham Bold Condensed (ITC)
Cheltenham Bold Condensed Italic (ITC)
Cheltenham Ultra Condensed (ITC)
Cheltenham Ultra Condensed Italic (ITC)

Franklin Gothic Book (ITC)
Franklin Gothic Book Italic (ITC)
Franklin Gothic Medium (ITC)
Franklin Gothic Medium Italic (ITC)
Franklin Gothic Demi (ITC)
Franklin Gothic Demi Italic (ITC)
Franklin Gothic Heavy (ITC)
Franklin Gothic Heavy Italic (ITC)

Futura Light
Futura Light Italic
Futura Book
Futura Book Italic
Futura Medium
Futura Medium Italic
Futura Demi
Futura Demi Italic
Futura Bold
Futura Bold Italic
Futura Extrabold
Futura Extrabold Italic
Futura Light Condensed
Futura Book Condensed
Futura Medium Condensed
Futura Bold Condensed
Futura Bold Condensed Italic
Futura Extra Bold Condensed

Garamond Light (ITC)
Garamond Light Italic (ITC)
Garamond Book (ITC)
Garamond Book Italic (ITC)
Garamond Bold (ITC)
Garamond Bold Italic (ITC)
Garamond Ultra (ITC)
Garamond Ultra Italic (ITC)

Helvetica Light
Helvetica Light Italic
Helvetica
Helvetica Italic
Helvetica Bold
Helvetica Bold Italic
Helvetica Bold No. 2
Helvetica Heavy
Helvetica Heavy Italic
Helvetica Black
Helvetica Black Italic
Helvetica Black No. 2

Old English

Oracle
Oracle Italic
Oracle Bold

Souvenir Light (ITC)
Souvenir Light Italic (ITC)
Souvenir Medium (ITC)
Souvenir Medium Italic (ITC)
Souvenir Demi (ITC)
Souvenir Demi Italic (ITC)
Souvenir Bold (ITC)
Souvenir Bold Italic (ITC)

Times Roman
Times Roman Italic
Times Roman Semi
Times Roman Semi Italic
Times Roman Bold
Times Roman Bold Italic
Times Roman Extra Bold
Times Roman Condensed
Times Roman Condensed Italic
Times Roman Bold Condensed
Times Roman Bold Condensed Italic

Univers Light (45)
Univers Light Italic (46)
Univers Light Condensed (47)
Univers Light Condensed Italic (48)
Univers Medium Expanded (53)
Univers Medium (55)
Univers Medium Italic (56)
Univers Medium Condensed (57)
Univers Medium Condensed Italic (58)
Univers Bold Expanded (63)
Univers Bold (65)
Univers Bold Italic (66)
Univers Bold Condensed (67)
Univers Bold Condensed Italic (68)
Univers Extrabold Expanded (73)
Univers Extrabold (75)
Univers Extrabold Italic (76)

Zapf Book Light (ITC)
Zapf Book Light Italic (ITC)
Zapf Book Medium (ITC)
Zapf Book Medium Italic (ITC)
Zapf Book Demi (ITC)
Zapf Book Demi Italic (ITC)
Zapf Book Heavy (ITC)
Zapf Book Heavy Italic (ITC)

While the page designer is not limited to these examples of typefaces, at most newspapers one style is used for the story text and two or three complementary styles are used for headlines, cutlines, subheads, and so on.

alone, it does not make a story important or unimportant. The reader is lured into the story not only by easily read type, but also by the clarity of writing in the headline.

Though it is tempting to mix type families, this should only be done with serious thought about the look of the finished page. Robert Lehmenkuler, while serving as business systems marketing manager for Compugraphic in Wilmington, Mass., made several points about mixing typefaces. In a *Communication Briefings* article on using type more effectively (and with reference to a booklet entitled "Type Awareness" published by Compugraphic), Lehmenkuler made four suggestions to designers:

- Mix and match typefaces carefully. Too many variations create confusion that turns readers off.
- Mixing two sans serif typefaces is usually not a good idea, especially if they have similar design traits.
- Avoid mixing typefaces with extremely contrasting shapes, pronounced curves, or exaggerated serifs.
- Create variety while preserving coherence by using different typefaces from the same family.

HEADLINE WRITING AND PLACEMENT

The headline must describe the story accurately; otherwise, the effort of the writer is lost on the reader. It is particularly important that, while developing a headline that will fit, editors be careful not to write a "cute" headline that then needs to be qualified with subheads.

In their 1983 study of newspaper front pages (see Table 6) Steve Pasternack and Sandra Utt found that, at 44.4 percent of the nonmodular dailies, there was no pattern to the location of page one's largest headline. But among the modular dailies, only 25 percent indicated a similar flexibility. Also, as the researchers said in a footnote, "Some responses [from editors] indicated the selection of rarely used type sizes such as 64 point, 84 point, 90 point, 100 point, 104 point, 108 point, 112 point and 160 point."

Table 6
Modular and Nonmodular Newspapers' Placement of the Largest Headline (in percentages)

	Upper Right	Upper Left	Across the Top	No Set Pattern
Modular	50.0	4.2	20.8	25.0
Nonmodular	26.7	0	28.9	44.4

Source: Sandra H. Utt and Steve Pasternack, "Front Pages of U.S. Daily Newspapers," *Journalism Quarterly* (1984):879–84.

In addition to honoring the informative relationship between the headline and the story, the designer must consider what kind of look will be created whether the headline is placed above or adjacent to the text. For best effect, alternatives to the standard headline placement should be used sparingly. Tony Majeri, of the Chicago *Tribune* cautioned against using deviations from the standard placement when he spoke to the Southern Newspaper Publishers Association (SNPA) Foundation seminar, "Layout, Design and Graphics." He made the following points:

- Do not use side heads; they trap white space. It would be better to drop the head into the first column of type and raw wrap the other columns. [A "raw wrap" is where columns of type do not have a headline extending over them. The "saddle dutch wrap," "straight dutch wrap" and "sunken dutch wrap" are all ways that headlines may be handled, as the figures in this chapter show.]

- Get rid of kickers, hammers and hanging indents. They create unnecessary white space that gets trapped if the makeup is modular. [These graphic gimmicks (explained under "Caps and Lower Case" later in this chapter) should be saved for stories that might benefit from special treatment, such as the packaging of a continuing news series or a special topic page.]

Page 4-C   ★★   EL PASO TIMES, Friday, January 10, 1986

By Julio Lujan
Times staff writer

NCAA stats show Ags 11th nationally in scoring defense

LAS CRUCES — A year ago, New Mexico State may have been the laughingstock of Pacific Coast Athletic Association basketball circles. Today, the Aggies continue climbing out of the dead.

The Aggies, 8-3 on the season and unbeaten after two road games, rank 11th nationally in scoring defense, allowing 58.7 points in 11 games.

Last season, the Aggies had a very soft defense in a 7-20 season, including a bleaker 3-11 mark in the Pan American Center. NMSU surrendered an average of 76.3 points — eighth-best in the 10-team PCAA.

Best on defense

The NCAA's college basketball team defense leaders through Monday's games

	G	Pts.	Avg.
1. Princeton	10	532	53.2
2. Indiana St.	10	548	54.8
3. St. Peter's	12	664	55.3
4. S.W. Missouri	12	665	55.8
5. N. Caro. A&T	6	339	56.5
6. UTEP	14	797	56.9
7. Ala.-Birmingham	15	866	57.7
8. Richmond	10	580	58.0
9. Fresno St.	13	758	58.3
10. California	12	704	58.7
11. NMSU	11	646	58.7

This time, NMSU rates second in the PCAA behind Fresno State's 58.3 clip that stands ninth nationally.

NMSU Coach Neil McCarthy was unaware his team compared that well defensively.

McCarthy attributes that early success to his team's development since winning four straight games.

"Our guards — Jeff Williams, Kenny Travis and Virgil Harris — have taken control," McCarthy said. "Gilbert (Wilburn) and Pierre (Smith) have established themselves as starting forwards ... I think all of that has helped."

Princeton and Indiana State rank 1-2, yielding 53.2 and 54.8 points, according to this week's National Collegiate Athletic Association statistics. UTEP is sixth (56.9 in 14 games).

NMSU plays Long Beach State

Saturday at the Pan American Center.

Aggie assistant coach Dan Dion was equally surprised that the team has made the turnaround that quickly.

"Gosh, that's great," Dion said. "Hopefully we can continue that trend. For us to be successful, defense is what it's going to take."

The Aggies have relied on speed, quickness and defense this season. Their tallest player is 6-8 freshman center Steve McGlothin, although McCarthy brings 6-9, 235-pound junior Brian Soistman off the bench. But Soistman has played an average of 10 minutes in five games.

Alabama knocks off LSU

As ... 'ed ...

Intimidation? Yes sir, Idaho found out about the big time

By Dave Boling
of the Tribune

LOS ANGELES · Perhaps the shadow of the two national championship banners hanging above the basket caused the poor Idaho shooting.

Certainly, the banners cast a reflection. They reflected the University of Southern California's tradition, its power and its tournament experience.

Relying on those attributes, the Trojans rather easily handed Idaho a 74-51 defeat at the Los Angeles Sports Arena in an NCAA tournament opening-round game.

And whether it was labeled intimidation or

simple nervousness, it caused the generally deadeye Vandals to connect on a paltry 36 percent from the floor Friday.

"We just haven't played that kind of competition all year and it showed," said Idaho Coach Pat Dobratz, whose club finishes with a 28-2 record.

"We're normally good shooters and we got some good shots but they just didn't fall," Dobratz said.

"The major fact is that we were intimidated the whole time," she said. Dobratz felt that the Vandals were far too slow adjusting to the level of competition.

"We've never seen a team that quick," she said. "They made us look worse than we are."

The net result was an amazingly poor start in a game that Dobratz labeled getting a fast start as the key.

"We just rushed our shots and changed our shots," Dobratz said.

Some of the shots were changed for the Vandals as all-American Cheryl Miller blocked four Idaho attempts - one against center Mary Raese early in the game.

USC Coach Linda Sharp rejects the idea that Idaho was intimidated.

"I can't believe they were intimidated; they came in here with a 28-1 record and facing the shot to knock off the defending national

See Intimidation, Page 2C

Saddle dutch wrap—placement of the headline to the left of the text, with type spread across the page columns—creates a design where the story text is the dominant element; this design is especially useful as a shelf across the top of a large advertisement or at the page bottom as an anchor. These examples show different ways the saddle head is used at the El Paso (Texas) *Times* and the Lewiston (Idaho) *Morning Tribune*. Reprinted by permission.

Wastes found in field apparently hazardous

By Joe Dowd

Democrat and Chronicle

BYRON — Preliminary tests on samples taken from steel drums found in a Genesee County field indicate that the barrels contain hazardous wastes, a state Department of Environmental Conservation officer said yesterday.

Jerry Sporer of the DEC's enforcement section said the 219 drums apparently contain organic solvents, which are considered hazardous under state law.

Organic solvents are usually petroleum-based materials used to dissolve other chemicals. They are commonly used to thin paint, but have other uses in industry. They are usually flammable, and can damage a water supply.

State police have not made any arrests in the case, and say they don't expect to until tests are completed.

After an anonymous tip, state police raided a Byron farm field Thursday on Transit Road and found the barrels.

The 55-gallon drums pose no immediate threat to public safety or the environment, Sporer said. The materials are believed to be flammable, however, and police have roped off the area.

Eric Seiffer, DEC's regional director in Avon, said the samples were taken to Buffalo for testing. He said the final results could be known in a week, or it might take as long as four months.

A form of straight dutch wrap—headline as the main first-column typographic element—is shown in an example from the Rochester, N.Y. *Democrat and Chronicle.* Reprinted by permission.

By FRANK WHELAN
Of The Morning Call

In the spring of 1910 the Lehigh Valley had more than enough news to read about. Most of it dealt with bloody confrontations between management and labor. The long, acrimonious strike at Bethlehem Steel was just drawing to a close, railroad engineers were planning a nationwide walkout and Philadelphia's bloody streetcar strike had finally been settled.

It was also quite a spring for funerals. Mark Twain had died on April 21, King Edward the VII of England joined him on May 5 and Noah T. Shaw, the undertaker who had embalmed Lincoln, left the world on May 15.

Washington, D.C.'s, polite society was still shocked over the suffragettes' hissing of President William Howard Taft. The president had suggested a woman's place was in the home and not the voting booth. But the ladies had other ideas and greeted the chief executive's suggestion with something less than enthusiasm.

In Allentown, William Roxberry, William Kennedy and William Boyle had more immediate concerns. They were serving time in the city's jail, paying the penalty for stealing cheese and crackers from a grocer's wagon so they would have something to go with their beer.

Meanwhile a traveler from the edge of the solar system was to pay a visit. Its arrival that year was expected. Ever since its 1758 appearance, mankind had Halley's comet on a timetable. So 75 years after its 1835 showing, astronomers confidently talke of Halle return

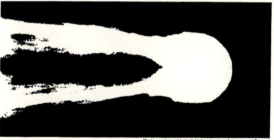

Photo courtesy of Lehigh Valley Amateur Astronomical Society

Dr. G.W. Ritchey took this photo May 8, 1910 at the Mount Wilson Observatory, Calif., during the comet's last appearance.

SPACE VISITOR

Valley citizens' reactions ranged from curiosity to fear

that the comet could be a danger to earth. It was said that cyanogen gas in the tail of the visitor from space would sweep over the earth and poison the atmosphere. Although most scientists pooh-poohed this theory, a lot of people around the world were not taking any chances. The Chronicle and News reported that in some parts of the country, particularly in the rural south, churches were full and police courts quiet. Postcard vendor New York City re said

sy a shower of rain." Others such as Harvard's Robert Wilson thought it might create an effect like the Northern Lights. He added, "there may be a shower of charged particles, very small but very numerous" that could, " affect wireless telegraphy." But Wilson's boss, Professor Edward C. Pickering, dismissed the whole thing. He declared simply, "I doubt if there will be any effect at all."

But the world wr ready t rel- ne H Co d r nt

In the Lehigh Valley, the Eagles party was in full swing. Out in the country Miss Mamie Moyer, daughter of Frank Moyer, proprietor of the East Macungie Hotel, had secured a ladder and was climbing up to the roof of her house to get a better look. On roofs all over Allentown hundreds of people with the same idea looked to the sky. In the city's bars and saloons others were getting generously "load and se more n one

stationed on the roof garden made heroic efforts to locate the comet," noted The Morning Call, "no result was obtained up to an early hour in the morning when members who had lingered for the end of the activity left for their homes well satisfied with the evening session."

Out in Macungie the ladder-climbing Mamie Moyer was not amused. She had never even reached her destination. "When she was almost to the top," said the newspapers, "the ladder collapsed and she fell to the floor. She declares she saw 50 comets and suffered painful bruises."

Some people said that they had seen something but these reports were usually attributed to one too many comet cocktails. "One young reporter," stated The Morning Call, "came back from the Sixth Ward and declared that he had seen three stars fall in quick succession; each of which broke into a thousand fragments. As no one else saw the same occurrence, it is likely that the reporter's imagination was a trifle too vivid."

Word had also come from Hackensack, N.J., of one poor woman that the comet had driven insane. She had been taken to the Morris Plains Insane Asylum by the local constable. According to the Chronicle and News, "the unfortunate woman was a victim of nervous collapse following the comet agitation. All the way to Morris Plains she continually said she would follow the comet no matter where it went."

The newspaper was not all despair. It reminded comet watchers that they still had a chance to catch the heavenly visitor on Friday night when it swung through the sky again. "There will then be no light from the ris in to the g of the

Sunken dutch wrap centers the headline between the columns of text type, as displayed in this Allentown, Pa. *Morning Call.* Reprinted by permission of Call-Chronicle Newspapers, Inc.

Nanette Bisher, design editor of the *Orange County Register* in Santa Ana, Calif., made suggestions for the application of two other types of headlines—feature, and the lead as headline—when she spoke to the same SNPA Foundation seminar. Regarding feature headlines, Bisher said,

> When laying out a feature page and using a big head for type attack, try to place it directly above the copy, rather than above dominant art or centered somewhere on the page. Readers' eyes fall naturally down the page, and the head is more likely to lead them into the story if it's directly above it.

Sometimes headlines for feature articles are not so specific about the topic as those placed with news stories. Often they are written in an intriguing manner to lure the reader into the story's subject matter, or are more of a "label" that only suggests the topic.

Concerning the lead as headline, Bisher said,

> If it is difficult to write a headline for a story, but the story has a dynamite lead, use the lead as the head. Set it in several lines—six to eight—of type in descending sizes, then let the next graf [paragraph] follow in regular type size.

WHAT A HEADLINE DOES: HOW AND WHY

An editor must take into consideration what a headline does and how it does it. A headline:

- provides a place for the eye to land. If all type were 10-point text, the news of the page would be lost amid column after column of gray.
- calls attention to why stories are being published; it sells the story.
- makes a statement, with a subject and a verb, to tell readers what the story is about.
- must be written from the lead paragraph of a news story, and from a point beyond the lead in a feature story.
- has integrity; accuracy in a head is no less important than in a story.
- reads like a sentence in down style—lower case letters, with upper case (capitals or caps) used only at the beginning of the headline and for proper nouns. Some papers use an up style—lower case, with caps for the first letter of each word except articles and all or some prepositions. Using all capital letters for headlines hinders readability and should be reserved for striking effect with only a single word or two (such as "SHUTTLE EXPLODES"). Also a section

flag—SPORTS or LIFE STYLE—which is seen everyday by the reader will work in all capital letters. (This is discussed further in the "Caps and Lower Case" section of this chapter.)

- grades the relative importance of the news so the reader will not be misled. This is done by headline point size, along with the story's length and placement on the page and in the paper.

- should not be in too small a point size for the number of columns and the depth of story that it covers. For example, one deck (line) of 18 point is sufficient for a 5-inch story spread over two columns, but this same point size would not be so attractive with a 12-inch story spread over three columns; and 24-point type will effectively cover a 12-inch story spread over three columns but would not work so well spread over four columns.

- should be written to fill at least three-fourths of the width of its allotted space. If it is not, the reader's eye will be attracted to the trapped white space. (White space is considered "trapped" when it is the first thing that a reader's eye is drawn to on the page.)

- is usually set in the same type family established for all the paper's headlines, except in special circumstances.

Because reading newspapers is a voluntary experience, anything that makes the reading difficult should be avoided. To quickly test the look of the headlines, the designer can hold the completed page upside down or at a cross-angle upside down so that the top of the page becomes the bottom, and then view it from a few feet away. This causes the eye to focus on any unattractive white or ashen-gray places, if they exist. If the page is attractively designed, it will be strong whether right side up or upside down.

HEADLINE PLACEMENT AND RELATIVE SIZE

Headline writers follow certain widespread, consistent design principles that have been proven to work well for broadsheet format papers. Additional decisions that they should make when designing a TPC newspaper include:

- whether headlines should be flush left, centered or flush right, and either up style or down style;
- how to avoid having too many horizontal—and sometimes too many single-line—headlines on the same page; and
- just how much kerning (the space between letters) will help or hinder legibility.

Majeri at the Chicago *Tribune* offers two design tips regarding headline placement and size:

- Do not allow editors to condense headlines to fit. This destroys uniform kerning.
- Flush everything left. Do not center any headlines or bylines for any reason.

While Majeri makes an important point about headline styling at his own paper, there are others who disagree and do things differently. Majeri is correct in terms of news pages; but when it comes to special pages, the occasional manipulation of kerning and the positioning of headlines other than flush left can give variety and enhance the Total Page Concept. When the kerning is adjusted manually, it can compensate with white space to make the words in a headline fit into a desired column width. While kerning can be done within the letters of a word, it works best between words. This is less noticeable to the eye because letters are not so likely to be crammed on top of one another, leaving the words difficult to read. As for position, since the headline is the passageway into a story, and because the eye reads from the left, headlines that are flush right should be used sparingly—and usually just for special feature story displays.

Taller Hoyas trump Friars' strategy switch, prevail, 69-54

By MIKE STANTON
Journal-Bulletin Sports Writer

PROVIDENCE — Rick Pitino tried to shorten the game, but unfortunately the Providence coach couldn't shorten the Georgetown Hoyas.

And that, Friar fans, was the lon° an⁴ sh⌐rt ⌐f i⁴ at ⌐he ⌐ivi⌐

problem is a lack of athletic ability among our frontcourt people."

Matters weren't helped any by the fact that centers Steve Wright and Jacek Duda, the only Friars over 6-foot-7, got into foul trouble. The slumping Wright finished with eight points in 18 minutes after rlayi⌐g j⌐st f ⌐r ⌐in⌐⌐es ⌐d ⌐il-

While most newspapers "flush left" the headlines, others have established a centered style, as used by the Providence, R.I. *Journal-Bulletin*. Reprinted by permission.

Headlines should be written as horizontal arrangements of type—not (if it can be helped) vertical that must be read down. Also, they should not always be set as a single deck of type in a point size too small for the story itself. For most typefaces, a two-column story—two single columns of type or a double-width column of type—should be no deeper than five inches under a single-deck headline. Use two decks if the story is six inches deep or more, and three decks if the story is 11 inches or more—up to 16 inches of text type. Stories that run any deeper than that as a single or double column of type should be arranged across more columns or continued elsewhere, for maximum readership.

Other considerations for the page editor include:

- how to design a page without burying headlines;
- deciding whether a headline is too large, too small, or a good size to fit the story; and
- whether a hood (a border over or alongside the headline) would help or hinder legibility.

Another use for headline type is in the display of overlines—headlines for photos. In the 1983 Pasternack and Utt study, overlines appeared on the front pages of 80.3 percent of the newspapers surveyed.

Of those newspapers using overlines, 27.9 percent use them with all front page photos. Most commonly they are set in either 18- or 24-point type (71.6 percent). Some dailies indicated that overline size depends on photograph size.

NEWS GRADING AND EVENT CHRONICLING

The task of grading the news always brings up related concerns as the editor and designer are faced with how to chronicle accurately the day's or week's events. While headlines should call attention to why stories are being published and why they are worthy of being read, the primary purpose of the newspaper—the news itself—will not be enhanced by important-looking headlines, but only by stories that are well written and tightly edited.

Therefore, in addition to the responsibility of writing accurate headlines or seeing that they are written and placed with the stories, the news editor and designer must avoid creating a beautifully designed newspaper that has few—if any—interesting stories. Newspapers published with numerous pages of "fluff" might as well set the alphabet in type as many times as necessary to represent each story and add black cutouts to designate photos—for the amount of readership that the paper will receive.

However, it is certainly possible that a newspaper staff may be doing its best and that still, for any given issue or edition, there are no significant stories to publish. It may be a slow day—or week. In such cases, using a headline schedule based solely on a story's value or impact on the reader becomes impossible.

STAN ALOST MORNING ADVOCATE

Safety in numbers

These four tame ducks in the Atchafalaya Basin may not be in danger, but their natural inclination is to stick together. Besides, solitude is not always what it's quacked up to be.

An overline may be used above a photo or—as in this example in the Baton Rouge, La., *Morning Advocate*—only above the caption. Reprinted by permission.

SERIF/SANS SERIF HEADS

Many of the early newspapers had only one typeface, usually one with serifs (fine lines projecting from the strokes of the letters); and the entire newspaper—stories, headlines and advertising—was set in that face. With Bodoni and other serif fonts, the type itself was clean and easy to read because of the flow created by the extra flourishes of the serifs. At some newspapers today, the headline typeface is sans serif (lacking the fine serif lines) so that the heads are clearly distinguishable from the story type.

Typeface selection sometimes comes down to a question of attractiveness vs. readability. Whatever the reason a publication decides to use a type font, it is best to select a style that is legible over a style that is attractive or beautiful but harder to read.

One serviceable typeface created especially for a specific newspaper is L.A. Times Roman, a face drawn for computer typesetting. This new typeface was created as the Los Angeles *Times* was entering the 1980s, when Sheila de Bretteville was called in to retool Times New Roman Bold. Dugald Stermer, writing in *Communication Arts* (1982), said that de Bretteville saw the retooling project as "a logical extension of typography determined by changing technology." In 1931, the *Times* of London had commissioned Stanley Morison through the Monotype Corp. to design the first typeface specifically intended for a newspaper. "When Sheila researched the history of newspapers, it became clear that the best—if obvious—choice of typefaces would be prototype versions of Morison's designs, but that the typeface fonts needed redesigning," Stermer said. "This she did, with amazing success, and with the collaboration of type designers Ronald Arnholm and Kenneth Williams."

Another designer who has researched the effects of various typeface choices is Lisa Vanco of Westlake Village, who spearheaded the redesign of the *News Chronicle* in Thousand Oaks, Calif. during 1982–84. Prior to the redesign, the paper's headlines had been set in Bodoni. Vanco's research led her to suggest the selection of Oracle. In Marvin Sosna's "View Point" column on June 17, 1984—the first day of the redesigned newspaper—he said, "We narrowed our field to what is called a 'square-round' effect, and came up with a type that is called Oracle. It is stronger than the headline type we have used for the last 19 years or so, that is called Bodoni; the difference consists largely in the width of the horizontal portions of each letter, which are darker in Oracle than they are in Bodoni and thus are more readable."

The key to choosing headline typeface is instant readability. Type such as Old English—which is really German script—works well as a corporate identity on a newspaper's nameplate because it is seen daily and is almost not even read every time. But so ornate a typeface will hinder—if not halt—the reading of a headline, especially if it is set in all caps.

CONSISTENCY OF FONTS

Since readers like to see the newspaper as a "family" or collection of material all coming from the same location, headline consistency can go a long way toward creating this image of TPC cohesiveness. Therefore, the same headline font—printing type of a particular face and size—or complementary fonts from the newspaper's established headline schedule should be used for all headlines. For instance, news and features might be set only in Helios or Helvetica; these and Times Roman Bold might be used for fast-breaking stories. These main headlines could be run with a Futura or Univers Condensed Italic kicker (small size; see "Caps and Lower Case" below) or drop headline, and an italic version of any of these faces might be used for a news feature or an editorialized story.

In addition to the consistency factor, there is at least one other point to consider: Headlines should be both energetically bold and of contrasting medium to light typefaces if there is to be any typographical depth to the page. While the reader may not immediately recognize how a headline characterizes a story as being straight news or a news or lighter feature, the size of the headline is taken as a clue to the importance of a story, at least of a news story. Usually headlines that are 24 points or larger should be used on all stories—except news briefs—to provide legibility. Staff-written or syndicated columns and occasional feature displays may be headed in a different way, as discussed earlier in Chapter 6.

CAPS AND LOWER CASE

Most newspapers use both upper and lower case letters for headlines, either in down style—like a sentence—or in up style—like the chapter titles in this book. The term "case" originated when printers used to take individual letters out of a case or font box and place them in a stock or galley to make a headline, compose a story and then assemble an entire publication.

Some newspapers use all capital letters for kickers—smaller size headlines set

SPORTS

Ted Blofsky
Executive Sports Editor

Skip Reager
Sports Editor

Chico Enterprise-Record
Sunday, March 17, 1985

1C

STATE CHAMPIONS!

Pleasant Valley girls top El Camino 63-49

By David Little
Sports Writer

OAKLAND — An hour after the state basketball finals, Tom Campbell was saying, "It's hard to believe."

Across the Oakland Coliseum, El Camino Coach Ray Johnson was in his locker room saying the same thing.

Pleasant Valley High School dealt El Camino a 63-49 beating for the Division II crown, and both teams were surprised by the ease of it.

"We were confident and thought we could win by five or six points, at best," said Coach Campbell, whose team completed a perfect 28-0 year. "I didn't expect to win by that much."

El Camino, and many of its followers, were in for a rude awakening. Seven of the mistakes were by far the most for the Wildcats this year. Pleasant Valley had 15 steals and played a tight man-to-man defense. Nobody had dared to run a man defense against El Camino — at least not for very long — but PV pulled it off. The Wildcats finished 40 percent from the field (24-for-60) after averaging over 50 percent this year.

Anderson spearheaded the defensive effort. She was assigned to Sharon Turner, the state's leading scorer at 34 points per game and an All-America candidate. Anderson hounded Turner all night. Turner finished with a season-high nine turnovers and an 8-for-21 shooting mark. She was held to 16 points, but showcased her passing skills with eight assists.

You can say all you want about Sharon Turner, but the Anderson did a great job.

While caps and lower case headlines are generally recommended, all caps may be more dramatic in some major story instances, as in this example from the Chico (Calif.) *Enterprise-Record.* Reprinted by permission.

over the main headline or over short, one-column boxed stories; or for the writer's name in a standing column head. Used sparingly for a specific reason with five or six words that are not more than a half-dozen letters each, caps— although not easy to read quickly—provide contrast to a full page of otherwise "C&lc" (capital and lower case) heads.

In any case—whether written with all caps or caps and lower case—kicker, drop (smaller size set under the main headline) and hammer (or reverse kicker) headlines must have a uniform relationship (half plus one point size greater, say) to the main headline combination. For instance, if the main headline is 36 points photoset on 37 points (allowing half a point of space for a descending letter of the alphabet—a descender—and half a point of space for an ascending letter—an ascender), it would be best for the kicker headline or drop headline to be at least 24 points, set in italic to contrast with the roman of the main headline. The relationship of sizes should be established in the newspaper's guidelines. The size combinations for the hammer headline—actually larger than the main headline—would have the hammer 36 points and the main headline 24 points (again, based on editor/designer preference), in medium-face type.

Drop heads contain additional information for the reader in what would otherwise be wasted white space. They are better to use than kickers or hammer heads because drop heads are directly under the main head. Careless placement of a kicker or hammer head above or beside the main head can be nonpurposeful and a waste of space, a precious commodity. If used at all, kickers and hammers should be on the top of a page, where they won't trap white space. Any placement works only if the eye isn't initially attracted to white space.

The pica indentation for the main headline can be measured in either picas or ems. (There are six picas in one inch. An "em" is the square of the type size; for instance, "18-em" means that the type is 18 points high and 18 points wide. Em is one of the space keys on some typesetter keyboards.) The main headline under a kicker or hammer headline should be indented the same number of picas each time the combination is used, thus creating a consistent style.

MULTICOLUMN AND MULTILINE HEADS

The use of more than one line of head type—horizontal stacking of type—becomes a convenience for the headline writer and also provides relief (air or white space) on the page. A designer can tell whether white space is "trapped" or whether it "gives relief" by determining if the white space is conspicuous by its presence; it should not be. Just as multicolumn headlines create horizontal variation, multiline headlines provide vertical relief.

Imagine how visually boring it would be if all headlines were only one column wide on one line. The reader would find it mentally impossible to grade the

Warriors OK after Baldi loss

Underclassmen set to fill void at Woodbridge

When you've lost the servies of a 6-9 all-league player with the physical dominance which Italian Marco Baldi provided last season, you might expect a wake to prevail for some time — but in the case of Woodbridge High basketball coach Bill Shannon, such a situation has not materialized.

Rather, Shannon says he's more excited now with the season approaching than had Baldi stayed.

Far-fetched? Not really. Although th' Wa 'ior 'nt 'th' 198 '-85 'eas 'n

New heart too late to save her?

Slow recovery worries doctor

Associated Press

MINNEAPOLIS — The first woman to receive an artificial heart grasped a doctor's hand Friday, but a spokesman for her surgeons said she is not recovering as quickly as they hoped and the implant may have come too late.

Mary Lund, 40, who suffered from a rare heart disease, received a scaled-down version of the Jarvik-7 hear† in a si '-ho:r o'era†ion Thurs-

The drop head—directly beneath the main headline—may be displayed across the width of the main head, as shown in the Mesa, Calif. *Daily Pilot* and the Everett, Wash. *Herald*, or only in the first column of text type. Reprinted with permission.

Feeding the needy for 10 years at Padua Dining Room

Times Tribune staff

For the past 10 years, the volunteers and staff at the Padua Dining Room in Menlo Park have trusted in providence to aid their efforts to provide the poor and needy with something to eat.

At St. Patrick's Day the donated cabbages start to roll in, and now the turkeys are being counted in anticipation of Thanksgiving.

It is the 10th anniversary of the dining room, which is located at St. Anthony's Church on Lower Middlefield Road in Menlo Park, and although it has seen many changes, for the hundreds that eat there, it is still the place to go for a hot meal.

Dennis Kent, now the manager of the dining room, started out as a dishwasher there a few months after it first opened in 1974.

Back in those days, he said, 175 people being served a meal was considered a big day. Now, an average of 300 people per day eat at the dining room, which is open from 11 a.m. to 1 p.m. every day except Sunday.

Kent said that one of the big changes over the years is the availability of donated food.

"We have pretty high visibility now," he said. "We have a greater variety and availability of donated food."

Still, the dining room is always looking for more volunteers, said the president of the dining room board of directors, Vince Bruno.

A dinner was held last weekend at the dining room to celebrate the 10th anniversary and also to show appreciation for the help of the many donors and volunteers.

The 200 people attending the dinner were treated to ham and turkey with all the dressings, and a volunteer who has worked there since 1975, Mrs. Phil Weston, was recognized as an outstanding volunteer whose service has been an inspiration to all at the dining room.

Actors Give Production Style, Humor

Carpenter Square's 'Ritz' a Hit

For a good time, check in at "The Ritz" down at Carpenter Square Theatre, 840 Robert S. Kerr.

This adult farce by Terrance McNally, which runs through Jan. 26, is full of wit, wisdom and plain old belly laughs.

The fun starts when Gaetano Proclo, a hapless garbage man from Cleveland, warmly portrayed by Shawn Greenfield, stumbles into a men's bathhouse in New York City.

Terrified because he is being pursued by his Mafioso brother-in-law Carmine Vespucci, played in a hilariously tight-lipped style by Mike Samples, Proclo hopes to find solace and a good night's sleep in the bathhouse.

No such luck.

The plot twists and turns upon mistaken identity, crossed purposes, a dash of mystery and the lure of big money.

Strong shots of visual humor — such as people crawling under beds, silly floor shows, outlandish costumes and men getting dragged into the steam room — are injected throughout the production, which is directed by Kelly McDonald.

The 14-member cast works well together with strong performances by the leads as well as the supporting characters.

Greenfield is chubby-cheeked and vul-

Review

nerable in the lead role which demands the ability to be silly, but emotionally believable.

Greenfield handles the role quite well with outstanding support from Sam Burris as Chris, the lean, swishy bathhouse patron with a heart of gold. Burris brings a good sense of timing and restraint to this role and his performance is one of several highlights.

Len Slater goes straight for the slap-

stick in his portrayal of Claude Perkins, a crazed bathhouse patron, and Michelle DeLong brings non-stop high energy to her role as Googie Gomez, a bathhouse singer who is in constant search of fame and glory. Scott Gordon is hilarious as the dim-witted detective who manages to misinterpret every situation and miss every clue.

Tim Treadway as Tiger and Ted Enlow as Duff bring a nice sense of calm to their performances as bathhouse employees and reluctant floor show performers. Their floor show with Gomez is a highlight and the amateur night performances brought down the house on press night.

Carpenter Square consistently presents the most provocative, risk-taking theater in town. With the organization of its new advisory board, which includes Central State University's Clif Warren and Broadway playwrights McNally, Lanford Wilson and Milan Stitt, Carpenter Square is well on the way to putting Oklahoma City on the regional theater map.

— **Mary Sue Price**

Kickers—smaller headlines above the main head—are used at some newspapers; but because of all the trapped white space created, they should probably be used only with stories at the top of a page. These examples show good use of the kicker: the *Peninsula Times Tribune* in Palo Alto, Calif. and the *Daily Oklahoman* in Oklahoma City. Reprinted by permission.

Luck smiles

It's Doby's Delight as lost check returned — and more

By Faye Fiore
Staff writer

At about the time Doby Marsellos was counting the number of days before he would run out of food, a Central American man named Fernando was picking up a employee on Lorne street

didn't get the man's name.

The next day the Treasury Department sent Doby a check for $122 and a letter saying he had been shorted about $4 a month since February 1983. It might have been the report of the lost check that uncovered

---

Hammers—reverse kickers—are an effective headline form if used for specially selected news or news features; they are best used if the hammer word or words carry a singular meaning, as shown in an example from the Torrance, Calif. *Daily Breeze.* Reprinted by permission.

From the world's soccer fields to the streets of Pasadena, Brazil's most famous export scores popularity

Grand Marshal Pele loves a parade

By DOUG CRESS
Staff Writer

Pele: To most Americans, it is simply a name synonymous with a sport played elsewhere.

Eleven years ago, a tiny, black man bounded out of a tunnel into a

you to pay attention to the young of the world, the children, the kids. We need them too much."

Tears mixed with the raindrops running down his face. Pele wiped his eyes and continued.

"Love is more important than what we can take in life. Everything pass.

When a short kicker is not enough, some newspapers use a "prelude headline" to take the reader into the story, as shown in this Pasadena, Calif. *Star-News.* Reprinted by permission.

Bucks tab Warrick and Lamp — SPORTS

Fashion: Crusading for the over-40 crowd — PAGE 6

Tosa: $2.23 tax rate hike recommended — PAGE 10

Series: Saberhagen cuts Cards' lead to 2-1 — SPORTS

Weather
Mostly cloudy, 60% chance of rain Wednesday. High 66 to 71. Low 44 to 49. Decreasing cloudiness Thursday. High 58 to 63. Maps and tables. PAGE 14.

MILWAUKEE SENTINEL

36 Pages, 3 Parts   Wednesday morning, October 23, 1985   ★ ★ ★ ★ Edition

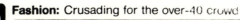

Maier hits chord on Bradley Center

By Mike Christopulos

Mayor Maier may have lost his pitch for a Downtown Bradley Center, but to prove he's still in tune, he has penned a new song.

To the tune of "Down in the Valley," the ditty celebrates the construction of the sports arena at County Stadium instead of Downtown — which Maier favored.

Maier also has cut a tape of his song. It features his baritone voice — known so well for annual renditions of "Summerfest Polka" — as well as piano accompaniment and appropriate sound effects.

Copies of the tape will be delivered to all area FM and AM radio stations early Wednesday morning, according to Roy De La Rosa, the mayor's director of communications.

Maier said he hoped his musical message would help "lighten the solemn atmosphere" that has surrounded the issue of where to locate the Bradley Center, estimated to cost $30 million to $40 million.

De La Rosa said the mayor's decision to make and circulate his tape had "nothing to do" with Gov. Earl's recent decision not to sing the state song, "On, Wisconsin," on NBC-TV's

"Late Night with David Letterman" program.

Maier and Earl aren't on the best of terms.

Maier's lyrics poke fun at the Milwaukee Bucks basketball team, the city's harsh winters and the ongoing attempt by the Earl administration to locate a prison in the Menomonee Valley near County Stadium.

Down In The Valley

A musical message from Mayor Maier

Down in the valley
When it's 20 below.
Go to a Bucks game.
Hear the wind blow.

Down in the valley
We'll go to and fro
To nail down a place
For our Bucks to go.

The top of our prison
Will surely be seen.
As arena built there
Will stand like a queen.

We'll hear the judge say,
"Son, dry up your tears.
You'll be near the arena

For some 21 years."

All said in fun fans,
However it blows.
We'll love the arena
Wherever it goes.

(Repeat last stanza)

Dragon surveys new domain

Saks sought

A headline should tell a story. Sometimes a more creative head can be designed to make sure that the reader knows what the story is about, as in this musical example from the Milwaukee *Sentinel.* Reprinted by permission.

news value of stories, and the page would be like a massive "tombstoning" of side-by-side headlines. However, in the writing of multiline headlines, it is important that each line be able to stand alone whenever possible.

REVERSES AND SURPRINTS

Occasionally a page design will call for a reverse headline or for a surprint. The reverse headline is one that appears as white type against a black background. A surprint head is one that appears black on gray, such as on top of a sky photo. Both can be effective if used correctly and not overused.

Headline type from 14 point up will usually work well as a reverse or surprint against the appropriate background shade. This device becomes a problem, though, when the black is not black enough for a reverse or when the gray is broken up with streaks or whole patterns of black, with black type trying to complete against the background.

WHITE SPACE

White space is created by the amount of space placed between headline decks and between the headline and the story. Both provide excellent breathing space. But the white space must be consistent and must follow the newspaper's design stylebook (for instance, no more than 1 point between descenders and ascenders in multideck heads, and no more than 2 picas above the ascender or below the descender of the head). The use of white space around body copy will be discussed in Chapter 8.

If headlines were set with virtually no space between the decks—a 24-point line space for a 24-point head—there would be no room for ascenders (capital letters plus "b," "d," "f," "h," "k," "l," and "t") and descenders ("g," "j," "p," "q" and "y"). Some breathing room can be created by setting the headlines at least 1 point size less than the space—such as a 24-point head with a 25-point space.

White space in headlines can also be made by the amount of space left between the main headline and the kicker or hammer above, or between the main headline and the drop head or nutgraph below—and between them and the byline or story. The "nutgraph" is used to summarize the story completely in a single sentence.

Like all other aspects of white space, the air between the headlines and stories must be consistent if the reader is to feel an orderliness in the design of the newspaper. For instance, if a 2-point space between a headline descender and the byline or first paragraph has been established as the standard in the newspaper's design stylebook, then that is the rule, and no situational standards should be acceptable. Regarding headlines, white space and all other graphic

U.S. strikes back at Libya

Terrorism spurred U.S. challenge

Gulf conflict sparks call for restraint

STATE

Actor treated

SANTA MONICA — Actor Jimmy Stewart has been undergoing radiation treatment for a skin cancer which has affected the left side of his face, his wife said Thursday.

The 75-year-old actor began the visits to St. John's hospital two weeks ago and should complete his

NATION

Only hibiscus

PARKVILLE, Md. — Whoever stole Norma and Linwood Schiflett's prize hibiscus this week probably thought they were getting some good weed — the illegal kind. Instead, Mrs. Schiflett said, they got a perfectly innocent plant covered with weed kill

NEWSBRIEFS

Justice clears Burford

WASHINGTON (AP) — The Justice Department on Thursday cleared former Environmental Protection Agency chief Anne M. Burford and five onetime aides of any criminal wrongdoing. A House subcommittee chairman said the action poorly documented and carries the aroma of freshly applied white paint."

"President Reagan will now likely renew his fictitious claim that no wrongdoing occurred at EPA. Nothing could be further from the

Occasional use of reverse headline type guides the reader into page designations, as shown in this strip used by the Kansas City (Mo.) *Times* about U.S. involvement with Libya, or the news-briefs section dividers in the San Luis Obispo, Calif. *Telegram-Tribune.* Kansas City (Mo.) *Times* © The Kansas City Times, all rights reserved. Reprinted by permission.

Mirror, mirror on the wall: Am I really ugly? Is my husband seeing another woman these days? How can I wipe away my stretch marks? Is there something wrong with my face? Does my teddy bear love me anymore? Is my laundry white enough? Is my nose shiny? Can I pinch an inch? Do I want those ugly liver spots? Can I make my skin softer? Am I too skinny? Will my husband still love me with age wrinkles? Does dry skin turn my friends off? Have I really come a long way, baby? Am I a binge shopper or a problem shopper? Can I control how well I age? Am I really ugly? Is my husband seeing another woman these days? How can I wipe away my stretch marks? Is there something wrong with my face? Does my teddy bear love me anymore? Is my laundry white enough? Is my nose shiny? Can I pinch an inch? Do I want those ugly liver spots? C

Headline-size type—12 or 14 point or larger—may be used for special purposes, such as the feature-story lead in this example from the *Florida Times-Union* in Jacksonville. Reprinted by permission.

elements, the underlying thought at a TPC newspaper must be to use only what is consistent with design guidelines and what best complements the news package. Designers need to visualize not only what they and the writers will see in the final product, but also what the design concept will do to guide the reader.

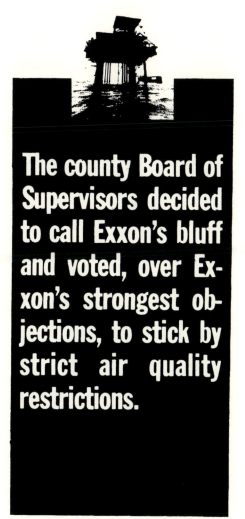

The county Board of Supervisors decided to call Exxon's bluff and voted, over Exxon's strongest objections, to stick by strict air quality restrictions.

In a nutgraph, reverse type is sometimes used to complement the story text, as seen in this example from the Santa Barbara (Calif.) *Independent.* Reprinted by permission.

8   Text Matter Elements

> Newspapers are changing typography every day . . . as computerization
> and cold type allow us more and more freedom and control.
>
> Ron Patel
> associate managing editor
> Philadelphia *Inquirer*

While headline typography and other display elements usually jump out at the
reader first, information in the stories is the underlying reason for purchasing a
daily or weekly newspaper. Therefore, to bring the predictably gray sea of text-
type columns of stories to life, the designer must arrange the type artistically
and functionally according to the Total Page Concept (TPC). Text-type considerations include height, letter fullness, justification of columns, column width
and other ways to make reading the stories more inviting.

TYPEFACE VARIATIONS

As discussed in Chapter 7, there are serif and sans serif typeface choices for
headlines, and the same holds true for text type. For the reader to stay with a
story—to read and absorb it—there must be an appealing typeface with intriguing
variations. Tony Majeri of the Chicago *Tribune* told the Southern Newspaper
Publishers Association (SNPA) Foundation seminar, "Layout, Design and
Graphics," that "effective use of typefaces and sizes tells readers many things
about how important stories are" and that "contemporary-looking typefaces
help 'lift' the paper and make it look fun to read."

Reading is—before anything else—an optical experience; readability depends
on a subtle blend of form and function in the typeface. The editor's selection
of typeface style imparts a sense of the words' meaning to the reader. If the
style is serif and if the hairlines that are part of the letters' strokes do not detract

from the form of the letters themselves, this can contribute greatly to the speed with which the writer's thoughts are relayed. But if the letters have conflicting or not enough ornamentation, the reader will have to deal not only with the message of the text, but with the typeface as well. Therefore, for readability's sake, a typeface should be carefully chosen, rather than selected quickly just because it is beautiful or traditional. Legibility is central to typography, especially on the porous newsprint page. Making the type readable is as important in the communication process as are the words themselves.

Robert Lehmenkuler, then with Compugraphic Corp., discussed in *Communication Briefings* (1985) how type is placed on the page in terms of "x-height," which "is the height of a lowercase 'x' in relationship to the height of a capital letter."

"Because lowercase letters predominate in typeset copy," Lehmenkuler said, "their size affects the overall appearance of a typeface." Understanding the x-height principle becomes especially valuable as the designer chooses typefaces for the text and headlines. "A typeface with a large x-height is more readable in text and gives added impact for display heads."

Lehmenkuler gave these guidelines in regard to text line spacing:

- Line spacing is measured in points. When the line space equals the point size, the type is considered to be "set solid."

- As a general rule, line space should be the point size plus 20 percent of the point size, i.e., 10-point type should have 12 points (10 plus 2) of line space.

- The current trend, however, is toward adding 10 percent of the point size for body copy, i.e., 10-point type with 11 points of line space.

The x-heights are determined by the height of lower case x, as shown in the top example. Different-sized x-heights of selected type families are illustrated in the bottom examples. Robert Lehmenkuler, "Type Awareness," cited in Compugraphic Corporation, "Bonus Item: How to Use Type More Effectively: Part 2." *Communications Briefings* 4:11 (September 1985): 8a-8b. Reprinted by permission.

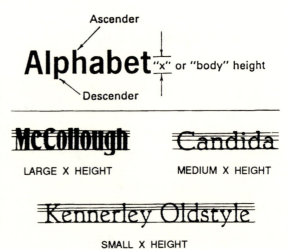

Increasing type to 10 point on an 11-point line space (allowing for half a point above and below ascenders and descenders of type) increases readability. Changing from 9-point type set on a 9.5- or 10-point line space will have less impact on readability.

Lehmenkuler then made suggestions regarding headline line spacing (see also the discussion in Chapter 7):

- When two lines have *different* point sizes, for instance a major head followed by a subhead, you can use this rule of thumb to calculate the minimum line space: one-third of the point size of the *current* line plus two-thirds of the *next* line's point size. For instance, when switching from 36-point to 24-point type, use a minimum of 28 points of line space (emphasis in original).

- Increase line space for long lines, heavy typefaces and typefaces with large x-heights.

Another contributor to readability is the use of a typeface in which the letter shapes are more open, instead of condensed.

Taking all these guidelines into account—while there is no one standard typeface for all newspapers—it has become generally accepted that, for readability, a serif type with minimal ornamentation should be used in most text type, except for classified advertising pages.

TYPESETTING VARIATIONS

There are many other things to consider in the treatment of body copy. A readable-size typeface set in unjustified or "ragged-right" columns can be very attractive to readers because of the consistent letter and word spacing. Furthermore, based on readability, the newspaper can style its end-of-line word-breaks either with or without hyphens. Although there has not been a rush to the use of ragged right, several newspapers have chosen it for the text of their entire publication. These papers include the *Morning Call* in Allentown, Pa.; the *News Chronicle* in Thousand Oaks, Calif., and the *Daily Record* in Morristown, N.J. The reason usually given for not making the switch away from justified right-hand columns is that "rag-right" is too informal. However, some professionals in the typography business disagree.

Allan Haley wrote about legibility and readability in a 1986 *U&lc* (upper and lower case), the international journal of typographics—which is printed in tabloid format and of which Haley is an editorial director. As Haley said,

> There are those of the opinion that whether type is set justified— lines flush at both left and right sides of the column—or rag-right— lines flush at the left and having an uneven edge at the right—affects typographic readability. For the most part, they are wrong.

By Lois Taylor
Star-Bulletin Writer

It's the middle of the social season at Rancho Mirage, Calif. The 45 golf courses of the Palm Springs area have been reseeded with winter rye, replacing the Bermuda grass that dries up and dies during the desert summer. Boutiques and French restaurants are opening again, their sales clerks, waiters and bartenders returning from summer work at Lake Tahoe and Yosemite.

Palm Springs, on the edge of the great Mojave Desert, is a winter resort for people with money. Million-dollar condominiums ring the golf courses and Rolls-Royces and Ferraris jockey for space in supermarket parking lots. The ultimate extravagance in the desert is useless running water, and most of the country clubs have built enormous waterfalls and fountains on their property. This would seem to be a place where the most serious decision is whether to have the lobster salad or the veal primavera for lunch. But at the intersection of Bob Hope Road and Frank Sinatra Drive stand four low buildings dedicated to reinforce a major decision. At the Betty Ford Center at Eisenhower, 2,000 men and women have completed programs to rid themselves of drug and alcohol dependency.

Type set ragged left is difficult for the eye to adjust to because it has to begin each line in a different location. Still, ragged left is acceptable if the type is no longer than in this example from the Honolulu *Star-Bulletin*. Reprinted by permission.

According to Haley, many studies have shown rag-right and justified type to be equally readable.

In fact, in most cases, readers are not even aware that they are reading one or the other. As a rule, readability only suffers when typestyles are not handled with proper care, allowing problems to occur in letter—or word—spacing. Sometimes rag-right copy can create unattractive contours along the right margin; this condition, while not particularly inviting to the reader, does not detract from readability.

Ragged-right columns, while infrequent among the nation's newspapers, are used throughout several, including the Allentown, Pa. *Morning Call* and the Morristown, N.J. *Daily Record.* Reprinted by permission of Call-Chronicle Newspapers, Inc. and the *Daily Record.*

Tom Goss, writing in *Print* (1985), quoted Maureen Decker, assistant managing editor for graphics at the Allentown, Pa. *Morning Call,* who said, "We talked to type consultant Rolf Rehe of the Herron School of Art, who had done research indicating that ragged-right enhanced legibility and made it easier for people to remember what they read." But the *Morning Call* was not immediately interested in making the switch. "Ed Miller, who was publisher at the time, was afraid our readers would be upset by the change and didn't want to do it."

Robert Lockwood, now of NewsGraphics, was art director at the *Morning Call* when the change from justified to ragged right was made. "It caused a lot of controversy at that time," Lockwood says. "It was seen as radical, but Ed Miller agreed that we should do it. He told me, however, to put it on hold for a while. I put it on hold for a few days and then introduced it into the paper without mentioning it to Ed." Miller later told Lockwood that, when he came in one day and saw the ragged right, "he was so angry that he was ready to get

The use of type set ragged right is also found at the Thousand Oaks, Calif. *News Chronicle* and at least one collegiate paper, the *Graphic* at Pepperdine University in Malibu, Calif. Reprinted by permission.

out of his seat, come back to the Art Department and fire me. He said on the way back he thought, 'I'd better look at a couple of days' papers.' " Miller looked through some back issues and saw that ragged-right had been there for a week before it caught his attention. "At this point, he thought he had a weak argument, but he didn't tell me until a few weeks later how close he came to firing me."

Another argument for ragged right—having nothing to do with readability—is that copy changes at deadline are easier to make on a line-for-line basis, and this can have a convincing effect when late-breaking news details arrive.

Ron Patel, associate managing editor of the Philadelphia *Inquirer,* tells of his frustrations in working with the "old back shop" of hot metal days. It is much simpler today to make text fit in the columns, to choose between a justified or ragged-right look and to design pages that are better organized—all with more control by the news department. As Patel says,

I have been designing newspaper pages since I was 12 years old, 26 years in all, and I know very well how restrictive the old hot-type was. At my junior high school and high school, we pasted up galley proofs in order to create a paper, since none of us could read upside-down and backward as was required in order to do hot-type makeup.

In college and at my first professional papers, I learned that the grind-it-out typesetting practices made even simple efforts at grace in page design frustrating. The old hot-type copy cutters laughed me off the floor of the Detroit *News* when I asked for flush left, ragged-right type on a textblock for a photo page in 1969. Their job was to produce a paper through the management of a hundred or so type-setters as fast and as accurately as possible. It was not to make the pages pretty, or to help any editor in that task.

Even if the copy cutters cooperated, as they did at *Newsday* when I worked there from 1970–73, it was still a major task of sawing and fitting to make any page with white space work, or a box of any significant design.

In addition to ragged right, another infrequently used form of typesetting in newspapers is block paragraphing—no indentation for new paragraphs. Newspapers that use this variation separate paragraphs with one line of white space.

Speaking to the SNPA Foundation seminar "Layout, Design and Grahpics," Nanette Bisher of the *Orange County Register* in Santa Ana, Calif. cautioned against too many changes in column width.

Don't use too many different widths on one page. They tire readers' eyes and compete with each other. Highlight one story with a different measure and set the rest uniformly. Run news stories in standard measure for efficient, fast reading. Set feature-type stories in wider measure to indicate a sort of slowing down and easing up.

The measure—length or column width—of a line is capable of encouraging or discouraging the reader. Most newspapers establish their own standard line measure based on typeface readability. Measure specifications are then printed in nonphotographic light blue on grid pasteup sheets or within a computer program's page layouts.

Writing in *U&lc,* Haley said, "Once the correct size of type has been deter-mined, the next step is to establish the number of letters and words to put on a line." Haley added that "contrary to what many may think, the eye does not read individual words, one at a time, but scans the line pausing momentarily to record groups of three or four words; in addition, the eye can make about three or four of these pauses on a line before it gets tired."

Lehmenkuler while at Compugraphic said that his guidelines for line length include:

- For text applications, nine or 10 words per line [of serif faces] work best, while sans serif faces require shorter line lengths—seven to nine words.

- In general, the body copy should be about twice as wide in picas as the point size of the type. For example, 8-point type should be set about 16 picas wide.

- Another rule of thumb—Line length should be no longer than two lower case alphabets of the typeface and point size you're using.

- Typefaces with strong thick and thin contrast in the strokes, such as Bodoni or ITC [International Type Corp.] Tiffany, require shorter line lengths.

- Typefaces with large x-heights usually lend themselves better to longer line lengths rather than small x-height typefaces.

Haley wrote that it is best not to have too many words on a line—which makes it difficult for the reader to reference the next line. "The extreme of this condition," he said, "is called 'doubling,' and occurs when the eye in its swing back to the left margin loses track of where it is and begins to read the same line again. This not only obstructs copy readability, it also introduces a nuisance factor that seriously limits audience attention."

As Haley points out, there can also be problems for the eye when lines are not wide enough, causing sentence structure to be broken. In regard to these short width lines—or "skews"—Bisher said to use them "sparingly and have a reason; try to keep them 10 picas or wider. Narrower than 9 or 10 picas makes for bad breaks, especially on a system that justifies copy."

In Chapter 7, the importance of white space between multiline headlines was discussed. In addition, an adequate amount of white space—called leading (pronounced and sometimes spelled "ledding")—must be provided between lines of type to make the text easily readable. Most newspapers allow for at least ¼–½

While the general rule for type width is that it should be set no wider than twice its point size (10-point type being set 20 picas wide), it is sometimes possible to set type less than the standard column width and still be effective, as in this example of 8.5 picas wide for a special page in the Cincinnati *Enquirer.* Reprinted by permission.

Back in the '60s, they called it "fun fur," and it was a budget alternative to the real thing. In the status-conscious '70s, real pelts were predictably preferable to plush. But now, for a variety of reasons, fake furs are fun again.

Indeed, many of them are so much fun that they may be worn not only by women who can't make it through the day without a mink, b⋅ ⋅ ᵃ ⋅ ⋅ ⋅ ᵗ ⋅ sᶜ ⋅ ᶠ

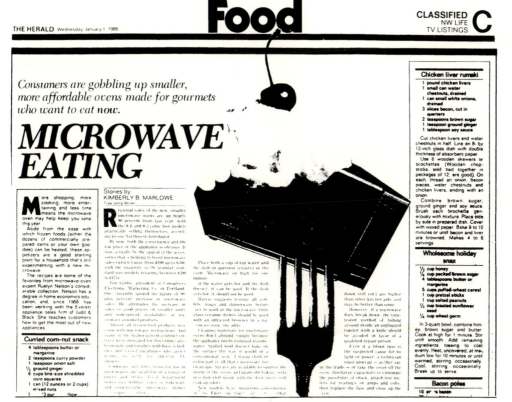

If the design calls for a skew, it should be done carefully so the story won't be hard to follow. This page from the Everett, Wash. *Herald* allows the reader to see what the story is about without the art effect hurting the text content. Reprinted by permission.

point of white space above and below the line of type to accommodate ascenders and descenders.

The implementation of bold and/or very light text type is another variation of creative design in the Total Page Concept. Positioning light and dark type allows the designer to evoke a mood. Used thoughtfully, it can provide a contrast that will encourage the reader to stay with the page. Done carelessly, it leads to graphic confusion, which will make the reader turn the page. Remember these three words: Keep design simple.

SUBHEADS AND OTHER GRAPHIC BREAKERS

In their 1978 *Journalism Quarterly* report, Gerald Stone, John Schweitzer and David Weaver wrote: "Few papers do anything to add graphic variety to story body type." However, the fact that this was their finding then is all the more

Awards likely winner in ratings war tonight

CBS' Emmy Award-winning, ratings-busting Monday night lineup of "Kate & Allie," "Newhart" and "Cagney & Lacey" finally meets its match tonight — **"The 58th Annual Academy Awards Presentation"** at 9 o'clock on ABC. No wonder CBS is telecasting reruns tonight. Alan Alda, Jane Fonda and Robin Williams are the hosts of the star-studded event.

To make a sweep of the evening, ABC precedes the Oscars with one of its most popular shows, **"The Barbara Walters Special."** With camera in tow, Walters traipses through the halls of the White House for an intimate little chat with President and Mrs. Reagan. "Just between you and me, Mr. President, I won't tell a soul."

Variation in light and bold type is effective for pulling out names or other reader keys, especially in roundup news summaries, as in this example from the Lexington (Ky.) *Herald-Leader*. Reprinted by permission.

reason why newspaper design editors now should use boldface subheads and other typographic elements to break up long columns of ashen-gray text. Set above every fifth or sixth paragraph, subheads can be either flush left or centered and either all caps or caps and lower case, with one blank line above and one below the subhead. Subheads may be the same size or one point larger than the text type size; if set any larger than one size above the text copy, they might be confused with regular headlines.

Another way to introduce variety into otherwise gray columns is to set the first two or three words of every fifth or sixth paragraph in boldface type. These words will serve the same purpose as subheads without making it necessary to write additional lines of type; they may be done in all caps or caps and lower case.

White-space breathers might be made to contain a meaningful phrase; they then organize the story into thought units and become valuable not only to enhance the look of the newspaper but also to provide guidance for the reader.

Some newspapers, in their effort to become different from or brighter than their competitors, have adopted TPC design elements that are more frequently found in magazines. For these papers, the most common change to the text copy has been the introduction of "initial caps" or "strikedown letters" (24- to 36-

embedded type at the beginning of a paragraph). These are usually found on inside feature-section pages.

Bisher at the *Orange County Register* said that "visual breaks (for example, lead-letter caps)" are "effective to break up a long story." She suggested using them "every nine inches or so, variable with copy width." It is important, however, to "make sure they are no bigger than the main head."

Some newspapers have used initial caps in news stories, either limited to the story's first word or sprinkled throughout. When used sparingly, this style can provide needed white space below and adjacent to the story. In any case, the pros and cons should be carefully considered since, while initial caps do create white space and make reading more inviting, their use will also slightly reduce the number of words possible in the story.

The use of "breakers"—also known as "breakout quotes," "quote breakers," "quote boxes," "quoteouts," "readouts," "pullouts," "blurbs" or "sandwiches"—can be introduced into longer pieces of copy by extracting quotes or statements from the stories, setting them in 14- or 18-point type and strategically placing them within the columns of text type. Ideally, these should precede the quoted material in the story so they will not have already been read when the reader gets to them. Breakers may be used to accompany a headshot photo.

White space is as important around text copy as around heads because it emphasizes whatever is adjacent. But trapped white space is dead space. Majeri at the Chicago *Tribune* emphasized that the spacing between typographical elements should be the same throughout the newspaper. "A consistent spacing system is imperative for a neat, professional-looking paper," Majeri said. "Establish standard margins, gutters, et cetera, and enforce them. Leave 18 points [1.5 picas] of white space between unrelated items."

If the need arises for white space adjacent to the text on a page layout, it is best to place it on the outside (top and bottom right on a right-hand page, and top and bottom left on a left-hand page). This creates the effect of a "half-bowl" on a single page or a "whole-bowl" on a double-page spread. Within interior columns, consistent margins of one pica—in the gutters between text columns, between headlines and stories, and between a photo and its caption—are generally accepted as a reasonable amount of white space.

ACCESSORY TYPOGRAPHY

In addition to the various considerations for making text type optimally readable, there are a few accessory methods of story identification and reader direction that are done with typography. Bylines, credit lines, cutlines, continued or jump lines, and tabular display of information are all ways by which stories can be expanded or given more clarity.

At or near the top of many stories is the writer's byline. It may be above the first column or centered above a two-column story, but is best positioned over

Process theology focuses on the process of love

By PAGE LAWS
Staff writer

PROCESS THEOLOGY.
The term is dry, intimidating — until you hear Dr. Marjorie Suchocki, dean of Wesley Theological Seminary, talk about it.

And you realize it means love.

Process theologians focus on relationships, between God and the world, but ʼso ʼʼ atʼ ʼerʼ ʼnaʼ ar hiʼ feʼʼ ws ʼArʼ

"How do you measure the well-being of the world?" she asks her audience. "Justice.

"Do not consider justice as the blind woman holding the scales," Suchocki advises, lifting her arms to assume the traditional pose of Blind Justice. "The measure of justice in the world is the well-being of the worst off."

In centuries past, that meant widows and orphans, lepers. Look for the contem- ʼorʼ ʼʼ ʼtiʼ s, ʼhe savʼ ʼ ʼʼʼnse wiʼʼ

If anyone knows how much power the Anaconda Co. press wielded in Montana, how far its newspaper empire extended or why it sold its papers after a half-century of ownership, it is James Dickey Jr.

But he's not talking. At least he's not talking much. And he certainly isn't giving away any secrets.

Dickey, one-time manager of all of Anaconda's non-mineral holdings, including most of the state's daily newspapers, will turn 97 in March.

He has the clear complexion of a much younger man. The thick lenses in his glasses magnify a pair of ʼparʼlinʼ broʼn eʼes. ʼnakʼng tʼem ʼopʼʼ ʼr ʼʼʼt of

Initial caps, or strikedown letters, may be placed at the beginning of a story or in other locations to provide bold type. Variations include regular type, as in the Norfolk *Virginian-Pilot* example; reversed type, in the Butte *Montana Standard;* and much enlarged type, in the Des Moines, Iowa *Register.* Reprinted by permission.

Vacations on dialysis
Patients learn to cope

By DEBORAH CUSHMAN
Register Staff Writer

Nurse practitioner, nurse midwife, nurse travel agent?

When Becky Liggett graduated from nursing school she may have considered the first two titles, but probably not the third.

Now Liggett, head nurse at Iowa Lutheran Hospital's renal dialysis unit, spends at least half a workday each week arranging for patients on kidney dialysis to cleanse their blood regularly while on the road.

The Des Moines nurse is probably the state's busiest health professional specializing in renal travel arrangements, but she is not alone.

Across Iowa, renal dialysis staffs have helped patients wing off to England, take gambling junkets to Las ʼʼ ʼʼ ʼʼ ʼʼʼʼ ʼʼʼ ʼʼ hʼ hʼ

The nation's economy drags along sluggishly. And with opinion split over its prospects, policy-makers must pick their way through political pressures and a changing global environment, balancing long-term considerations with short-term needs. Many conventional tools can't be used — lower taxes or higher federal spending to spur growth would deepen deficits. And other tactics — like cutting interest rates — seem to have lost their effectiveness.

Today: "Global economy" blunts traditional economics tools.

Text type may be used to extend the understanding of a story, as in this *Investor's Daily* perspective paragraph. Reprinted by permission.

Soviets say U.S. wavering on SALT

Reagan administration officials gave confusing statements about the treaty.

Tribune Wires

WASHINGTON — Amid confusing statements by Reagan administration officials, a top Soviet diplomat declared Friday that U.S. policy-makers were having "second-thoughts" about abandoning the 1979 Strategic Arms Limitation Treaty.

Secretary of State George P. Shultz said President Reagan's top spokesman never described the SALT II pact as dead, which Larry Speakes had been reported as having said Thursday. But Edward L. Rowny, a senior U.S. arms control adviser, said Friday, "SALT is be-

The nutgraph, written as a complete sentence in this Tampa (Fla.) *Tribune* example, is set in headline type size as a graphic element and used to extend the story's meaning. Reprinted by permission.

Applications are now being taken from colleges, businesses and individuals interested in the money.

Candy Lightner, who started Mothers Against Drunk Drivers a few months after her daughter's hit-and-run death, fumed when she heard about the new arrest of Clarence Busch, 52.

Dixon claimed post-Vietnam combat stress as a defense, but a jury convicted him.

The evaluation was based on government tests and private data.

For a readout, a sentence or a paragraph is pulled from the story text and set in type larger than the text type, as shown in several papers: the Little Rock *Arkansas Gazette*, the Fresno (Calif.) *Bee*, the St. Paul (Minn.) *Pioneer Press and Dispatch*, July 8, 1986, and the St. Petersburg (Fla.) *Times*. Reprinted by permission.

"I am not sure that we have learned much from the history lessons available to us in Watergate. There has been little real change in political, corporate, social or individual behavior in our nation."

— Harry Dent

Quoteouts may be printed with the quotes alone, as in the Columbia (S.C.) *Record*, or with a photo of the person quoted, as in the Merced (Calif.) *Sun-Star*. Reprinted by permission.

"We got too relaxed in the middle quarters. We need to play a more complete game."
———DON ODISHOO

ABRAHAM Melzer has a credential rare among acousticians: After earning a physics degree, he studied music in a conservatory.

'**S**OME people—especially the highest-paid people—may be looking at their lowest tax rates ever,' says one compensation consultant.

These two examples from the *Wall Street Journal* show variations of a readout and a quoteout, and how the wording relates to the story text. The readout, about acoustician Abraham Melzer, touches on the subject's credentials for remodeling the 1891-built Carnegie Hall in New York City. The quoteout was with a story about how executive pay plans would change if a bill passed as proposed; it uses a job title for the attribution, to simplify for the reader the position referred to in the story as being held by Richard Raskin, a consulting actuary with Wyatt Co., a New York–based compensation and benefits consulting company. Reprinted by permission of the *Wall Street Journal,* © Dow Jones & Company, Inc. 1986.

only the first column of a story spread over three or more columns. Centering a byline above a story of more than two columns allows too much space for it to "float."

Some papers use boldface caps for bylines while others have them set in italic caps and lower case; some include a reference to the writer below the name to designate the staff position held or the news or syndication service that the individual represents. No particular byline style is better than the others; what is important is consistency: All bylines for the newspaper should be set in the same typeface, degree of weight or style (bold, medium or italic), and size; and all should be placed in the same relative position to the story.

Credit-line styles are established at newspapers for photographers' and artists' names, with the line often being a point size or two smaller than text type, sometimes set in a bold or italic sans serif typeface and placed just under one side—usually the right-hand side—of the art. All bylines and credit lines should be set in legible type, should not be buried in the story or photo, and should not be confusing to the reader who wishes to know to whom credit is due.

Cutlines—so named when captions were set in metal type and used with artwork engraved on zinc—are used to describe or identify the people or subjects

Bylines may appear with the reporter's name alone, as at *Newsday* in Melville, New York, or with the name and either the staff position or newspaper identification, as at the Knoxville (Tenn.) *News-Sentinel* and the Yakima (Wash.) *Herald-Republic. Newsday* copyright 1986, Newsday, Inc. Reprinted by permission.

By Emily Sachar

by BARBARA ASTON-WASH
News-Sentinel staff writer

By GARY E. NELSON
Of the Herald-Republic

in a photo or illustration. They should be set wide enough to cover the width of the photo or other form of art, but no wider—preferably according to uniform column widths. An exception to this rule occurs when the caption is positioned adjacent to the art.

For a news page, cutlines or captions should always be set in accordance with established column widths. For a photo or display layout, the width may vary, but in any case the pica width should be no more than twice the point size. Breathing room for the caption can be provided by setting it a pica less than the accompanying photo or other art. This, too, is a good use of the Total Page Concept—so long as the rule of consistency prevails and the width is the same for every caption.

Newspaper editors know that using continued or jump lines for stories discourages readers from finding—or looking for—the remainder of the story. However, those newspapers that do jump stories have to follow a style when doing so.

The fact that a story has been continued, and where, should be obvious to the reader. Jumps need to be proofread carefully to make certain that they follow from the originating page to the jump page. A key word and the page number are especially important if more than one story has been jumped. The "continued from" reference must have a headline that matches the key word and then below that—in text type, usually boldface—a line that indicates the originating page of the story.

Some newspapers try to jump stories only in the middle of a paragraph, and others make the jump wherever it happens to fall. Usually at least one line of white space is placed between the story line and the jump-line reference. Stories less than 5 inches in length should not be jumped; rather, they should be edited tightly to fit the space.

Tables can be used to display vertical listings of facts and figures. Given a consistent style of type, the organizing and categorizing of information into tables can provide a valuable service for the reader. However, if a graphic is confusing to the staff at the newspaper office, it will not—as though by magic—become

Dave Shippee/Statesman

Purrfect kitty Spittin' Image looks up at his owner, Dolores Johnson, Oregon City, Ore., after being examined by judges on his way to winning the Best Kitten of Show overall award at the Idaho Cat Fanciers' annual championship Saturday at the Western Idaho Fairgrounds. Spittin' Image, a 4-month-old white Persian, joined more than 200 other felines in the competition.

Captions for photos that stand alone—without an accompanying story—usually have an overline above the photo, or at least directly above the caption, in headline-size type, as in this embedded type head with caption in the Boise Idaho *Statesman*. Reprinted by permission.

start s..net..ne ...te. .ni. .ugh.. Te...-
peratures today are expected to be
near 30 degrees so road crews should

.u. .e. .e. si. ju. p. in. .. ..u.,
River and fought Friedman and his 15-year-
old friend, Ernst Fleischer, as they struggled
to pull her to the riverbank.

"All the various crises that have come to

See **SNOW/BACK PAGE**

Please see **HERO**, Page **C8**

Stories jumped to other pages need to clearly indicate where the remainder of the story is continued, as in these examples from the Norfolk *Virginian-Pilot* and the Owensboro, Ky. *Messenger-Inquirer*. Reprinted by permission.

Elway proves he's a top dog

JARES / From Page 1

"You know, he's extremely competitive and it really hurts him to hear the criticism that people throw at him, and I could see a determination in his eyes today like I've never seen before. He w? ?te? to · 'ay ?o v ?ll ?n b? ?ly"

"Even on the 2-yard line (in overtime) we believed in ourselves. We've seen things like that happen too much here on Denver.

"John and the offense have done some magical things, and he did it today."

"He's done it so many times"

Reagan

(Continued from Page 1)

Reagan, then an actor, campaigned for Truman in 1948, but he drifted away from the Demo- ?rat? in ?he '950? an? em?rg?d a?

said. "We were born to be a special place, between these two great oceans, with a unique mission to carry freedom's torch. To a tired, disillusioned world, we have always been a light of hope where all things are possible."

De?oit? th? ?or?ide ?tr?e? hi

Stories continued from other pages need an immediate reference source if the reader is to easily find the continuation; possible methods include those from the Los Angeles *Daily News* and the Stockton (Calif.) *Record*.

instantly understandable to the reader. A poor tabular listing of information may cause the reader to lose interest not only in the graphic element, but in the article as well. (See Chapter 11 for more details on graphic display.)

Bylines, credit lines, and (at some newspapers) cutlines and tabulated material are set in the same typeface as headlines. This practice creates a subtle consistency throughout the TPC page. Such consideration pleases readers, who can sense the unity even if they cannot articulate it.

Story text is seen by the reader as the foundation of information in the newspaper. The news is told through variations in typefaces and typesetting techniques. These variations make the otherwise bland offering of type palatable. Complementary to this in the TPC newspaper are graphic breakers and accessory typographical elements that identify information and give direction to readers as they browse through the paper. The newspaper designer who effectively applies these text matter elements also provides an important service to the staff members, who will be pleased to have their work displayed to its fullest advantage.

IV DESIGN CREATIVITY

A newspaper provides a creative source of news for its readership, whereby the relationship of text and graphics is clearly stated. The designer should be news trained and able to direct the art staff so stories will be told in both written and visual ways that work together to help readers understand the news. Specifics of how text and graphics work together as one in design creativity are explained in the next three chapters.

Special topic sections, such as this "Viewpoint" section front in the Miami *Herald*, provide many creative possibilities for newspaper design. Reprinted by permission.

9　Creative Design

As far as we are concerned, quality content also implies quality presentation. The specifics of that on a day-to-day basis always fluctuate, but with proper pre-planning, an organized set of procedures and a very strong commitment to the inclusion of the Photo and Graphics departments in every story and layout decision, it makes it much easier to insure that you have both.

Randy Cox
director of photography and graphics
Hartford (Conn.) *Courant*
(Quoted by George Tuck in *APME News*, 1985)

Editors who develop the news budget and assign stories must pay attention to a number of things: "story slugs" or file names (two- or three-word working titles or descriptions, based on subject, such as City Council meeting or 49er game), story lengths, and art—and as to art, whether it is to be included with a story or to stand alone as a "floater." When the Total Page Concept (TPC) is applied in bringing all these elements together, the look that the newspaper presents to the reader becomes determined by the news budget as well as by space planning. Both should operate according to a news philosophy that fuses story and graphic considerations under one ultimate goal: effective communication. Dramatic changes are taking place these days as the process by which the news is printed continues rapidly to evolve.

Tom Kennedy, assistant graphics director of the Philadelphia *Inquirer* (quoted by George Tuck in the *APME News*, 1985) sees change in the communication media to be an ongoing process. Kennedy said,

I believe we are living in an age of emerging communications technologies that will profoundly alter the way human beings process information. In my gut, I feel that people are learning to process information based primarily on visual images far more readily. Graphic presentations of information will prove to be as useful and accepted a means of communicating as text.

LINKING STORIES AND ART

In an effort to encourage a link between story and art, some newspapers—in this graphic journalism decade of the 1980s—have created the position of "assistant managing editor for graphics" or "designer." Certain news editorial people have become art/editorial people or "graphic journalists." These individuals are trained to operate with both a spatial design sense and news judgment. Ideally, they work in offices where the art and news departments are adjacent to one another, with the department heads being equal. Maureen Decker, assistant managing editor for graphics at the *Morning Call* in Allentown, Pa., applauded newspapers that take such a cooperative position. As quoted by Tuck in *APME News*, Decker said, "I cannot emphasize enough the importance of people working together well. Designers at the *Morning Call* work with reporters, editors and photographers as early as possible to determine the best means of communicating the information at hand."

Decker was also quoted by Tom Goss in *Print* (1985) as saying, "Our interest is in good composition, readability, and the same sense of quality we learned in school." Goss declared that such "goals are realized" at the *Morning Call* through its "stunning use of photography" and also at the Seattle *Times* by its "exquisitely illustrated feature pages and both papers' crisp informational graphics." This "is as much due to the influential positions designers hold at their respective papers as it is to the skills of the designers themselves." Goss pointed out that "designers at both papers work side by side with editors on a daily basis, and perhaps more significantly, designers at both papers attend the weekly budget and strategy meetings that determine a newspaper's overall direction and content." Rob Covey, former design director of the Seattle *Times* and now art director at *U.S. News & World Report,* was quoted in the same article, with reference to the role of designer: "I see a designer's role as being a leader in guiding a paper—in content as well as graphics." Goss quotes Decker as saying, "We're journalists. We just use a different set of tools than editors and reporters."

The long-range result of the new staffing is a workable interaction of graphics and editorial specialists who, as a team, create attractive pages that will take the reader to and through an organized tapestry of pages—a visual and verbal look seen by the reader as one single entity.

Walter E. Mattson, president of the New York Times Co., referred to the importance of this point when he addressed the Southern Newspaper Publishers Association (SNPA) annual convention in 1983 on the topic "What Do We Do

Next in the Newspaper Business?'' Mattson said that pages should be designed "in an attractive manner" and the newspaper should "be well organized, so that a reader will know where to look in this supermarket of ideas. Illustrations will be used extensively to help the reader better understand the accompanying article."

David Owens, graphics editor of the Albuquerque (N.M.) *Journal*—also quoted by Tuck in *APME News*—said that an essential aspect of a newspaper's success lies in planning. Owens claimed that *Journal* editors "think through a story all the way to the page and reader. Once a story idea is conceived, it is time to ask how best to present it to the reader. What page is best, position, type of art, color, headline, how much play." The stories are packages on the pages "where the quality and quantity of content to reach the reader is directly related to how we present the information. If presentation is poorly planned, the reader may receive very little of our message. We cannot communicate good content without good presentation."

Matt Moody, editorial artist at the Los Angeles *Times,* gives an example of how this works:

I try to ask, "What is it that you want this graphic to show?" The editors are putting it to the reporters, "We want more graphics." A reporter comes to me and says, "I have this idea for a graphic" or "I want some graphics with this story,"—he may have worked three months on it; I try to understand what is being said in the story. Sometimes the reporter will say, "I don't know, I just want some graphics, I've got these numbers here."

I was doing a little chart on Los Angeles Pierce College and how the agriculture program has changed. It used to be more of an ag school, and now it is not. The story showed the declining enrollment. There were these figures of the declining enrollment in the agriculture department, which pretty much showed the department was getting smaller. I suggested looking at the enrollment figures for the school across-the-board. We got those numbers and they almost paralleled the decline in enrollment for the ag department. So, even though the enrollment for the ag program is declining, overall enrollment was also declining. A chart would not substantiate what the reporter was trying to say.

A lot of times you have to feel out the reporters and see what it is they want. If the editor is on top of it, this person will do it for you. I have found it to be pretty good. They respect our opinion and they like our input; we are an objective source. The editor and the reporter have been so close to the story that they sometimes can't see that a graphic won't do what they want it to do. On the other hand, sometimes they say, "I want this, and this is what I want," and you can't say anything about it. Usually it is a negotiation; you feel like your input is worthwhile. The editors who come down and say, "This is what I want,"—you do it, but you'd rather feel like you have some negotiation power.

Indeed, effectively bringing art and news people together in a harmonious relationship will lead to the success of the Total Page Concept in the computer age.

PAGE ORGANIZATION

Newspapers have to get the reader to the top of the story; if not, even the best-written stories will go unread. Nigel Holmes, executive art director of *Time* magazine, says, "Graphics play an important role in the paper. They help the readers to get involved in the story. They shouldn't just become decorations, although they do, in fact, look good on the page. They help people to read."

Not all newspapers have one or two dozen art department personnel assigned to present stunning graphic information. Holmes says that "editors have to be convinced that while their reporters are writing, they should also be collecting information for a graphic on the subject."

At *Time,* Holmes is in "the luxurious position of having people to draw, and people to research, and they are both separate from people who are reporting." Newspapers must "be convinced that there is some real use for graphics, and not just run them because they see other papers doing it. The use of graphics is very specific: to put into pictures things that are better done in pictures than words."

To attract the reader, each page should ideally have a dominant story, one that is more important than others. This assists the reader in quickly appraising the key events and people of that edition. Nanette Bisher of the *Orange County Register* in Santa Ana, Calif. told the SNPA Foundation seminar, "Layout, Design and Graphics," that "good design should employ a two-pronged approach—'art attack' and 'type attack.' Art and type should be used together to balance the page and draw readers' attention from start to finish."

Another method of attracting readers is for all pages to include news stories, even on the so-called specialty pages such as lifestyle, religion, real estate and sports.

Pages are most attractive if they have a piece of large, informative art—an illustration, an informational graphic, a map or a photo. A small photograph or illustration will help the design even if the page happens to be dominated by a six-column by 18-inch advertisement.

Dominant graphics have news potential, provide a strong signal of importance for the newspaper's photography and art display, and make a more readable publication. Even before it has been decided that art should accompany a story, an exchange of ideas among all involved art and news department participants—the graphic journalists—is necessary. This can be carried out by having routine assignments placed on storyboards and discussed by members of the art and editorial departments present at daily meetings. The two departments have the common objective of effective communication, and their intimate cooperation is imperative to develop a successful news or feature story and art package.

Sandra White, graphics editor of the Detroit *Free Press* quoted by Tuck in *APME News* said, "We're in a period of stretching the limits of what can be done graphically. It may seem to some people at times that the emphasis in newsroom has shifted to graphics, but what's really happening is that the emphasis is shifting to include graphics."

From the editor on down, all must fully understand the story itself before there can be an effective use of accompanying art in any form. Randy Cox, director of photography and graphics at the Hartford (Conn.) *Courant*—also quoted by Tuck—said, "Editors have to learn that picture editors, designers and art directors are not miracle workers and they, as a general rule, cannot pull rabbits out of their hats."

Furthermore, if news/graphics efforts are to be successful, the graphics editor should not be part of the advertising services department. Graphic elements are an integral aspect of the news process, and people who work with news art should work as part of the news department on a small newspaper and on the art—or editorial art—department on a larger paper.

Brian Steffens of the Los Angeles *Times* Orange County Edition says that "Ad art and news art are two different disciplines. One is to sell and one is to inform. You approach them from different mindsets. You don't want to sell or color the news. You want to be as objective and as informative as possible."

The designer ought to report to the editor, the managing editor or the news editor, depending on the size and editorial organization of the newspaper. Also, the copy editor must be part of the art department's team in order to review the informational graphics and other art elements that include editorial text or information. A close relationship between the art department and the news department establishes the idea that the news staff decides what is to be in the newspaper that day or that week, but not without the able help of art and copy-editing people.

According to Susie Eaton Hopper, graphics director of the St. Paul (Minn.) *Pioneer Press-Dispatch* (quoted by Tuck), the role that news executives play in the relationship of the news and art departments determines the possibilities for a strong graphics newspaper. Further, Hopper said, "Our executive editor sometimes attends these (critique sessions) just to see what's up. She always gives us her 2 cents worth and supports the changes that need to be made. It makes everyone aware that top management is in on the fix: to be the best paper, both in looks and content that we can produce."

Thomas Trapnell, editorial art director of the Los Angeles *Times,* reviews his newspaper with a special interest in two areas. "I look for accuracy and clarity," Trapnell said. "Most of our people are pretty good at achieving that. We communicate extensively with editors, so we don't have too many factual errors, unless the reporting is wrong to begin with. News graphics and page layouts should be clean, legible and factually correct; if something requires several steps to explain it, it should be done in the fewest number of steps."

THE ROLE OF THE GRAPHICS EDITOR

When the paper is being designed according to the Total Page Concept, the role of the graphics editor is to design and package the news as a multifaceted form of communication. This means having pages that complement one another; it means setting some stories inside boxes for easier reading, and showing dynamic photos, a balance of headline sizes, consistent byline column heads and a variety of other graphic elements that organize news and advertising for the readers. After all, readers are the ones who subscribe to the paper, look at the news and advertising columns, consider the editorial matter and may purchase the products advertised. For the newspaper to be profitable, design time must be thoughtfully spent in attracting and keeping readers.

David B. Gray, managing editor/graphics at the Providence, R.I. *Journal-Bulletin,* made a presentation during the 1987 sessions of the Ninth College Press Convention of College Media Advisers and Columbia Scholastic Press Association in New York City. Gray gave a 10-point editor's guide to graphics that was adapted from tip sheets put out by the Society of Newspaper Design, the *Orange County Register* in Santa Ana, Calif., and *USA Today,* with special thanks to Dave Miller (Kansas City (Mo.) *Star-Times*), George Rorick (Detroit *News*), Howard Finberg (Arizona *Republic* in Phoenix), Nigel Holmes (*Time* magazine), and Phil Nesbitt (Hackensack, N.J. *Record*). Gray's guide to graphics for editors follows:

- Don't use graphics for graphics' sake. Put graphics in the paper because they are news. Do not use them for window dressing. Our objectives as editors should be to put information into the paper in its best possible form. Sometimes that is the written word. Sometimes it is a photo. Sometimes it is a graphic. Sometimes it is a combination of all three.
- Think of graphics as you think of stories. They can stand alone, be sidebars or second stories. Sometimes they illustrate the story. Sometimes they add additional information. Think of them as ways to relieve the copy of burdensome material. Remember: some things are very difficult to explain in writing but are simple in graphic form.
- Kinds of graphics to look for as you edit:

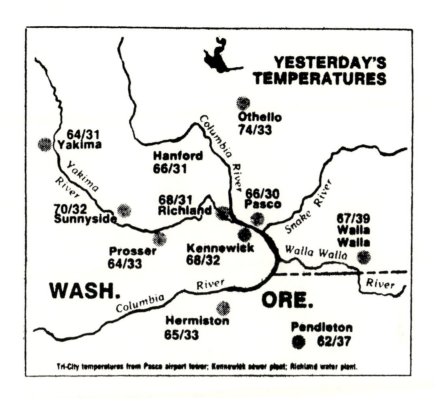

YESTERDAY'S TEMPERATURES

Othello 74/33

64/31 Yakima

Hanford 66/31

Columbia River

66/30 Pasco

Snake River

67/39 Walla Walla

68/31 Richland

70/32 Sunnyside

Prosser 64/33

Kennewick 68/32

Walla Walla River

WASH.

Columbia River

ORE.

River

Hermiston 65/33

Pendleton 62/37

Tri-City temperatures from Pasco airport tower; Kennewick sewer plant; Richland water plant.

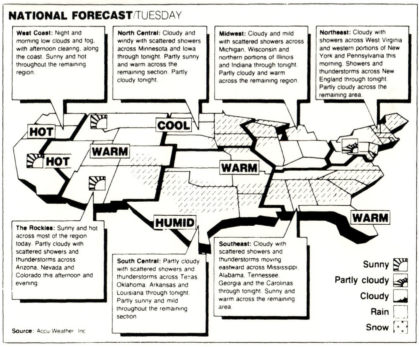

NATIONAL FORECAST/TUESDAY

West Coast: Night and morning low clouds and fog, with afternoon clearing, along the coast. Sunny and hot throughout the remaining region.

North Central: Cloudy and windy with scattered showers across Minnesota and Iowa through tonight. Partly sunny and warm across the remaining section. Partly cloudy tonight.

Midwest: Cloudy and mild with scattered showers across Michigan, Wisconsin and northern portions of Illinois and Indiana through tonight. Partly cloudy and warm across the remaining region.

Northeast: Cloudy with showers across West Virginia and western portions of New York and Pennsylvania this morning. Showers and thunderstorms across New England through tonight. Partly cloudy across the remaining area.

HOT

HOT

WARM

COOL

WARM

HUMID

WARM

The Rockies: Sunny and hot across most of the region today. Partly cloudy with scattered showers and thunderstorms across Arizona, Nevada and Colorado this afternoon and evening.

South Central: Partly cloudy with scattered showers and thunderstorms across Texas, Oklahoma, Arkansas and Louisiana through tonight. Partly sunny and mild throughout the remaining section.

Southeast: Cloudy with scattered showers and thunderstorms moving eastward across Mississippi, Alabama, Tennessee, Georgia and the Carolinas through tonight. Sunny and warm across the remaining area.

Sunny
Partly cloudy
Cloudy
Rain
Snow

Source: Accu-Weather, Inc.

The weather map is a creative informational graphic that shows readers what temperatures and other atmospheric conditions are, as in this regional illustration from the Tri-City (Wash.) *Herald* and this national example from the *Orange County Register* in Santa Ana, Calif. Reprinted by permission.

THE WALL STREET JOURNAL.

Some nationally circulated newspapers publish for a specific market and may be designed creatively with little or no art, as in these examples for readers with financial interests: the *Wall Street Journal* and the *Investor's Daily*. Reprinted by permission.

Trend graphics: Numbers that show what has happened over a period of time. (Examples: housing sales, jobless rate, deficit's growth.) In order to plot them, however, you need *all* of them.

Comparisons: A bar chart comparing the difference between numbers, but sometimes a pie chart showing what percentage of the whole something is. (Examples: almost all budget figures can be charted.)

Unusual comparisons: Often a comparison chart is simply comparing something out of the ordinary with things that are commonplace in our lives. (Examples: if you stacked up the federal deficit

using $1 bills, it would reach a third of the way to the moon. Americans snort a bathtub full of cocaine—325 pounds—each day.)

Maps: It's not always important to show where things occur. Not just locators. The best maps are the ones which add information. (Examples: the president's trip to Europe, the downing of a jetliner.)

"How" Graphics: How it happened, how it works, how it should have worked, how to do it. Requires a lot of resources, but one of the most valuable types of graphics for the reader. (Examples: what caused the Connecticut bridge collapse, the Galaxy plane crash, the shuttle disaster.)

Tonight's agenda

- ✔ Superintendent will recommend which elementary schools should close.
- ✔ Administration will recommend sale of Adams School to computer service firm.
- ✔ Board will hear about parties interested in Squaw Creek, including investors eyeing it for drunken driving prison.

Calendar

	MONDAY AUG. 13	TUESDAY AUG. 14	WEDNESDAY AUG. 15	THURSDAY AUG. 16	FRIDAY AUG. 17	SATURDAY AUG. 18	SUNDAY AUG. 12
BRONCOS						INDY COLTS 7 P.M.	
BEARS	WICHITA 7:35 P.M.	WICHITA 7:35 P.M.	WICHITA 7:35 P.M.	WICHITA 7:35 P.M.	OKLA. CITY 6:30 P.M.	OKLA. CITY 6:30 P.M.	OMAHA 5 P.M.

HOME GAMES ▨   MOUNTAIN DAYLIGHT TIME

BROWARD LEADERS

Top Boston Marathon finishers from Broward County:

Bill Harvey, 140th overall, Coconut Creek, 2:35:56.

Bobbi Rothman, 14th among women, Coconut Creek, 2:43:36.

THE WINNERS

Men — Rob de Castella, Australia, 2:07:51.

Women — Ingrid Kristiansen, Norway, 2:24:55.

Wheelchair — Andre Viger, Quebec, 1:43:25.

Sooners

Blue Devils' big lead stands up for 93-84 win over Oklahoma

DURHAM, N.C. (AP) — David Henderson scored 28 points, 18 in the second half, and Johnny Dawkins added 20 to lead second-ranked Duke to a 93-84 victory over No. 10 Oklahoma Saturday.

#2
#10

The Blue Devils, 27-2, cruised to a 23-point lead in the first half, but had to fight off an Oklahoma charge that began in the first half and continued into the first 10 minutes after intermission.

Duke grabbed a 23-8 lead by outscoring the Sooners 15-2 and added a 16-4 run to take a 39-16 lead with

---

Informational type extends a story—sometimes alone, and at other times with type and a small ornamental graphic—as illustrated in examples from the Cedar Rapids (Iowa) *Gazette*, the Denver *Post*, the Fort Lauderdale, Fla., *Sun-Sentinel* and the Syracuse (N.Y.) *Herald-American*. Reprinted by permission. Fort Lauderdale, Fla. *Sun-Sentinel* reprinted with permission of the News and Sun-Sentinel Company.

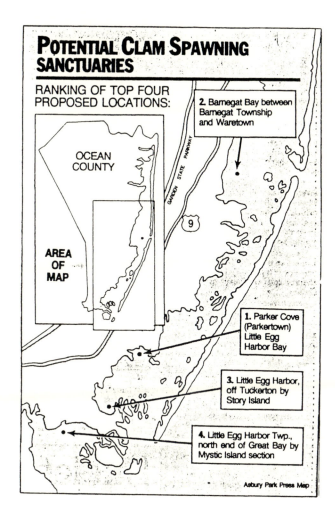

POTENTIAL CLAM SPAWNING SANCTUARIES

RANKING OF TOP FOUR PROPOSED LOCATIONS:

2. Barnegat Bay between Barnegat Township and Waretown

OCEAN COUNTY

AREA OF MAP

1. Parker Cove (Parkertown) Little Egg Harbor Bay

3. Little Egg Harbor, off Tuckerton by Story Island

4. Little Egg Harbor Twp., north end of Great Bay by Mystic Island section

Asbury Park Press Map

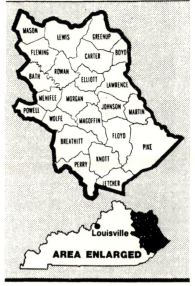

7TH CONGRESSIONAL DISTRICT

MASON, LEWIS, GREENUP, FLEMING, CARTER, BOYD, BATH, ROWAN, ELLIOTT, LAWRENCE, MENIFEE, MORGAN, JOHNSON, MARTIN, POWELL, WOLFE, MAGOFFIN, FLOYD, BREATHITT, KNOTT, PIKE, PERRY, LETCHER

Louisville

AREA ENLARGED

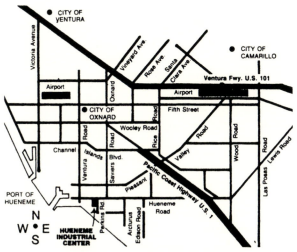

CITY OF VENTURA

CITY OF CAMARILLO

Ventura Fwy. U.S. 101

Airport

CITY OF OXNARD

Airport

Fifth Street

Wooley Road

Channel Islands Blvd.

Valley

Pacific Coast Highway U.S. 1

PORT OF HUENEME

Hueneme Road

N W E S

HUENEME INDUSTRIAL CENTER

This map shows where the Hueneme Industrial Center is going up in Oxnard

Locator maps are used frequently to show readers where the news is, as these examples do in the *Asbury Park Press* published in Neptune, N.J., the Louisville *Courier-Journal & Times* and the Ventura (Calif.) *Star-Free Press*. Reprinted by permission. Louisville *Courier-Journal & Times* copyright © 1984 by The Courier-Journal and Times Co. Reprinted with permission.

- Write the headline first. It helps to clarify your thinking and allows you to focus the graphic. If you can't write a crisp, clear head, you can't do the graphic.
- Make a news judgment. What's the story worth? By that judgment we'll know what the graphic is worth. Is it a two column by five inch graphic or a five column by nine inch graphic? The size of the graphic should be proportionate to the amount of information in it.
- Make sure you have all the numbers. Not just for graphics, but for yourself. . . .
- Remember: interesting isn't enough. The encyclopedia is interesting, but nobody is going to print it.
- Make sure the Graphics Department [people] get all the resource material they need. They should have access to the reporter, notes, photos, sketches, the editorial VDTs [Visual Display Terminals], etc.
- Get the information to the graphics department early. Don't wait until the story is written. If you have a graphic idea, share it. Don't keep it a secret. Let the graphics editor or art director know about it.
- Don't judge a graphic after it is done. It is too late. It's easy to rewrite a lead on deadline. It may take two hours to redo the graphic. Make sure that the graphic is edited to the same standards you apply to all other copy.

The publication should allow freedom to experiment with design graphics; but if the Total Page Concept is to work, the news and art departments must be fused so that everyone understands the goal of completing graphics projects on time to be published with the rest of the paper. The best piece of art delivered late is of no value to the news department. Whether the news story is breaking or is a feature, the editor should provide the photographer, illustrator or artist with text—or as many story particulars as possible—along with sample pieces of art so that it will be clear exactly what kind of visual material is desired and how the art will be used. Taking the time to do this makes it more likely that all the components will be used intelligently, even if they are not always innovative. Originality comes across to the reader in how the elements are brought together to make the paper easier to read.

According to Steffens of the L.A. *Times* Orange County Edition,

A lot of reporters say, "If I have these graphics or photos, that means I don't get all my text in; I have to take what ought to be a 60-inch opus [extensive literary composition] and make it a 40-inch story, or whatever." I think there is value to tight writing and tight editing, regardless. But you need to consciously sell the idea that a 60-inch story that isn't read isn't as good as a 40-inch story that is, if the art helps you get to and through it.

Also, Steffens said,

> You should use a multi-faceted approach to get the reader hooked. Sixty inches of story may be intimidating. But a graphic that might serve as a sidebar in normal terms might help get the reader all the way through the main story. Rather than treat them as competition, you might try and sell the concepts of graphics as sidebars.

Steffens suggested that, instead of—say—the main story and a six-inch sidebar being written by the reporter, a two-column by six-inch graphic should be created from data not covered in the story.

Three other journalism professionals whose thoughts parallel those of Steffens regarding the value of using purposeful graphics are Susan Miller, director of editorial development for Scripps Howard Newspapers; P. J. Erickson, design director of the *Arizona Republic* in Phoenix and J. Ford Huffman, managing editor of the Rochester, N.Y. *Times-Union.*

Miller, writing in *APME News* in 1985, said that "For every editor who rejoices in the ability of his staff to produce smashing graphics on deadline, there's another editor who thinks smashing graphics will get in the way of his story." Interestingly enough, the two-way proposition involved here is shown in the fact that "some of the newspapers that place the most emphasis on graphics and design are the very same papers routinely cited for the quality of their reporting. At these papers," Miller added, "editors have come to the conclusion that visual presentation is an integral part of telling the story."

However—according to Erickson—mechanical preparation can be taken too far, if the art is used to make up for a mediocre story. As quoted by Tuck in *APME News,* Erickson said, "The greatest danger in enhancing content unworthy of such (effort) is losing the impact of good packaging when the material *is* exceptional" (emphasis in original).

Huffman—also quoted by Tuck—said that "a good story will never get read if it looks like still another city council story. A bad story won't get read long if it was sold to the reader as the Second (graphic) Coming, and isn't."

PREPARATION MECHANICS

The mechanics of preparing art for a page or a section should be detailed on a standardized form or chart from the originating department or bureau. This form should accompany the design throughout production, providing documentation for analysis in the event of missed communications or missed deadlines

The *Arizona Republic* in Phoenix and the Cincinnati *Enquirer* are two newspapers where graphics and text complement one another to tell stories in greater depth. Reprinted by permission.

or both. While not all news can be planned for, some can be anticipated—in which case, space requests should be made specific, well ahead of the deadline. In every case, the elements used—whether illustrative or photographic—should be such that they are feasible in terms of the newspaper's deadlines.

The paper's graphic staff and related departments should design the standardized form with help from the news editorial staff so that all graphics/news concerns can be mutually considered. The form can be printed in triplicate, and it should specify the time covered by the story—if a scheduled event—and other art and assignment details. Also, it might include comments from the initial planning meeting of editors, photographers, illustrators and artists. Throughout the process, enough time must be allotted to review the art in draft, as completed, and finally alongside the story with which it is to be published.

Separate forms might be filled out for the different types and stages of production: for example, one form for features and section pages, and another for straight news stories and photos. Having forms to cover every part of the process—says Steffens of the L.A. *Times* Orange County Edition—might solve the

The Rochester, N.Y. *Times-Union* frequently uses a large photo
as a dramatic graphic element to extend a news story. Reprinted
by permission.

problem faced by editors of morning newspapers who, at 8 o'clock at night when
a map or some other graphic element arrives, have been heard to remark, "I
didn't know this was coming: I've already moved [sent out] the page."

In any case—whether a feature or a news page is on the agenda, cooperation
and respect for others is the key. Success accompanies a staff that (1) orders
only what is needed and then picks it up as soon as it is completed, whether
needed at the moment or not; and (2) checks the element's dimensions so that
the reproduced (and probably reduced) graphics will be correct initially, avoiding
a waste of materials and time.

The San Diego Union **GRAPHICS REQUEST** Artist

To be filled out by assigning editor		Sketch of idea and/or page layout
Tentative story slug		
Deadline day/date	**Publication** day/date	
Size	**Color** _____ full or _____ spot _____ B/W	
Section	**Page**	
Assigning editor	phone	
Layout person	phone	
Reporter	phone	
Photographer	phone	
Story idea with copy and/or photos attached to form (include suggested headline and text block/cutline)		
To be filled out by art department		
Approved by Art Director		
Special Instructions		

FORM #421 501

2001

Speedi-set ® Moore Business Forms, Inc.
MCP X Moore Business Forms, Inc. Powers 1224 Oik 4 J.x 2

As newspapers add a news graphics staff, assignment forms are developed for better communication between staff members. The example shown is from the San Diego *Union* and is printed in triplicate by Moore Business Forms, Inc. Reprinted by permission.

Steffens suggested that newspapers establish internal deadlines for both story text and graphics production. "You do it on the composing room floor," he said. "If you want the page to get out by (d), you have to have the copy set by (c), which means you have to have it to the copy desk by (b), which means you have to have it to the editor by (a)." The graphics and news deadlines should not be the same, Steffens added. "A lot of stuff needs Veloxes [that is, chemically treated paper on which halftone photos or line art are printed], and it takes maybe 30 minutes to an hour to turn around a Velox, so you have to build that time into it as well as proofing and checking [the graphics]."

All members of the photo, illustration and art staffs should be familiar with how the department or section functions regarding story production, photo art processing, art preparation and bringing the package together as a whole. Members of the news editorial and section staffs should be familiar with the photo, illustration and art staffs' work procedures. All graphics/news staffers need to be involved in the team as soon as a graphics department is established; this includes the art director, editors, illustrators, photographers, statisticians, research people and writers.

Coordination in production can extend the way a news or feature story is told to the reader. To illustrate this point, Steffens gave an example:

You have a headline, the lead of your story, a picture, and a caption: four areas. It's amazing how many editors want them to all be the same.

The headline says, "Fouts Scores Winning Touchdown." The lead says, "Dan Fouts, in an act of desperation, scored the winning touchdown..." The picture shows Fouts dashing across the line on a quarterback sneak. The caption says, "Dan Fouts wins game with quarterback sneak." Why read the rest of the story?

On the other hand, if the headline says, "Fouts Wins Game," and the lead says, "Dan Fouts, in spite of an injury, led the [San Diego] Chargers to..." the picture shows maybe another part of the game— maybe that a key block set up the score, and the photo caption says, "Defense (or lack of it) kept this a high-scoring game so Fouts had to win it," you've given the reader three or four reasons to read the story. All of a sudden Fouts' injury is of interest; the defense is of interest; the blocked kick is of interest.

To bring about the best marriage of graphics and editorial people, it is recommended that artists learn about photography and writing, news editors and reporters take instruction in art and photography, and photographers study drawing and writing. Such a crossover into the other skills probably won't result in writers becoming accomplished illustrators, or photographers becoming outstanding writers. However, it is possible that they will develop an appreciation for what the other team members are trying to do and that their guidance and instructions for projects involving art, writing and photography will be improved. It is also possible that, as views and talents are shared among these enlightened team members, a broader vision will be created: The illustrator might see value in spending more time reading a story to comprehend its meaning before rendering a drawing, or a writer might provide better direction for a photographer who is to take the photo that will accompany a story.

C. Thomas Hardin, photo and graphics editor of the *Courier-Journal* & Louisville (Ky.) *Times,* said that "on a large project, the photographer should be involved in the story as soon as possible. If not in on the inception of the story," he added, then "when the first planning begins. That allows the photograph to communicate to the reader—to advance the reader—as much as possible." Hardin said that photographs, charts or any other form of graphics should "keep the reader going along in the story" because "when that stops, the reader stops and goes on to the comics or to the weather or whatever."

Certainly, news work is imperative for all involved in enhancing the overall newspaper product. When each person has a clear understanding of what the others do, and how the system is set up to work, there is a greater likelihood that these individuals will freely discuss and become more interested in the published work. A system that positively engages individuals with a common

Two newspapers that are similar in design but for entirely different audiences are the New York *Times,* circulated nationally, and the *Litchfield County Times* in New Milford,

goal can go a long way toward creating a climate whereby the talent that each staff member brings to the publication is understood and complemented by the others. Mattson, president of the New York Times Co., agreed with this when he told the 1983 SNPA convention delegates that "news coverage and the organization and design of newspapers will be the constant concern of owners as well as editors."

Roger Black, former editorial art director of the New York *Times*—quoted by Tuck in *APME News*—said that his paper "continues to value content over presentation—even at the cost of 'good design.' However, we are aware that readers are increasingly bombarded by visual information on television and in

THE LITCHFIELD COUNTY TIMES

advertising everywhere." Black said that the *Times* uses graphic elements with its news story text as often as possible; but for news breaking at deadline, a variation of this policy remains in effect. "Our art directors and graphics editors endeavor to bring graphics into stories in all sections of the paper," he said. "Still, with breaking news and tight space, the *Times* will favor the text to the exclusion of prepared graphics."

Dan Turner, executive vice president and creative director for AMS Advertising, New York, has noticed visual improvement in the New York *Times*. Quoted in *Communication World* (1983) by Bill Hunter (a New York–based free-lance writer), Turner said, "Lots of people don't realize how the *Times* has changed over the years. Its graphics in various sections—Living, Home, Science, Arts and Leisure—are exceptional for a daily news publication."

Fundamental to design at the New York *Times* are three considerations, according to Louis Silverstein, former assistant managing editor, corporate art director, and presently consultant to the New York Times Co. These design purposes are:

- content enhancement;
- making the newspaper as a whole more inviting and more richly textured, and using all possible tools to give the reader more information and service; and
- level of typographic, graphic and artistic sophistication.

In *Print* (1985), Goss cited a poll commissioned by *Advertising Age,* in which members of the Society of Newspaper Design in Reston, Va., ranked the New York *Times* as the best-designed newspaper in the nation. Ranked two through four—in order—were the Allentown, Pa. *Morning Call, USA Today* and the Seattle *Times.*

With reference to *USA Today,* which began publishing in September 1982 as "the nation's newspaper," Hunter in *Communication World* said, "A new dimension to American journalism was added by the Gannett Co." Hunter added,

> Whoever is providing the lead—*USA Today,* the European press or the videomaniacs—organizational communicators are tightening their copy whenever appropriate, running more graphs, charts and other visuals. For today's busy readers that trend can't be all bad.

In 1985, Charles T. Brumback, president of the Chicago *Tribune,* also referred to the quick rise of *USA Today.* Speaking at the Inland Daily Press Association convention on the future of newspapers in the United States, Brumback said that *USA Today* represents the first major change since the introduction of color. Listing what some people had called "many reasons why it wouldn't survive," Brumback commented that "Advertising agencies showed their conservativism by not embracing what they took to be a new media with an ill-defined, changing, day-by-day readership." But the stand off attitude did not last for long, he said. "Advertising revenue and linage are up sharply [and] circulation continues to grow in spite of a price increase to 50 cents."

John C. Quinn, *USA Today's* editor, told an Arkansas Press Association audience in 1987 that the newspaper is truly a product of technology.

> Each evening the news pages are reported, written, edited and produced at our news center just across the Potomac River from our

nation's capital. Pages are moved at the rate of one every four minutes, bounced off American Satellite's ASC I about 23,000 miles into space and delivered simultaneously back to 30 print sites across the USA.

This means that the last page of tomorrow's *USA Today* must leave our newsroom a few minutes after 11 p.m. [Eastern time], be off the satellite about 15 minutes later and will be turning on the presses across this country 15 minutes or more before midnight. And all of those pages can be updated hourly throughout the night.

Referring to the reaction of other newspapers to *USA Today* and how it quickly became established across the nation, Quinn said, "At first they questioned why anyone would start a new newspaper just like all the others; then they complained that it was not like all the others."

Philip C. Geraci, associate professor of journalism at the University of Maryland, compared graphic design and illustration in three Washington, D.C., daily newspapers and then reported in *Newspaper Research Journal* (1983) that "*USA Today* is the most visually varied paper from the design standpoint. This newspaper uses more color, more maps, charts and graphs, more capsulization and teasers with the result that it has a bright 'modern' image." Geraci also said, "The shortened text and lavishly illustrated design of *USA Today* will surely have an impact on American journalism."

Rob Covey—formerly the design director of the Seattle *Times*, which ranks in the "best-designed" group along with the New York *Times*, the *Morning Call* and *USA Today*—said that these and all other newspapers recognized as design leaders

have a sense of architecture or space; the newspaper has a way of presenting itself in the layout of the spaces. It pays some sort of attention to the reader. It has advertising built into it. The reader is not cheated out of the news when he turns inside the paper. There's a sense of structure, but it is not so structured that it prevents anyone from still reacting strongly to the news.

Editors responding to the 1983 study by Steve Pasternack and Sandra Utt were asked to evaluate the appearance of seven prominent dailies. Pasternack and Utt reported that top scores were given to the Miami *Herald* and *USA Today* (see Table 7).

As part of the Pasternack and Utt study, an overall "most attractive" daily paper was selected by open-ended response. Among the 78 editors responding, the St. Petersburg (Fla.) *Times* was the clear winner, with 21 votes. The researchers said in their report that a phone interview with Frank Peters, artist for the *Times*, "indicated he was pleasantly surprised at the 'vote' " and that

A national newspaper that has influenced many other publications with its tight writing and lavish design is *USA Today*. Reprinted by permission.

Table 7
Editors' Opinions on the Attractiveness of Seven Daily Newspapers

	Percentage Giving High Rating	Percentage Giving Low Rating	Mean Score[a]
Des Moines *Register*	45.8	54.2	2.67
Denver *Post*	42.3	57.7	2.57
Los Angeles *Times*	25.4	74.6	3.02
Miami *Herald*	80.3	19.6	1.98
New York *Times*	33.7	66.7	2.87
USA Today	70.9	29.1	2.08
Washington *Post*	52.8	47.1	2.48

[a]The highest rating was 1; the lowest rating was 4.

Source: Sandra H. Utt and Steve Pasternack, "Front Pages of U.S. Daily Newspapers," *Journalism Quarterly* (1984):879–84.

"he said graphics are vital to newspapers in a competitive situation; while Peters said he finds the *Times* extremely attractive, he said the majority of American newspapers are unattractive."

The study also showed that "other dailies receiving more than one vote in the 'most attractive' poll were *USA Today*, 6; the Boston *Globe*, 4; the Allentown *Morning Call*, 3; the Minneapolis *Tribune*, 2; and the Chicago *Tribune*, 2."

Actually, newspaper editors who represent news and art departments are frequently asked by polling organizations and academicians what they think about the look of their own and other papers. Putting all studies and categories

The Boston *Globe* presents a clean, uncluttered arrangement of news supporting graphics. In this case, there is even a silhouette of a tire to lure readers into one of its stories. Reprinted courtesy of The Boston Globe.

aside—"best designed," "most attractive," or whatever—graphics employed within the Total Page Concept must support the way the news is displayed. Creative design should not be undersold. However, it should not be oversold at the expense of good news content.

A statement by N. Christian Anderson, executive editor of the *Orange County Register,* substantiates the need for attractively displayed news with good content. As quoted by Tuck in *APME News,* Anderson said, "If you don't have good content, readers ultimately will be turned off by spiffy looks. If you have great content poorly presented, it may not be read by anyone."

At the *Orange County Register* in Santa Ana, Calif., the readers' need for timely, accessible information is clearly represented in the design of the news. Reprinted by permission.

10   Photographic Design

I don't know that photographs, per se, contribute to the design. But it's how they're used. How they're used with graphics and how they're used with type, and what the photographs say. Frankly, that's the most important contribution. Photographs can take the reader there and freeze the moment and hold it for the reader. It's not a fleeting thing; it's there forever.

C. Thomas Hardin
photo and graphics editor
Courier-Journal & Louisville (Ky.) *Times*

Photographs are an important communication tool within the Total Page Concept (TPC), and in every other system of design. Philip Geraci at the University of Maryland observed in the *Newspaper Research Journal* (1983) that the use of photography to illustrate the news has "varied little in recent decades." As part of his study comparing graphic design and illustration in three newspapers in the nation's capital, Geraci examined the element of photography itself and concluded that the use of photographs to illustrate the news has been the dominant display choice of editors and graphics directors for more than 100 years.

To arrest the reader's interest and complement the typography, photos should express an emotion and be of the best possible quality. This is because a photograph has a greater potential for instant impact on the reader than any other element. Photos can serve as an extraordinary contribution to or distraction from a page, so every designer must learn how to select and effectively use them to tell the news.

Photos that can serve as stand-alone pieces of art give the publication a special feeling, whether they are pictures of elation—a local team, say, winning a relay event at a track meet—or somber—for example, the assembly of world leaders at the funeral of one of their peers. A photo with great emotional impact has an ability to steal the reader's attention from all other elements on the page.

A photo can quickly document the devastation of a disaster, as does this example from the Newport (R.I.) *Daily News*. Reprinted by permission.

Speaking about the photograph's importance on a page and the value of a designer fully understanding its significance, Geraci mentioned that "Designers regard photographs and other illustrations as shapes and sizes, patterns of dark and light, large and small, as related to the shapes, sizes and dark/light patterns of headlines and body type." At the same time, Geraci added, "Designers must constantly keep in mind the physical constraints imposed by the production process." Photographers must be aware of the designer's concerns and also understand the value of effectively and artistically documenting news events with spontaneous photos that will cause the reader's memory of the event to be lengthened.

The basic black-and-white photo with a headline tells the story in this example from the Seattle *Times*. Reprinted by permission.

The photographers are part of the news-gathering staff—not a service department used to supplement the news department. For this arrangement to work satisfactorily, the graphics editor must be assigned to the picture desk, where he or she can establish guidelines for the staff photographers that will show their work to its best advantage and also realistically address the news-value kind of decisions faced by news editors.

As Brian Steffens—graphics editor of the Los Angeles *Times* Orange County Edition—says, editors need to understand that photos should never be used in lieu of telling a story in text. If the story was not worth writing about in the first place, using a photo instead will only waste the photographer's time, talent and energy. For example, a city editor might receive a press release from an organization about a ground-breaking ceremony—or some other routine event— look at it, and say, " 'That's not even worth my intern doing a three-inch brief on. Let's assign a photograph. That's how we'll deal with this.' They'll send a top-scale photographer out in a company car with all the insurance they pay on this guy and all the equipment."

The result, says Steffens, is that the photographer will spend an hour on the assignment and—since there is no obvious news angle to the story—come back frustrated because of his inability to get a good picture. "The city desk will run a three[-column] by five[-inch] photo and caption. Something that was not worth three inches of text type has all of a sudden" taken up 18 inches of news-column space. "Where is the sense in that?" Steffens concludes, "Personally, I think the three-inch brief would suffice—maintaining the paper's image of the paper of record, noting the event in an efficient manner."

So, precisely because photos are dramatic, fast and dominating, they should be placed throughout the paper with care. They represent significant news judgment—choices that should never be made on the basis of ease, but through the same substantial principles applied to the evaluation of news everywhere else in the paper. The design policy on photographs must fall within the newspaper's ongoing understanding of what its readers expect to see. Photos have an integral role to play in design; they are the core of the Total Page Concept.

UNDERSTANDING THE GRAPHIC POTENTIAL OF A PHOTO

The relationship of all the parts of a page are quickly discerned on TPC pages that include photos. Faces are at the heart of the Total Page Concept: They mirror events; they tell to whom the events are happening; they take a message to the reader; and, packaged with stories, they provide a whole picture of the news of the day.

Steve Pasternack and Sandra Utt found in their 1983 study of the nation's front pages that "mug shots are still widely used by daily newspapers"; an overwhelming 98.7 percent were displaying the usually single-column photo of a face to illustrate a front-page story. However, this is still not universal. Reid Sams, former editor of the St. Helena *Star,* a weekly in California, does not often see any reason to publish a mug of a news source. "We, as a general rule, do not run thumbnail mug shots—mainly because they are so small and must be very clear," he said. "Because they are hard for the reader to figure out, we don't bother with them." There is one spot where the *Star* does print mugs, however, and that is with the "question man" feature: Mug shots are shown with the answers to the question. "Many newspapers use varied layouts to give local people a chance to see themselves and their friends in the paper," Sams noted. "When laying out the features, it is best to keep the answer and photo close together and clearly marked so it is easy for readers to see who is saying what."

The St. Helena *Star* notwithstanding, most newspapers do use mug shots freely. Geraci's 1983 study revealed that "the predominant illustration was the black and white head shot. The second most used illustration was a black and white medium-range photograph of people."

Through no fault of the photographer, even an excellent photo can lose its impact because of a bad design decision. For that very reason, it is not unusual for newspapers to establish a standard position for the dominant page-one photo. As Pasternack and Utt found in 1983, "When a modular newspaper finds a permanent spot for its dominant photograph, it is most likely in the upper left section of the page; at non-modular newspapers, the preferred location is in the middle of the page" (see Table 8).

As would be expected, the photos on page one are most frequently used to support a story on that page. Pasternack and Utt's research confirmed that tendency among a little more than half the respondents (55.4 percent), but it also uncovered very interesting variations—ones with a significantly alternative approach to their photo display. Their report showed that "many front page pictures serve as an 'index' to some inside content—19.2 percent—or are not related to any other item in the publication—25.4 percent."

Knowing how to look at photographs with a sense that they need to be part of an organized mosaic will foster TPC relationships. Steffens at the L.A. *Times* Orange County Edition says that deciding which photo to run is easy: "Run the picture that will get people to read the story." But the designer should not "run the lackluster shot of this important guy—because he is important"—in a prominent position on page one or on another display page in the newspaper.

Table 8
Modular and Nonmodular Newspapers' Placement of Dominant Photo (in percentages)

	Upper Right	Upper Left	Middle of Page	No Set Pattern
Modular	2.4	21.4	14.3	61.9
Nonmodular	8.7	17.4	34.8	39.1

Source: Sandra H. Utt and Steve Pasternack, "Front Pages of U.S. Daily Newspapers," *Journalism Quarterly* (1984):879–84.

Run him smaller, or secondary on a jump page. I'm not saying that
if the guy earned recognition, highest scoring guy or MVP [Most
Valuable Player], he's not worth a picture, but is he worth four
columns by 10 inches, or is he worth a one column by four or a two
column by four? If it's that important, why can't you find a way to
make a second picture in the paper? Just like it's worth it in a story,
you make a sidebar [photo].

The results from thoughtful selection, sizing and cropping of photographs in
the Total Page Concept should be twofold: (1) more page layouts displaying
photographic art to complement other page elements and (2) the potential for
greater readership of those pages.

Concerning the appropriate size of a photo for a newspaper page, the possibilities are limited only by the production capability for making a halftone. As
to the reality of photo sizes in use, Pasternack and Utt asked editors to describe
the sizes that they would normally publish. The researchers reported that:

Most editors, 62.5 percent, said the photograph would be four columns wide, although several indicated photos occupying three, 12.5
percent, five, 11.1 percent, or even six, 8.3 percent, columns. The
length of the horizontal photograph was most likely to be either six,
25 percent, or seven, 19.4 percent, inches. However, responses on
this ranged from five inches to 13 inches.

Previous research on how the size of a photograph draws readers to a page
was cited in a study of newspaper images with relation to readership that was
conducted by Rita S. Wolf, director of student publications, and Gerald L.
Grotta, associate professor of journalism, both of Texas Christian University
(TCU). Writing in *Newspaper Research Journal* (1985), Wolf and Grotta said,
"The data support previous studies showing that a large photograph attracts
readers to a story, and that certain types of photographs are especially effective
in enticing people into a story." They studied responses of 95 students in a Mass
Communication in Society class at TCU. Three alternate front pages of a regular
issue of the TCU *Daily Skiff* were printed and used for the study. Each front
page featured a different four-column photograph and cutline. Two of the photos, taken by student photographers and judged to be of acceptable technical
quality by three professional photographers, pertained to a local news feature
about a student who had received a scholarship to study ballet in New York
City, and the third photo had nothing to do with the story. Noting that the study
in part showed that their own results concurred with the research of others,
Wolf and Grotta reported, "More students read the text of the 'TCU Dancer'
story, and more read it thoroughly"—over stories not accompanied by a piece
of art.

QUALITY PHOTOS

Most photo assignments are routine, but the photographer who approaches all assignments as though they are going to be routine will take only routine—and boring—photos all the time. The fact that many photo assignments are not exciting provides the biggest challenge to editors on the assignment desk and to the photographers themselves.

While generic photos—a beautiful sunset or a fresh snowfall, perhaps—may have all the quality in the world, these are not examples of news photos and should never be substituted for news photos, although sometimes they are appropriate illustrations for a feature story or to document an unusual weather condition like the first time it has snowed in an area in many, many years. Many times a photographer may be tempted to take that sunset or some other photo cliché, such as a "for the record" check passing between donor and worthy recipient, a "lineup" of torsos, a speaker shot or a driver's license-style mug. Equally unattractive are photos with poor composition or poor lighting. Craig Harrington, publisher of the *InterMountain News* in Burney, Calif., added that a photo's highlights are also important. "The eye is immediately attracted to the white portion or highlights of a photograph," Harrington said. "Make sure those highlights lend themselves to your main subject, or are part of the main center of interest." Habitually poor composition, poor lighting, and lack of concern for highlights will cause readers to pay little attention to the photos—and text—on a page.

Although photographers do undeniably take lots of pictures, they would make editors much happier if they printed more of them that were usable. In turn, the pages of the newspaper would be much brighter. For starters, Harrington said, those who design pages might use fewer photos and publish them larger. "Publishing almost every picture taken means they can't be run very big," he added. Harrington suggested editing the page so that one piece of artwork will dominate.

If a picture is a quality photo, the design editor has more choices to make regarding size, especially when the event tells a significant news story. Harrington gave the example of the 1980 volcanic eruption of Mount St. Helens in Washington state. When the volcano "blew its top, some West Coast newspapers ran just one photograph on page one—as a matter of fact, that's all they ran. The photo took up the entire front page." Something similar happened at the InterMountain News late in 1987 when fires raged throughout Northern California. "We ran just one photograph five columns wide by 13½ inches tall. This was packaged with a one-column story on the fires—running down the left side of the page."

The photo staff that seeks to take the most creative photographs possible in any event and that completes assignments on time and stays within budget is a quality photo staff. Quality of success at deadline usually begins when the assignment is made. Newspaper reporters and photographers work together to

84 Tuesday, March 25, 1986   THE TIMES HERALD **RECORD**

Army basketball: wait until next year

By TERRY EGAN
Staff Writer

season in review

Record file photos

Coach Wohtke looks toward guard Kevin Houston, and the team's future

Muscle and brawn like Mom used to make

By ROB SWIERSKI
Record Correspondent

sports briefs

SCHOLASTIC VOLLEYBALL
Miniink sweeps Burke

Port Jervis downs VC

Comeback propels Goshen

Middies defeat Monticello

O'Neill outlasts Washies

RECREATION BASKETBALL
Middletown League

GYMNASTICS
Two qualify for state meet

A more creative alternative to the for-the-record photo is to show the subjects in action, as displayed in the *Times Herald-Record*, a tabloid in Middletown, N.Y. Reprinted by permission.

make certain that the captured art accurately represents the story. Tom Maurer, reporter with the Bakersfield *Californian*, said, "Reporters and photographers make the best teams, largely because they are both cynical and stubborn. Both want to make the best of every story assignment. However, they sometimes can go in separate directions."

Maurer said that the best way to avoid confusion is for the reporter to communicate to the photographer exactly what he or she wants taken. The reporter cannot assume that the photographer is able to read minds. The process should begin with an assignment slip that carries specific information on it—and includes the reporter's name so that the photographer has a contact for checking back. "It also helps if they go to the assignment together," says Maurer, "I often tell

This edition of the Bakersfield *Californian* provides a page-one example of obvious communication between the reporter and photographer. Reprinted by permission.

the photographer what I want before we leave so he or she can get the right lenses. Then we can talk more about the story in the car. By the time the assignment is over, we both usually have what we want."

PHOTO EDITING TECHNIQUES

Harrington at the *InterMountain News* said that photographers frequently do not help pictures because they pay little attention to the first level of photo editing: that done in the camera. "One of the biggest problems I see in the use of photographs is the publishing of pictures with distracting or uninteresting elements. Not enough attention is paid to eliminating busy backgrounds that lend nothing to interesting pictures." The photographer can begin the editing process "by taking more than a snapshot of his subject; sometimes this means nothing more than getting a different angle of the subject instead of straight on—move up on your subject." Harrington suggests that the photographer use a ladder, chair or car fender to become taller and shoot down on the subject, or kneel or lay down and shoot up so the sky provides "a simple background free of telephone wires, buildings and the like." However, Harrington cautions, "When shooting people, make sure the low angle pictures are taken so you aren't looking up your subject's nose, a very unattractive position."

Pages are easiest to design when the photos are the first element placed on a wide-open page, or placed second on a page with advertising on it. The order in which photos and other art are placed on a page is an indication of their importance in the Total Page Concept. Forms of art are placed on the page first because art is difficult to edit, beyond cropping, and also because they are the first page elements to catch the reader's attention. Merrill Oliver, while assistant graphics editor of the Cincinnati *Post,* said that, at the *Post* "pictures are inseparable from page design. We use a single dominant image on our pages and this image is the starting point for the modular design of the page." He added that the goal at the *Post* is "to communicate with words and pictures, with neither being subservient to the other."

Locating an individual or individuals qualified to understand the photojournalistic goals of the newspaper is not an easy task for some papers, especially small ones. Wayne Welch, managing editor of the Tulare, Calif. *Advance-Register,* claims that "photo editors at small papers are about as common as editorial cartoonists, which is to say there aren't any." At the *Advance-Register,* the contact sheets from the negatives are handed directly to the news desk or page editors "in almost all cases, all the while encouraging photographers and reporters to make recommendations on which photos we use." Welch said that "it is absolute policy the final determination be made by the page editors; that's the person with the best overall sense of what the story is about and the amount of space and positioning the picture or pictures will likely get."

In any case, the photo editor or page designer must be skilled in sizing, cropping, doing markup for the printer, proportioning and keying photos for layouts. These skills are defined as follows:

• **Sizing**—Photo size should complement the story in such a way that readers do not wonder whether they are looking at a photo with a story or a story with a photo.

• **Cropping**—Short of going to extremes, photos should be cropped tightly. This means that the page editor should cut out extraneous parts of the photo, including unnecessary background and foreground areas and unessential parts of the body—being careful not to "saw" body parts except at the shoulders and waist.

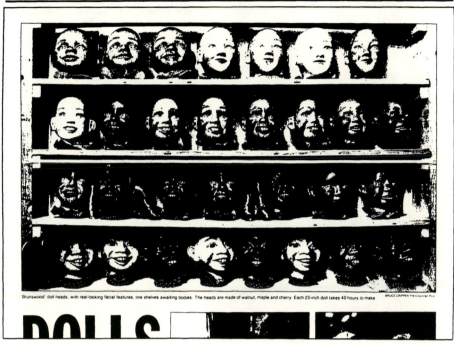

A doll collection is the single dominant image in this photo on a Cincinnati *Post* section page. Reprinted by permission.

According to Harrington,

> The photo editor or page designer can sometimes save a picture that has distracting backgrounds by using a tight crop on the final print. Even check passing or award pictures look much better if you get rid of unnecessary space around the subject by cropping it tightly.

Sizing and cropping are done from a contact sheet of prints made the same size as the negatives—usually with an entire roll printed on one piece of 8x10-inch photographic paper.

• **Markup for the Printer**—The printer should be able to understand just which parts are to be left in and which are to be cut out, according to grease-pencil marks on the photo.

• **Proportioning**—Some photos work better as horizontals; others are better as verticals. Using a "proportional wheel," the gauge for reduction should be set to include the best part of a photo for the desired column width. Measuring

WILD BET

He has a scream like a primal-therapy patient, a laugh like a perverted chipmunk, and a routine guaranteed to enrage people of all creeds and persuasions. SAM KINISON is brutal when it comes to the bleaker side of marriage, sex, religion, world problems. The preacher turned comic has been married twice, and the highlights of those experiences still burn in his memory. He taunts, cajoles, stabs. And audiences love it. They come to be shocked and overwhelmed. Santa Barbarans will have their opportunity to see "The Beast," as his fans affectionately call him, on Saturday, September 26, at 8 p.m. Tickets are available at the Arlington Ticket Office. Call 583-8700 for more info.

Sparky Anderson

Bill Scherrer

A tight crop is the key to bringing a reader to the photo immediately; this includes the single-column picture of the face, as in these examples from the Santa Barbara (Calif.) *Independent* and the Muskegon (Mich.) *Chronicle*. Reprinted by permission.

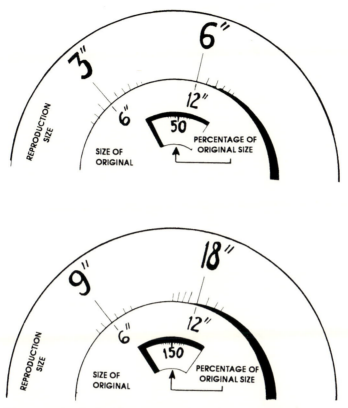

The proportional wheel is a gauge used to reduce or enlarge photos by matching the outside and inside rims of the device. Illustration by J Archer. Reprinted by permission.

to enlarge a piece of art is done by lining up the original size on the inner scale of the proportional wheel adjacent to the desired size on the outer scale. The percentage of reduction or enlargement will appear in a window opening on the wheel.

• **Keying Photos with Layouts**—Photos and pages must be marked so that the individual responsible for placing the photos on the pages will be able to place them quickly and accurately.

It is at this point that black-and-white glossy photos are converted into half-tones—reproductions made with a special "stat" (photostat) camera through screens to convert images into dot patterns, and then printed from the screen negative onto Velox paper or directly onto an aluminum plate. The same procedure is used to prepare line art for publication—although in that case it does not result in a screen or dot pattern. Some papers have started using a good-quality office copy machine to accomplish the same task; this method is usually quicker and less expensive.

ENHANCING THE PHOTO

Photos must have integrity. For hard news stories, cutting away parts of the photo will weaken its credibility—as well as the credibility of the news itself. Photographers seldom take photos for hard news with the thought that they will be enhanced by editing with a brush or knife.

Patrick Lynch, editorial artist at the Los Angeles *Times,* has been in the business of creating editorial art for more than 30 years. Lynch—who began at the Kansas City (Mo.) *Star-Times* and was there 5 ½ years before moving west— says that when he started out, the backbone of the newspaper art department was photo retouching.

> We had relatively poor reproduction; we had newsprint that was gray, we had type that was dark gray. What we did was basically try to enhance photographs. With the advent of superior printing, photo retouching has pretty much fallen by the wayside. I don't want to give the impression that we don't use it anymore. We do [but] we are far more selective; we use it far less.

For soft news subjects on an inside page, it is sometimes effective to cut away the original background, creating a photo silhouette against white or a gray screen. Special consideration should be taken not to cut away arms or legs, thereby creating a contrived appearance. Areas where there are darks against darks or lights against lights, or curly or wavy hair, must be examined closely. The person in the photo could be caused much embarrassment if incorrectly given a crew-cut hairstyle or if part of a shirt or blouse is cut away or incorrectly included, making the person look larger or smaller than he or she really is. The importance of learning and carefully executing these photo enhancement techniques should not be taken for granted.

• **Airbrush Editing**—Delicately touching up with a special airhose and spray; an artist can apply brush strokes of paint to crop out unwanted parts of the photo.

• **Silhouette Editing**—Creating a "photo dropout" or "pop-up" also requires great care so as not to mutilate the photo; a knife blade is applied to separate the useful part of the picture from that which is to be thrown away.

Other techniques used to enhance photo quality are:

• **Printing Compensation**—In some cases, photos may need to be printed lighter or darker to compensate for a newspaper plant publication process that muddies the pictures or renders in flat tones what would otherwise be crisp prints. Other photos may need special attention because they show light building interiors or a dark gray sky. "Burning in" or "dodging out" certain areas during printing may also be used to compensate for imperfections in some photos.

• **Use of Border Tape**—One technique that will enhance or point special attention to photos is called "key-lining," "scoring-lining" or "tool-lining"—en-

A photo silhouette is sometimes appropriate in telling a story, but should be used sparingly—and preferably with an inanimate object, as in this example from the Akron (Ohio) *Beacon Journal*. Reprinted by permission.

closing them inside half- to 1-point black border tape. This may be done by applying tape directly to the photo, being careful that the tape does not overlap or underlap the photo edge and that the knife blade does not cut the photo; it may also be done with a mechanical application to the photo in the halftone production process or on a computer screen.

PHOTO PAGES

Even before a photo page is designed, the photos destined for the page are evaluated and judged individually. Donna E. Hicks, a free-lancer writing in *Editors' Forum* (1987), referred to unity as being the key to perfect picture-page layouts. Hicks added, "Of course, you need good photos to begin with—photos good in substance and print quality." Each photo should be strong enough to stand on its own; to use a bad photo just because it is part of the photo story is a lame excuse.

Photo pages that are worth their space have several inherent characteristics. These include:

ALBUQUERQUE JOURNAL, Sunday, July 20, 1986 H3

This striking example from the Albuquerque (N.M.) *Journal* is a photo page with a beginning, middle and end; in addition, all the photos would be able to stand on their own as single pictures. Reprinted by permission.

- An organized positioning of the photos into a story line, including a beginning, middle and end. Hicks said that, "in order for a picture page to be effective, . . . its layout must have unity. The photos, headline, text and cutlines all must stand together as an appealing unit."

- Generally, a clockwise arrangement will be easier for the reader's eye to follow. Hicks said that "most editors know that the focal person in a picture should be facing toward the inside of the page, yet this is an easy rule to forget when doing a layout." Furthermore,

- "Flopping a photo is not always a good way to correct this over-sight." Printing a photo backward "not only reverses any lettering in a photo, it can also change a person's characteristics; a person writing with her right hand will be left-handed in a flopped photo."

A photo story is just like a written story; the reader expects to know where to "read" next. The editor's arrangement can guide the flow of photos in the mind's eye of the reader.

Hicks suggested that the designer "select a combination of vertical and horizontal photos and use tightly-cropped pictures of various sizes." She recommended a procedure that would ensure creativity in the photo-page design:

- Sketch several rough layouts with the photos in different sizes and positions. At this stage, just approximate the size of the photos.

- When you get a basic design that you like, then use the proportional scale to see how the pictures actually fit. This is the tedious part.

- Have a dominant photo. It need not be the first or last photo in the arrangement, but the photo story will have more impact if the dominant photo is the best one in terms of eliciting human emotion. "A layout with one dominant photo looks best," Hicks said, "but sometimes the limelight may need to be shared by two or more photos since not all photo stories lend themselves to only one main photo."

- Put equal space between the art and copy block shapes. Photos may be separated by white space—the same throughout the photo story. Differences in the spacing between photos can distract from the story itself. Hicks commented that, although white space "looks good on the outside, it should not be trapped between photos" because "photos and text should be placed close together—about 1 to 1.5 picas, or a quarter inch, apart." She said that the designer is challenged in a picture-page layout by the absence of columns. "The hardest part about designing a picture page is throwing away your concept of columns." The standard column format should never be used, she added.

- Add copy with a headline. While it must never overshadow the photo part of the story, a short block of copy should be written to cover aspects of the story that the reader cannot infer or that need expansion beyond photos and captions. As Hicks said, "On a picture page, let the photos carry the story. Try to keep the text to a minimum, if possible. You may want to do the layout first, then write the text to fit. Always do the writing for a picture page with the photos in hand."

- Place captions below each photo. This method is preferred to printing all caption material in a single box. The latter forces readers first to identify which photo is which, and then to bob their heads up and down and back and forth to figure out who is who.

Harrington at the *InterMountain News* has his own list of suggestions for the photo page:

- Use no more than five photographs for a full-page broadsheet layout; make one dominate in size, surrounded by smaller ones.
- Do not trap white space. Do not surround a blank area with photographs on all sides. Use white space effectively. Work your layout with photos in the center, moving outward. Be careful also not to let the white space encircle your package of photos and copy like a fence.
- Make sure all captions or cutlines touch some portion of the corresponding photograph. Do not use one caption to tell all and then, compounding the problem, place it at the bottom of the page. A well-placed cutline underneath or to the side of the photograph is what counts.
- Do not have your subjects looking out or off the page.
- If the photographs lack a natural frame, outlining them with border tape or using a 20-percent gray background screen helps hold the picture together.

Once the photographer has been allowed sufficient time to shoot the story idea, the editor should edit the photos for the layout. "I have used as few as one picture in telling a story, but find from three to five usually works well," Harrington said. "If you have a sixth, really fantastic photo that you want to publish, run it on page one to tease your readers into this photo essay or story you spent the extra time on." Finally, "after you have narrowed your selections to five, choose the one that will dominate the page; all other photographs will work in smaller sizes around this one."

Calling for more photo pages, Harrington said, "A commitment must be made to publish them. I've heard from some daily editors the excuse that weeklies have more opportunity and flexibility to run photo pages than dailies. I've also heard just the opposite from weekly editor/publishers." Harrington claims that, based on his own experience at both dailies and weeklies, this is simply not true.

It's making the decision that you want to feature photography and good graphics. A small, five-days-a-week daily, publishing just six pages per day is still producing 30 pages per week, more than the 12 to 16 pages my weekly...publishes every seven days; there is no reason one of those daily pages couldn't be freed to feature a story once a week.

PHOTOS/TEXT IN PERSPECTIVE

C. Thomas Hardin of the *Courier-Journal* & Louisville (Ky.) *Times* says that "the photograph can take the place of type and get the reader into the page, get the reader into the story—entice the reader, if you will."

Oliver described the method by which photos and text are aligned at the Cincinnati *Post* so that they will complement one another:

> Since placement of the dominant image—most often a picture—is the first design step, it helps set the design course for the entire page. We normally run three-column vertical or four- to five-column main pictures on the front page, with a standard story count of five, and we frequently use secondary art in the form of a picture, locator map or informational graphic.
>
> We choose to edit a smaller number of pictures that we use prominently instead of using our space to run a greater number of smaller pictures. We feel that some pictures are more important to our readers than others and that it's our job to pick those most important and to use them large enough to give them the impact they deserve. The same reasoning is used in deciding to cut one story to give a more important story the space it deserves.
>
> Editing this tightly allows us to give our best stories and pictures adequate space in a clean, direct page design that's easy for the reader to attack and digest. This philosophy is followed throughout the paper and is especially apparent on section fronts and other display pages.

Words and photos need to work together to provide one idea that the busy reader can grasp. To harmonize a TPC layout, the design editor must determine appropriate sizes for each of the photos. According to Welch, "At a small newspaper with access to dozens of wire photos and prolific staff photographers, space is at a premium." He said that editors at the Tulare *Advance-Register* try to run as many photos as possible on as many pages as they can be placed.

> We accomplish that with one important rule of thumb: "Bigger is not necessarily better." In many cases, especially on inside pages, we run many small photos. However, when a photo is really strong, we are quick to pull out the stops to run it as big as we can. Mini-photo features—small two and three picture layouts—also are a valuable tool for small papers.

Mirroring Welch's idea are these words of Harrington at the *InterMountain News*:

> Treat each page special. Work to improve the inside pages using photographs. For inside pages at the *InterMountain News,* we try and run a four-column—standard advertising width—photo whenever possible.

Learning how to tie the pictures and text into a purposeful blend is an art in itself. Methods to carry this out were suggested by Nanette Bisher of the *Orange*

On the same day, two newspapers halfway across the nation from one another may publish the same news-wire photo and story with quite similar design, as in these examples from the Sacramento (Calif.) *Union* and the St. Louis *Post-Dispatch*. Reprinted by permission.

County Register during the Southern Newspaper Publishers Association Foundation seminar, "Layout, Design and Graphics." In regard to dominant art, Bisher said, "Try to use art related to a story to dominate a page, especially page one or a section front. It gives it better credibility." Regarding cluster photos, she said, "When using several photos on a page, cluster them and push white space toward the outside. Each photo should have its own cutline. If you need to use a copy block cutline to give more information, place it as near the photo as possible."

Another method to keep the photos and text in perspective is to place the main photograph above the fold of the newspaper's front page. According to Harrington of the *InterMountain News*, page designers should "follow the same pattern writers use with the inverted pyramid—place your most important or dominant piece of artwork at the top and work down." It is not unusual to see newsstand copies of newspapers where the main photo has been placed in such a way that the subject of the art—if there is any art—cannot be recognized above

the fold. "People aren't hoping you have good photography inside; they want
to see it from the beginning, above the fold on page one," Harrington said. "A
four- to six-column photo is advisable." Welch of the *Advance-Register* agrees:
"If you have a commitment to quality photojournalism—and we do—the photo
has to be a crucial element of page design. In the event of major stories, photos
may have to play a close second fiddle in determining how a page is laid out.
But more often than not, the page design can be built around a strong photo
or photos."

At the Tulare, Calif. *Advance-Register*—and most other newspapers—
editors try to place several photos on the top and bottom of each page.
Reprinted by permission.

When the words of text do not match a photo story, the words can be rewritten; but when the photos do not fit a written story, they must be retaken—at the cost of precious time and money. Oliver said that at the Cincinnati *Post* the process of matching photos and words is monitored constantly. "During all phases of the design process, there is give-and-take between those involved on the news desk and in graphics," he said. "The process I've explained is the standard, but there are days when the person designing the Local front [page] runs into a severe space crunch, so we offer to drop the secondary picture." The offer is based on an exchange. "We do this," Oliver said, "because another day we will want some extra space to run an extraordinary picture a column larger than normal, or we'll design a picture combination for the Local front that's larger than normal."

Maurer says that at the Bakersfield *Californian*—as at most other papers— design does figure into the planning of photography. "Metro desk editors rarely think in terms of large, creative art unless it is staring at them," Maurer said. "So, photographers will shoot color art as often as possible and look for the unusual shot. They often recruit the reporters to help them sell the art to the desk. Reporters are all too willing to help because good art will often elevate a story into more prominent display." At the Cincinnati *Post,* Oliver says, editors will also usually support the case of the photographer who brings in good art. "We feel our design practices motivate photographers and artists to go the extra step to get the very best picture possible and to create the best piece of conceptual art or information graphic possible, because they know we will give their work the space it needs to have the impact it deserves."

While having the writer and photographer work together on a story or a long-term project is not the only solution to bringing words and pictures together, it is certainly worth trying whenever possible within assignment and time constraints. This might be satisfactorily planned by the news and art editors meeting frequently to talk over and mesh their ideas. At these meetings, editors might also find ways to encourage photographers to approach stories as reporters do: Photographers should look with their cameras to see how best to tell the story— whether the photo is to stand alone or be connected to a written story on the TPC page.

11   Illustrative Design

Part of the process in attracting artists to the newsroom has to do with providing an environment that will speak for itself about our commitment to help artists grow into an important part of the newspaper.

James T. Robison
managing editor
Orange County Register, Santa Ana, Calif.
(Quoted by Joseph A. Weiler in *APME News*, 1985)

Line drawings and illustrations—once used mainly on the opinion and editorial pages—are now finding a wide audience through the Total Page Concept (TPC). Such art work is effective for soft sections and inside-page stories when there is sufficient time to produce the drawing and no suitable photographic art is available.

ILLUSTRATIONS

Illustrations are an important element used by news editorial staffs as page art. As complements to hard-news coverage, illustrations usually provide less credibility but more drama than photos. Whether the editor sends an artist to the news assignment location to do a sketch or the assignment is from an idea or an already written story, very specific instructions should be given to the artist for drawing according to the editor's needs.

Donald N. Clement, staff cartographer at the Los Angeles *Times,* emphasized that the artist is better prepared to work with the reporter if both are knowledgeable of one another's needs. "The essence of what we do in Editorial Art is to take maybe two ideas in a story, an editor's idea and a writer's idea as depicted or portrayed in a story, then you have an artist who has a concept and certain talents, abilities and limitations. Those elements have got to come together," said Clement. However, "often that communication is lacking." The

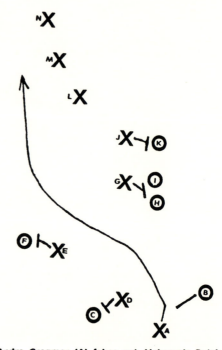

Andre Creamer (A) fakes out Alabama's Butch Lewis (B), then gets by Rory Turner (C), with help from Tommy Sims (D). Charles Davis (E) screens Bama's Ed Pugh (F) to the outside. Dale Jones (G) slows Tiders David Valletto (H) and Desmond Holoman (I). Jesse Messimer (J) then flattens an unidentified Bama player (K), sealing off the inside and allowing Creamer to reach the wall formed by Wes Rakestraw (L), Tim Welch (M) and Reggie McKenzie (N).

The Knoxville (Tenn.) *Journal* used this simple illustration to extend meaning about the outcome when Tennessee beat Alabama, 28-27, in the final seconds of a football game. Reprinted by permission.

artist must also know in advance how large the finished art will be and how it will be used.

Other complications arise when artists are asked to complete art "on demand." "It's easier as time goes on," Clement said. "In the days of the old hot [letterpress] type, why, it was a lot different. The pressure was even greater because you had only one crack at it—it was either right or wrong." Today, the artist may have to work much faster and still produce quality illustrations, but there is also more opportunity for making corrections. "We can make things and put them on the page at the last moment. There was a time when we couldn't do that; so, the pressure has eased up in many respects. It gives you more time to do a better job."

Bringing the artist in at the beginning of discussions about the art's place on draft page layouts helps to develop still another type of TPC designer, who will quickly prove more valuable to the newspaper than a mere decorator or creator of graphic shapes used to break up columns of gray type. The artist starts to think like a graphic journalist.

To enhance the Total Page Concept, illustrations should be:

- appropriately sized and carefully colored;
- attractive and strong, not crude or inexplicable;
- clean or simple and uncluttered;
- imaginatively drawn, not stale;
- informative and complementary to the story;
- large and detailed enough to provide a more complete understanding of the story; and
- used effectively to explain the focus of the story.

Some stories are not so suitable for graphic expression as others. A fashion feature may be an excellent spot for an illustration; a serious news story about crime may or may not be the appropriate place to put a drawing. The graphic artists must make their work credible for use in newspapers. It is their duty to produce line art that is exact in proportion and scale. This should be achieved by using a template of metal or some other firm material as a guide to make the finished work's contour correspond to the assigned dimensions. Computers also can be programmed to accomplish this process.

This piece of art accompanied a story in the Fort Lauderdale (Fla.) *News* to show the types of business consultants from which company executives have to make a selection. Reprinted by permission.

Illustration by Robert Barkin – The Washington Post

This drawing was published in the Washington *Post* to illustrate a story about buying U.S. goods. Reprinted by permission.

ILLUSTRATIONS AND THE COPYRIGHT ACT

Illustrations may be the work of a staff artist or a free-lance artist, or from an uncopyrighted clip art book or a copyrighted clip art source. In the latter case, appropriate permissions and credit must be displayed according to the 1976 Copyright Act. Copyright information may be secured from:

Register of Copyrights
Copyright Office
Library of Congress
Washington, D.C. 20559

or by leaving a message on the Copyright Office Hotline, 202–287–9100. The office provides a free copyright kit that includes information about copyright registration of books, manuscripts and speeches; copyright coverage basics; the copyright notice; and a booklet, *Copyright Law of the United States of America.*

The best approach to using material covered by copyright is to obtain permission in writing from the source. However, as Clement of the Los Angeles *Times* pointed out, it is not always possible to secure the written permission. "If you can't get permission, and often you can't, you still have to be attentive to the problem," Clement said. "What you have to be sure you do, and this is what our lawyers give us—we've had occasion to deal very specifically in this, especially in maps, not so much in other artwork—is to be careful if we do some copy work to represent it as our own work in the sense that it is not a direct lift. The essence of the original source data must not be retained."

Public information from government sources—free of copyright—is the safest material to reproduce. If a map he wants to use is copyrighted, Clement says, "the way to overcome it is composition—you compose from different sources."

Computers have so completely influenced the nation that they are now a part of sports decision making, as this story illustration portrays in the Phoenix *Arizona Republic.* Reprinted by permission.

Working with multiple data sources, the artist would—for instance—take the land boundaries from one and superimpose the highway system from another; make the outline of an island a different way; use city data from several maps and information listings; or create different symbols for the mountains on a regional section isolated from the map of a continent. "You don't misposition things, but you do alter it with your own technique, with your idea. Maybe your streets will be single lines instead of double, or you can even go on the color route."

After all, it is not necessary—and may not be possible—to go out and survey the area for each map. Most of the sources being studied by the newspaper artist were also studied by those who went before. "The people who made the map probably got it from somebody else and they have to put their own character into it; you may use theirs as a reference as long as you don't make a direct lift."

According to Clement, a "direct lift" is a case of merely making a photocopy and printing it as is. When cases of possible copyright infringement go to court, the piece of art is examined, and then one major question is posed. " 'Is this a direct copy?' That's what they're questioning," Clement says. " 'Is this a direct lift or the essence of someone else's work?' "

If permission to publish is refused by the copyright holder or if the source cannot be located, "at least give a source credit—sometimes that's a way to cover," says Clement, cautioning that even this strategy is not foolproof. "If there's a question," he admits, "we go to the lawyers and ask them."

INFORMATIONAL GRAPHICS

Informational graphics—which can be charts, maps, graphs, illustrations, and photos—are used in TPC page design to explain the story through a visual image.

Nigel Holmes, executive art director of *Time* magazine, is an informational graphics artist whose presence has been felt in the United States since he arrived in this country from England in 1977. When he first started at *Time,* his experience had prepared him to be an illustrator involved with information, rather than a statistician or mathematician employed to do charts. "So," Holmes says, "I made it clear to *Time* that if they were expecting to get straight-forward charts from me, then they should look somewhere else because I wasn't interested in doing that." Actually, there were plenty of historical precedents at the magazine for more illustrative charts. Reviewing *Time*'s illustrations over a 60-year period, Holmes noticed many maps, including "a lot of metaphors," made during and since World War II. "They drew the Red Devil approaching from the communist countries—things that right now we would have taste or racial problems with." Nevertheless, people could read and learn easily from such informational graphics. "They [*Time*] used images in a very telling way that helped people understand the information," says Holmes.

This illustration was drawn for ''Cover: The Graphics Revolution—A Special Report,'' *APME News* 155 (August 1985), to depict the response of some editors to the graphics revolution. Illustration by John Beshears. Reprinted by permission.

A decade or so later, informational graphics have become commonplace on metropolitan and many suburban and smaller newspapers. Nancy Tobin is a designer at the *Asbury Park Press* in Neptune, N.J. In 1985, while an instructor in the S.I. Newhouse School of Public Communications at Syracuse University, she conducted a survey for the Society of Newspaper Design. In her report, Tobin wrote,

> The mushrooming growth of well-designed newspapers punctuated by provocative, often colorful informational graphics has become something of an American industry legend. The demands of newspaper editors for modern-looking, visually exciting newspapers have created a ripple of minor revolutions in newsrooms across the U.S.

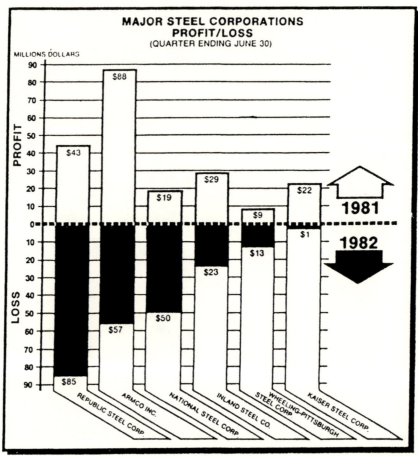

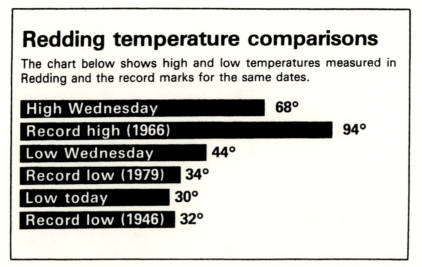

The bar graph can be easily created to explain stories, as in the Cleveland *Plain Dealer* and the Redding, Calif. *Record Searchlight*. Reprinted by permission.

Most area high school students surveyed think nuclear disarmament is unlikely, and neither the U.S. nor the U.S.S.R. is serious about it.

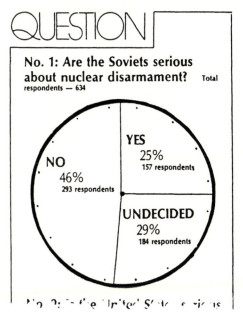

QUESTION

No. 1: Are the Soviets serious about nuclear disarmament? Total respondents — 634

YES
25%
157 respondents

NO
46%
293 respondents

UNDECIDED
29%
184 respondents

No. 2: Is the United States serious

The pie graph emphasizes the percentage of opinion difference in this example from the Thousand Oaks, Calif. *News Chronicle*. Reprinted by permission.

Weekly Earnings

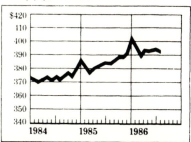

Weekly pay, in dollars.

$420
410
400
390
380
370
360
350
340

1984   1985   1986

AVERAGE WEEKLY PAY of factory workers in July fell to $390.74 from $395.76 the preceding month, the Labor Department reports.

The fever graph—so named because this type of graph is used to chart a medical patient's temperature—is used in this example from the *Wall Street Journal* to indicate the change in average weekly pay. Reprinted by permission of the *Wall Street Journal*, © Dow Jones & Company, Inc. 1986. All rights reserved.

Air quality

Pollution scale represents ozone (oxidents)

West Valley smog forecast for today: Pollutant Standard Index 42

Another form of informational graphic is the use of a meter to indicate—in this case—conditions of the atmosphere, as printed in the Ontario, Calif. *Daily Report*. Reprinted by permission.

Prior to 1980, Tobin reported, the art department at most newspapers "existed only to provide specific services to various 'real' newsroom departments—'Give me an arrow on this hockey photo—can't see the puck.' Or, 'I need a fast cartoon to go with this story on problems of newlyweds—her pouting while he plans to go out with the boys; two columns by three inches.' " Then in the early 1980s, the art department for most newspapers included a cartoonist or two, an illustrator and several retouchers. However, "if there was any formal leadership of the art department"—Tobin said—"it most likely was the position of 'chief artist' who had responsibility for ordering supplies and scheduling." The art departments of today seldom resemble the old ones. "They have undergone both major surgery and phenomenal growth as editors have become increasingly aware of the importance to readers of well-designed, appealing newspapers."

Reflecting further on her survey, Tobin added that today's art department remains

> for the most part outside the sphere of influence over hard news, except in the area of news graphics production, but the continued concern for and about informational graphics by all editors underlies the basic editorial interest in improved packaging of the news in ways that are journalistically sound and visually appealing to readers.

Tobin said there are indications "that informational graphics will be the bridge that eventually crosses the gap between 'art' and 'news.' "

Thomas Trapnell, editorial art director of the Los Angeles *Times,* claims that the biggest impact he can have in his position on a daily metropolitan newspaper is in informational graphics. "That's the most important thing we do," Trapnell said. "Taking a complicated subject and presenting it in a visual way that makes it easier for the reader to understand what's going on" is the major responsibility of the art department. He said that overall design of the newspaper is next in importance—specifically, the organization of the paper and the presentation of articles with photographs and graphics "in a cleaner, more readable, better-organized manner."

Charts and the complementing display type and illustrations are "reader aids, because they all make the job a whole lot easier for the reader," says Ernest Hines of the *Contra Costa Times* in Walnut Creek, Calif., adding that his newspaper is at the "very basic level of charts without the integrated art work." Integrated art work—"making a graphic a graphic"—is the next step up from making a graphic "just a breakout of numbers."

As Hines says, even a simple numbers breakout for budget stories serves the reader better than printing the article without the number chart. A format for breaking out a budget has been developed at the *Times,* and "clearly those stories with the breakouts were far better for the reader and more effective use of space for us than a traditional way of trying to jam all of those numbers into the body type."

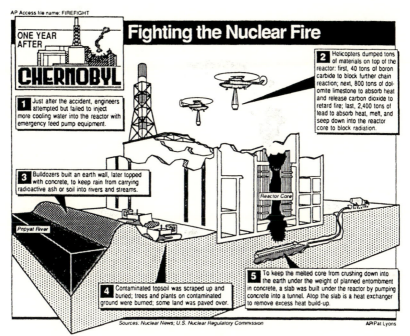

AP Access file name: FIREFIGHT

Fighting the Nuclear Fire

ONE YEAR AFTER
CHERNOBYL

1 Just after the accident, engineers attempted but failed to inject more cooling water into the reactor with emergency feed pump equipment.

2 Helicopters dumped tons of materials on top of the reactor: first, 40 tons of boron carbide to block further chain reaction; next, 800 tons of dolomite limestone to absorb heat and release carbon dioxide to retard fire; last, 2,400 tons of lead to absorb heat, melt, and seep down into the reactor core to block radiation.

3 Bulldozers built an earth wall, later topped with concrete, to keep rain from carrying radioactive ash or soil into rivers and streams.

Reactor Core

Pripyat River

4 Contaminated topsoil was scraped up and buried; trees and plants on contaminated ground were burned; some land was paved over.

5 To keep the melted core from crushing down into the earth under the weight of planned entombment in concrete, a slab was built under the reactor by pumping concrete into a tunnel. Atop the slab is a heat exchanger to remove excess heat build-up.

Sources: Nuclear News; U.S. Nuclear Regulatory Commission   AP/Pat Lyons

This AP informational graphic explains the first year of cleanup after the April 1986 Chernobyl nuclear power plant accident in the Ukraine, USSR. Reprinted by permission.

Infographics are most effectively used at papers where the news reporters are continually anticipating, preparing and collecting—when not in a crisis situation—information that will be essential but unavailable when they are working against a deadline. If informational graphics are to be valuable and usable, said Don DeMaio, director of graphics at the Associated Press in New York—quoted in the *California/Nevada AP Report* (1986)—"Give as much lead time as possible. If there's something coming up you know you'd like to have a graphic on, call ahead."

Informational graphics should never be used only as an alternative to a photo or illustration, or as something thrown in to break up an otherwise gray page. Effective informational graphics (also called "factgraphics" or "infographs") require the same degree of accuracy as the stories that they accompany.

Michael Hall, an editorial artist with the Los Angeles *Times,* says it is important for the reporter to supply sufficient information so that the artist can adequately explain the story. "Good journalists can write around the unknown details of a subject," Hall explained. "Graphics can't do that. [Graphics are] a very exacting, very unforgiving approach to journalism." He gave the example of a story about a tunnel used in a bank robbery. The reporter might not have to explain all the details of where the tunnel was dug, where it went, where it came from or turned, and what the soil composition was like. "But in a graphic those details become necessary," Hall insisted.

Tracking the Bull Market

Here's the Dow Jones Industrial Average for the last trading day of each year since 1979.

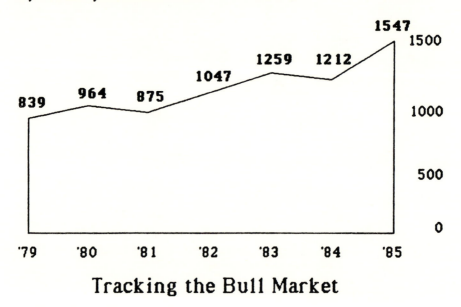

Tracking the Bull Market

Here's the Dow Jones Industrial Average for the last trading day of each year since 1979.

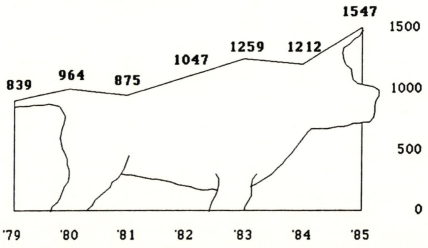

The informational graphic can sometimes take on the look of a ''chartoon,'' a term introduced by James W. Tankard Jr., professor of journalism, University of Texas at Austin, to describe the hybrid of a chart and a cartoon. His chart for a bull market, based on a graphic used in *USA Today*, is shown above in standard form and then below with the line indicating changes in the data becoming the bull's back. His research on quantitative graphics in newspapers was published in *Journalism Quarterly* 64 (Summer-Autumn 1987):406-15, and was presented as a paper, ''Effects of Cartoons and Three-Dimensional Graphics on Interest and Information Gain,'' to the Visual Communication Division of the Association for Education in Journalism and Mass Communication's annual convention in Portland, Ore., July 1988. Reprinted with permission.

The infograph should truly reflect the news, and its content should be available for quick retrieval just moments after a news story breaks. For this to occur, an art staff—or perhaps "infographers"—must keep a constantly updated and cataloged library of source materials that should include advertising logos, brochures, building diagrams, charts, clip art, copyright-free and original graphics, floor plans, maps, page layouts from other newspapers, pamphlets, photos, postcards, reference books and statistical data. The idea is to collect and file by subject a vast "swipe file"—background clippings from periodicals, newspapers and other resources. David Gray, managing editor/graphics at the Providence (R.I.) *Journal-Bulletin* told a 1987 College Press Convention in New York that such materials are many and that a conscientious effort should be made to save graphics from any number of sources:

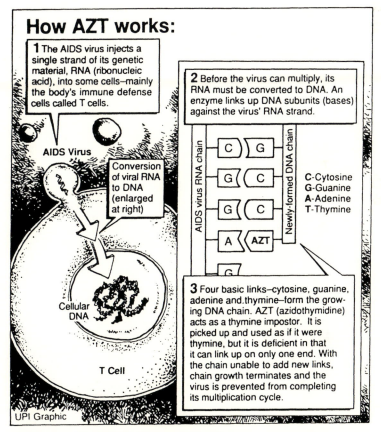

An explanation of Azidothymidine and its use to ease the suffering of AIDS patients is given in this United Press International informational graphic. Reprinted by permission.

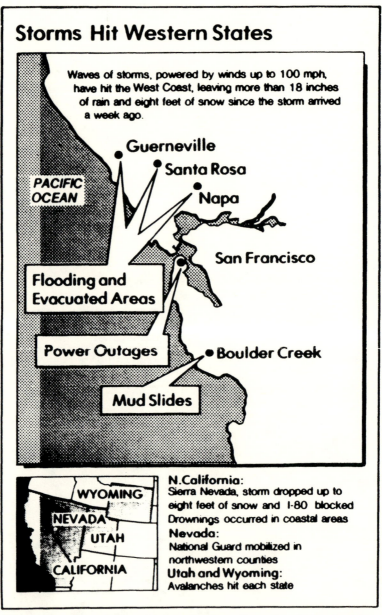

Storms Hit Western States

Waves of storms, powered by winds up to 100 mph, have hit the West Coast, leaving more than 18 inches of rain and eight feet of snow since the storm arrived a week ago.

Guerneville
Santa Rosa
PACIFIC OCEAN
Napa
San Francisco

Flooding and Evacuated Areas

Power Outages
Boulder Creek

Mud Slides

WYOMING
NEVADA
UTAH
CALIFORNIA

N. California:
Sierra Nevada, storm dropped up to eight feet of snow and I-80 blocked
Drownings occurred in coastal areas
Nevada:
National Guard mobilized in northwestern counties
Utah and Wyoming:
Avalanches hit each state

This Associated Press informational graphic shows the reader where a storm has hit and the extent of damages. Reprinted by permission.

- Instruction manuals for equipment and other manufacturer's hand-outs. The *Sunday Times* of London has its art department save all of these that can be found. They come in handy for spot news illustrations about things and how they work—or why they did not work.

- Models. The *Sunday Times* also encourages its art staff to purchase plastic models of items such as airplanes and ships. When the Falkland Islands were invaded, the artists had a ready-made reference library of all the types of missiles, planes and ships involved.

- Anything—or anybody—from the promotion and advertising departments that can help out.

- State and local government publications from highway planning departments for maps and diagrams, and tourist/promotion departments for photos and maps (which are also worth collecting from local tour groups and historical societies).

- Statistics, charts and diagrams at the state and local level. Make sure the reporter shares all of these with you; they are probably already on his desk, and he never thought to tell the story in graphics, the way the "source" has done.

- Travel agency fliers. We learned a valuable lesson during the Grenada invasion. A local travel agent called that morning and offered us a map of Grenada. It was a British topographical map, complete with each and every road and building on the island, as well as elevations of the mountain ridge.

- Publications of tourist boards and chambers of commerce. Tapped them lately for the latest maps?

Howard Finberg, assistant managing editor of the *Arizona Republic* in Phoenix, made suggestions on how to get information for graphics, when he spoke to the Southern Newspaper Publishers Association (SNPA) Foundation seminar, "Layout, Graphics and Design." Finberg's tips included these:

- All reporters should be encouraged to gather all possible information related to their stories, especially visual information. If not used with that particular story, it can be filed for later use.

- The *CIA Facts Book* is helpful in creating sidebars to world stories. For example, to help illustrate a story about Kenya, an artist could use a map of Kenya and set type within it giving the country's vital statistics. This kind of graphic is an attractive element to run with an international story because it gives a lot of information quickly.

- No government books, maps or charts are copyrighted; they can be reproduced and adapted with no fear of plagiarization problems.

- Many agencies and organizations are glad to provide visual information for publication. For example, NASA provides intricate

drawings and charts of the space shuttle program free to newspapers
that ask for them.

- Write to the Superintendent of Documents in Washington, D.C.,
  and ask for a catalog; then, request any information you might need
  for your files.

Gray's and Finberg's guidelines underscore the value of collecting statistical
material for charts, maps or other graphic materials that will help the reporter
write a more complete story. This file then becomes a source for future ideas—
not for reuse of the graphics themselves, except by explicit permission.

The infograph may be created in one of several forms, including the bar chart,
cluster chart, fever or line chart, pie chart, tabular chart, line graph, list, map
or table. Marvin Sosna of the *News Chronicle* in Thousand Oaks, Calif.—recognizing the value of more fully telling news stories with illustrative materials—
claims that newspapers provide the fullest information link for the reading public.
As Sosna points out,

> In the media-saturated society confronting us, journalists have al-
> ready recognized the need to ease the path of the public in its quest
> for information. Good graphics are like good maps: They help you
> get there. And in a world filled with perils, good maps become more
> than a convenience—they are a necessity for survival.

On the subject of maps, Finberg said that

> If a map is of an event in a small area in your circulation, it's usually
> a good idea to run another map pinpointing where the small area is
> in relation to the bigger one. The map showing the activity at the
> smaller area can be inset, or vice versa—use the bigger map to il-
> lustrate the activity and inset the map that shows the relative location.

Clement, the Los Angeles *Times* cartographer, considers maintenance of an
up-to-date map system to be necessary to the operations of any editorial art
department. The map library should be kept either in the art department itself,
in the newspaper's library or in both locations. "In the past," Clement said, "I
have used worldwide correspondence just to get information, because often you
can't get things out of Africa, for example, that weren't published by the colonial
powers." It is also helpful to have access to a university map depository. As
Clement says,

> You anticipate. I can't keep a city map of every city in the world,
> but oftentimes we'll need a small city and who knows where it is?
> You need some contacts. You do the best you can with this, but it

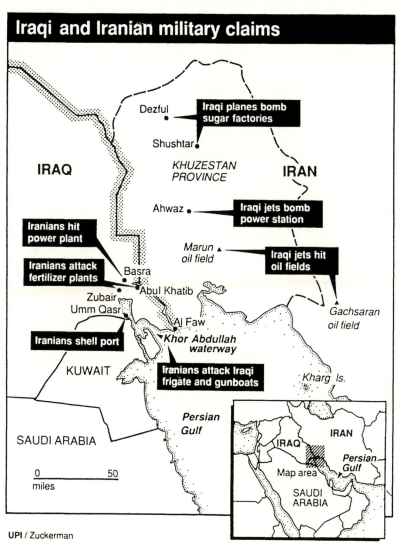

Iraqi and Iranian military claims

Dezful

Iraqi planes bomb sugar factories

Shushtar

IRAQ

KHUZESTAN PROVINCE

IRAN

Ahwaz

Iraqi jets bomb power station

Iranians hit power plant

Marun oil field

Iraqi jets hit oil fields

Iranians attack fertilizer plants

Basra

Abul Khatib

Zubair

Umm Qasr

Al Faw

Gachsaran oil field

Iranians shell port

Khor Abdullah waterway

KUWAIT

Iranians attack Iraqi frigate and gunboats

Kharg Is.

Persian Gulf

SAUDI ARABIA

0   50

miles

IRAQ   IRAN

Map area   *Persian Gulf*

SAUDI ARABIA

UPI / Zuckerman

WAP081916-8/19/87-UNDATED:Iran's forces shelled industrial and military targets in Iraq 8/19 in retaliation for Iraqi air attacks against Iranian oil installations, Tehran's official radio service said.   UPI   (GULFWAR)   smh/Zuckerman

This locator map by United Press International enhances certain Iraq-Iran battle sites. Reprinted by permission.

is a problem area and something that has to be maintained constantly; the communication, the correspondence, the liaison, the cooperation between libraries—that kind of thing is very critical.

All infographic forms can be executed quicker and with a subtle continuity in style if the art staff designs a base format with specifications at each assignment, photocopies the original and saves the copy for later reference. Such formats can also be used in computer graphics; where the pagination is already available, the format on file can be sent directly from the visual display terminal (VDT) screen to the page position where the piece of art has been assigned by an editor. (Using the computer to compose graphics is discussed further in Chapter 14.)

Referring to the vitality of graphics, Finberg of the *Arizona Republic* suggested that stories be treated visually to help readers. "Information is the key to good graphics," he said. "A graphic is a visual portrayal of data; newspapers are loaded with data, but it's important to distinguish a simple chart or grouping of data from a graphic."

Historical and current data should be included, Finberg said. "Good graphics show the historical trend as well as the current information. For example, a graphic to illustrate a story about SAT [Scholastic Aptitude Test] scores should show not only this year's scores but also scores from the last five years so readers can visualize the relationship."

According to Finberg, editing graphics and stories require similar treatment. "Apply the same standards to editing graphics as to editing stories. Graphics with missing information should be fixed, just as an editor would plug a hole in a story." Then Finberg made these recommendations to the *SNPA* audience regarding what every graphic needs:

- a headline to tell what the illustration is all about;
- a subhead for additional information, if necessary;
- a scale line to tell what the information is in terms of measure;
- consistent X and Y axes—when designing a graph, the X axis is more nearly horizontal and the Y axis is more nearly vertical—and
- some source—where the information came from.

Whatever informational graphic form is chosen, accuracy and clarity are the keys to credibility and good Total Page Concept. To avoid misinformation, the infograph must be checked before it is published to see that the facts and sources are correct. Some readers may not read the story but only look at the infograph. The accompanying story will be effectively explained if numbers have been taken from the text and inserted into the infograph so that the reader immediately sees the number and information relationship—which, in fact, may not have been easily comprehended by reading the text alone.

George Rorick, assistant managing editor/graphics at the Detroit *News*, said

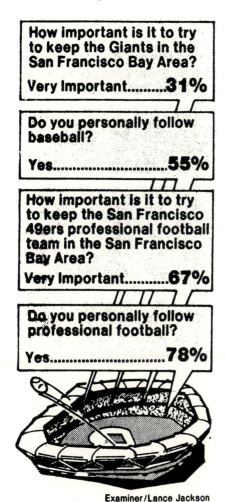

How important is it to try
to keep the Giants in the
San Francisco Bay Area?

Very Important.........**31%**

Do you personally follow
baseball?

Yes............................**55%**

How important is it to try
to keep the San Francisco
49ers professional football
team in the San Francisco
Bay Area?

Very Important...........**67%**

Do you personally follow
professional football?

Yes............................**78%**

Examiner/Lance Jackson

A generic illustration with a statistic will often assist readers to recognize a story's substance, as in a San Francisco *Examiner* story about how the San Francisco Giants, the San Francisco 49ers and other professional sports teams are vying for the same sports dollar. Reprinted by permission.

in *Design* magazine that it is important to "get all the numbers when reporting, not just for graphics, but for yourself." The reader will know more about the story if the reporter provides a sufficient amount of number information, Rorick said.

> If a source tells you that there has been a 30 percent increase in population since 1980, that's super. Then back it up with the numbers—your editor should be asking for them anyway. But don't get just 1980 and 1985 numbers. Get 1981, 1982, 1983, 1984 too. You may even need to get 1975 through 1979 to show the trend. Remember, you are on the scene and have easier access to the numbers.

Rorick's suggestion can be taken even further. The reporter should remember that what is not included in the infograph is just as important as what is included. If parts are missing supposedly to simplify the graphic story, the infographic will not explain, but instead confuse or detract from the story text. DeMaio at the Associated Press made this recommendation: "In the case of a plane crash, better graphics can be produced if the artists know exact distances, precise directions—north-northwest instead of just north—and specific descriptions of the plane and surrounding area." DeMaio also said that the reporter on the scene can give valuable assistance to the art department by making a sketch of the situation—so long as it includes such details as whether an accident occurred on a four-lane or six-lane highway.

Clement at the Los Angeles *Times* insists that experience and judgment are the best tools for executing, say, a one-column drawing of a map on deadline for the next day's paper. "You plan it before you even get anything going on paper," says Clement. "You design it in your head. You add or subtract data according to time, and you know if you have to make single lines for roads as opposed to double lines. You have to have that kind of experience to make those kinds of compromises." The pressure of deadline work can be heavy, indeed. It is "something you have to control—if you don't, it will master you."

Gray of the *Journal-Bulletin* provided a list of methods for improving graphics:

- Keep the idea simple; the drawing can be complex—but not the idea.
- Use human elements/scale/comparisons whenever possible.
- Typography should be clean and simple: no more than two type fonts. Use bold and light faces within a type font to provide emphasis, contrast and scale.
- Get an agreement on size first, and keep things in proper scale to the finished size: You cannot enlarge and reduce graphics like photos.
- Develop resource files: The kinds of image materials you need in order to do informational graphics are different from what regular libraries have.
- Add depth to simple charts and maps for greater interest, but not to the point where the art gets in the way of the data.
- Understand color theory. Use it to convey information, not just decorate.
- Appreciate space. An effective graphic does not have to be big. Some stories and circumstances should be illustrated with a photo, some with a "flavor" graphic and some not at all. Informational graphics are news, not fluff.
- Develop speed. Computers can help.

- Understand, in detail, all the production techniques at your publication.
- Be versatile in technique and approach, and consistent in style.

The infographer must read and understand the story text, talk with the reporter, and then draw numbers and symbols from the story's words that are easily recognized and that do not leave the reader guessing. The infograph should clarify the story and not add confusion by just taking up space on the page. The best infographs:

- put the story into perspective with timely news information;
- are aesthetically attractive and consistent in style;
- include pertinent information told through a visually valid metaphor; and
- entice the reader into the story text.

The sequence of data on the infograph must be arranged logically, with simple drawings and type in a readable size—preferably to be read clockwise or from left to right, and not superimposed on a dark 50-percent to 100-percent color. The typography in the art should be as consistent in style as the headlines in the publication—typeset, not hand lettered. In addition, the source of information should always be identified. If these needs cannot be satisfied, it is best not to use the infograph.

According to Finberg of the *Arizona Republic*, there are at least three pitfalls that the graphic journalist must avoid:

- Making an incorrect assumption about what readers know and then excluding necessary information from the graphic.
- The opposite extreme—using information that readers do not need or data that will confuse them. Cramming too many figures into a graphic is as bad as not giving enough information.
- Depending on cartoons too much as graphics. Cartoons can provide some information, but they provide no frame of reference for it and should not be overused.

As a final test before publishing it, the infograph should be shared with someone not connected with the story—perhaps someone down the hall in another editorial area of the newspaper. If that person understands its meaning, the infograph is usable; if not, the piece of art should go back to the drawing board for revision.

In his 1987 College Press Convention presentation Gray provided an informational graphics checklist that he had adapted from various journalism industry

Sonics preview

—————— vs. Philadelphia 76ers ——————

WHERE: Seattle Center Coliseum
WHEN: 7:40 p.m. tipoff today
RADIO-TV: KIRO-Radio (710 AM), pre-game 7:06 p.m.; KJR-Radio (950 AM), pre-game show 7:20 p.m., quarterly and post-game reports; no television
TEAM RECORDS: Seattle 16-28 (tied for fourth in Pacific Division), Philadelphia 29-15 (sec-ond in Atlantic Division)
STREAKS: Seattle one-game winning streak; Philadelphia one-game losing streak
SERIES RECORDS: Philadelphia leads all-time series 41-30 after Seattle won season opener between two teams, 105-100 at Philadelphia Dec. 8. Philadelphia has won 10 of past 12 meetings
PLAYERS TO WATCH: For Seattle — Forward Tim McCormick, coming off 19-point, 7-rebound effort; Danny Young, whose 47 turnovers are the fewest in the NBA for point guards who have played more than 800 minutes; center Jack Sikma, averaging 17.7 ppg and 9.5 rpg.
For Philadelphia — Center Moses Malone, among league leaders in scoring (23.5 ppg), re-bounding (11.8 rpg) and drawing fouls (11.4 free-throw attempts per game); forward Charles Barkley, NBA Player of the Week for averaging 24 ppg and 15.8 rpg last week.

FIRST TEXAS SAVINGS 1981 FINANCIAL SHEET

Total Assets	$2.181 billion
Total Liabilities	$2.1156 billion
Total Net Worth	$66.2 million
Total savings	$1.6 billion
Total mortgage loans	$1.7 billion
Gross operating income	$110 million
Total operating expenses	$21.7 million
Cost of money	$115 million
Net Income	-$28 million

SOURCE: Federal Home Loan Bank Board

The Dallas Morning News: Clif Bosler

sources (see Chapter 9 for detail of credits on this and other Gray lists). Gray's composite checklist included the following:

- Graphics should simplify, clarify, summarize, be accurate, restate— not duplicate—the main point, and/or be supplements—not dupli- cations—to words and photographs.
- Infographs can show comparisons, metaphors, trends, locations, processes, who, what, when, where, why and how.
- Flavor graphics are illustrations. Infographics are logos, tables, maps, diagrams and charts.
- The chart types of infographics are: pie—to show portions of a whole; fever—to show trends over time; area—to show comparisons over time; bar—vertical to show how specific quantities add up to

Television tonight

Complete daily television highlights appear in the Entertainment section of Friday's Telegraph Herald

Times	abc 4,9,34	CBS 2,33,34	NBC 7,34	PBS 12,30
7:00 30	American Music Awards "/	Scarecrow and Mrs. King	Movie: A Masterpiece of Murder	WonderWorks "
8:00 30	" "	Kate and Allie Newhart	" "	American Playhouse "
9:00 30	" "	Cagney and Lacey "	American Almanac "	" "
10:00	News	News	News	Wild World of Animals

6:00
8,9,27,40,2,3,4,
WKBT,6,7,KTTC,15 News
13 Newlywed Game
12 Business Report
'1 P'scʰ ʰll ʰeʰ ʰarʰ ʰaʰ ʰhoʰ ʰ

efforts to extract information from former government employees in nursing homes.
6,7,KTTC,15 Movie "A Masterpiece Of Murder." (Premiere)
12 ʰ1 "Wonʰerʰorkʰ "Boyʰ Wʰo

WGN Greatest American Hero
CBN 700 Club
NIK Movie "The Inspector General."
SPN Looking East
ʰjrʰ ʰPʰ ʰisʰ ʰhilʰ ʰnʰ ʰlifeʰtylʰs

Olympics '84

In some cases it is appropriate to use corporate art—an identifiable trademark from a business concern—for immediate recognition, as in these examples from the Bellevue, Wash. *Journal-American,* the Dallas *Morning News,* the Dubuque, Iowa *Telegraph Herald* and the San Bernardino, Calif. *Sun.* Reprinted by permission.

a whole during time; and horizontal—to show comparisons at the same time.

• When editing graphics, these questions should be asked: Who says so? How do they know? What's missing? Did they change the subject? Does it make sense? Does it have a beginning, a middle and an end?

EDUCATION FOR GRAPHIC JOURNALISTS

Graphics journalists working as newspaper artists need a strong foundation as illustrators. It is best when they have also worked on a newspaper as a reporter or have a college background in art and journalism.

Matt Moody, one of the editorial artists at the Los Angeles *Times,* comes

Rutgers women rip Penn State, in Eastern finals

By SUE ESTERMAN
Home News sports writer

PHILADELPHIA — The Rutgers women's basketball team, led by captain Kris Foley in its first NCAA post-season ap-pearance, advanced to the Eastern Regional finals last night by defeating Penn State 85-72 at the Palestra here.

Rutgers meets No. 5 ranked Western Kentucky tomorrow at noon for the championship and a trip to the Final Four in Lexington, Ky.

The Lady Knights, ranked 10th nationally, used a 25-12 scoring spurt with less than 10 minutes left in the game to break a 60 point tie in t' is,

Suzie McConnell led the game in assists with 17 for the Lady Lions. She is second in the nation in that category. She, along with four teammates, scored 10 points. Laura Hughes hit a career-high 13 points to lead Penn State.

Penn State, after taking a 59-58 lead at 9:24 of the second half, went into a field goal drought for the next seven and a half minutes.

The game, however, didn't turn into a blowout until Rutgers used the momentum of their scoring and the electricity of the fans in red and black with 10 minutes left.

The Lady Knights took a 41-40 edge into the locker room at the half, and aside from the free throw shooting percentage, the statistics didn't give either team much of an advantage. They were even in assists (14), turnovers (10), steals (5) and under the boa ds. Per St te nd 7

from the journalism rather than art side. He believes that the word about dual training is slowly getting out to those who would like to become graphic journalists. But, Moody says, "I think there really aren't a lot of people who know how to get to be a newspaper artist. There aren't a lot of schools that are doing this kind of work and there isn't a lot of understanding between artists and journalists."

Rob Covey, the former design director of the Seattle *Times,* stressed that graphic journalists should prepare themselves academically and professionally as much as possible if they want to work in newspaper art. "There's no substitute for being able to draw extremely well," Covey added. "By that, I mean being able to draw and handle the figure, being able to draw the figure in natural ways. All of the things that you see that are drawn exceptionally well are by people

Miller shows who's the best

From the start, USC blasts Idaho

By Dave Boling
of the Tribune

LOS ANGELES – On the night she was proclaimed the finest women's basketball player in the nation, Cheryl Miller took the opportunity to prove why.

Miller, who was named winner of the women's Naismith Trophy shortly before game time Friday, paced two-time defending national champion Southern California to a 74-51 win over Idaho Friday at the Los Angeles Sports Arena in the opening round of the NCAA tournament.

The loss brings down the curtains on the most successful season in Idaho history as the Vandals finish with a 28-2 record, a Mountain West Athletic Conference championship and their first post-season tournament appearance.

The least impressive element of Miller's game was her point total – 21 – which fell six points below her average.

The 6-foot-3 junior was also held below her rebound average of 16 as she pulled down 13 missed shots.

But no facet of the game was outside her reign Friday as she shelled out five assists, blocked four shots, stole five passes and committed just one turnover in 34 minutes of play.

"She's what everyone says and more," said

IDAHO (51)					
	FG-A	FT-A	R	F	TP
Kris Edmonds	6-9	4-6	7	2	16
Mary Westerwelle	2-8	0-0	6	4	4
Mary Raese	7-17	1-2	10	1	15
Robin Behrens	3-6	0-0	0	5	6
Paula Getty	0-6	0-0	1	0	0
Lynn Nicholas	1-4	0-0	3	1	2
Krista Dunn	2-5	0-0	1	3	4
Kristen Browitt	0-0	0-0	1	0	0
Susan Deskines	1-4	0-0	3	0	2
Kim Churnecki	0-0	0-0	0	0	0
Netra McGrew	1-5	0-1	0	0	2
Team			5		
Totals	23-64	5-9	37	16	51
SOUTHERN CALIFORNIA (74)					
	FG-A	FT-A	R	F	TP
Cheryl Miller	7-15	7-8	13	2	21
Tracy Longo	2-9	0-0	3	2	4
Holly Ford	9-12	2-2	8	0	20
Yolanda Fletcher	5-9	0-0	3	2	10
Rhonda Windham	2-6	1-2	2	1	5
Kalen Wright	3-8	0-0	1	1	6
Paula Pyers	1-1	0-1	1	1	2
Donna Carter	0-0	0-0	0	0	0
Wendy Brown	0-1	0-0	1	0	0
Melissa Ward	1-1	0-0	1	0	2
JaMalla Bond	0-1	0-0	3	2	0
Liz Hirn	0-1	0-0	1	0	0
Cyndie Thomas	2-4	0-0	3	3	4
Amy Alkek	0-1	0-0	0	0	0
Team			5		
Totals	32-69	10-13	45	14	74

Halftime score — Southern California 42, Idaho 23
Attendance — 1,500

Idaho Coach Pat Dobratz of Miller, who led the U.S. Olympic team in scoring and rebounding on her way to the gold medal last summer.

"What really impressed us was the way she passed," Dobratz said. "You get her covered and she dishes off. Every time we made a mis-

See *Idaho,* Page 2C

A display of corporate art may be embedded in the story text, as in these examples from the New Brunswick, N.J. *Home News* and the Lewiston (Idaho) *Morning Tribune.* Reprinted by permission.

who know how to draw natively very well." In addition to drawing well, it is important that the newspaper artist learn how to think.

> You have to learn how to draw and understand journalism from a journalist's perspective so you can come into the business and understand the kind of thinking journalists go through, their thinking process. You need to be able to think independently—think for yourself—and also, to be able to draw very well.

Covey advised the artist to learn a method of problem solving—a method that will be equally serviceable in designing a chair, a freeway system, a circulation path through a restaurant or hotel, or an airflow system through a building. "If you apply it to newspapers, you apply the same methodology," he said. "As a discipline, I think it's terribly important to have that kind of open approach to problem solving. Otherwise, what you get is a regurgitation of the same thing that everybody else is doing."

A design sequence or a design program within an academic setting would be helpful preparation for a career in graphic journalism, according to Covey. "I think people taking a broad perspective of humanities courses learn how to think better—learn how to be inquisitive; the scientific method of observation can be studied."

Given that a liberal arts education and opportunities as a writer and artist amply prepare the individual for graphic journalism, the best candidates for editorial art seem to be those who—as Moody says—are "involved in journalism" and "like the whole process," but find themselves "not asking the tough questions and writing the tough stories." Moody explains that in his work he teams up with a reporter to present the news attractively. "He [the reporter] does the leg work and then you do the work that makes his hard work a little easier for the reader to understand," says Moody. "Sometimes that reporter is so wrapped up in that, he can write a story, but as far as presenting some information that maybe will help—a graphic—it is difficult for him to do."

Newspaper artists support the editorial needs of the paper and never fail to draw readers to the stories that contain their illustrations and informational graphics. For those who succeed, the rewards are more than intrinsic. In today's market, graphic journalism professionals are sought after in every region of the country. An indication of the income that can be enjoyed by these specialists comes from William W. Lemmer, graphics director of United Press International in Washington, D.C., who says that the money is available for those who have talent:

> In 1987, my staff starts at annual salaries of $28,000, peaking right now at about $36,000 for my most experienced artist. For artists trained on two or more digital production systems, recent placements have been between $40,000 and $60,000 annually. The $60,000 went to a 25-year-old whose assignment was in Paris. Attractive enough? Management can obviously expect more [from such computer-savvy artists].

V   FINISHING TOUCHES

The reader can recognize and appreciate art beyond photos and illustrations. The finishing touches of the building block process are those elements that grab attention and highlight a TPC newspaper. Attention-getting elements and the use of color also provide an indication of the importance that a piece of text or art may have. Not every element on a page can be highlighted with a graphic device; the page needs contrast so that the reader will know which stories are especially noteworthy. The next two chapters show how attention elements can be used in the Total Page Concept.

Chapter 12   Reader Attention Elements
Chapter 13   Color

Washington State's wonder

Cougars' Mayes makes his mark

By Jeff Faraudo
Staff writer

Coach Jim Walden knows that if running back Rueben Mayes had come from the heartland of Texas or Big City USA, he'd currently be setting records at any of a number of schools other than Washington State.

But Mayes, the fleet and powerful junior who two weeks ago established a single-game NCAA record with 357 yards rushing against Oregon, did not come to Washington State from the kind of high school program that typically spawns prep legends.

Mayes, who will lead an exciting and potent Cougars offense into Memorial Stadium Saturday for a 4:10 p.m. televised game against California, played his high

Continued on Page 52, col. 2

Record-breaking Washington State runner Rueben Mayes cruises in the Cougars' come-from-behind win over Stanford.
Vern Mendes — staff photo

Time running out for 49ers to sign Dean

By Bill Soliday
Staff writer

Fred Dean

REDWOOD CITY — Eleven, 10, nine... the Fred Dean countdown is ticking away on the clocks at the San Francisco 49ers headquarters.

The 49ers are 8-1 but the fear lingers that their Super Bowl hopes could end as fast as their Dean imp pass rush could disappear without warning.

Continued on Page 49, col. 1

Hey, Tom, there's more to 49ers than Joe Montana

IT IS TO bring now to think of Tom Landry's words as he blurted them out on Jan. 10, 1982.

Bill Soliday

Joe Montana

FAUST

Irish coach's stiff upper lip belies pressure

By Hal Bock
Associated Press

SOUTH BEND, Ind. — The handshake is firm, accompanied by an arm around the shoulder, a warm greeting just a step short of an embrace. Gerry Faust is glad to see you. Step right in.

Hernandez makes it a sweep

Tigers pitcher edges Hrbek in balloting for A.L. MVP

By Hal Bock
Associated Press

NEW YORK — Relief ace Willie Hernandez of the world champion Detroit Tigers was named the Most Valuable Player in the American League Tuesday, completing a sweep of the league's major post-season awards.

Willie Hernandez

☐ **Davis lambastes Rozelle**
Al Davis says NFL Commissioner Pete Rozelle wasted time and energy on his 'vendetta' against the Raiders' move from Oakland to L.A.
Please see Page 48

☐ **Gomez advances; Jarryd, McEnroe won't**
Andres Gomez advances and Anders Jarryd is upset in Wembley tennis action, while John McEnroe waits out a 42-day suspension.
Please see Page 52

☐ **Pac-10 basketball preview**
Marv Harshman and Walt Hazzard grab the spotlight as Pacific-10 Conference basketball coaches preview the upcoming season.
Please see Page 47

The Hayward, Calif. *Daily Review* built its design during the mid-1960s around a campaign slogan: ''I'm a rectangular revolutionary.'' This page shows many stories and dramatic art, along with a mortice inset used for the photo caption. Reprinted by permission.

12   Reader Attention Elements

You've got to "fool" your readers a little and make them think a story is shorter than it really is. There's nothing wrong in making your pages more attractive to the reader any more than it is for a restaurant to dress up the main entree with a sprig of parsley. The content is the same, but it looks better.

Les Helsdon
former editor, *Navy Civil Engineer*
Port Hueneme, Calif.
(Quoted in *Ragan Report*, 1984)

The Total Page Concept (TPC) designer has available many special art and typographic effects to enhance the readability of the newspaper. While reader attention elements can be used alone or in combinations, the designer must understand how and when to employ them most effectively to direct the reader through the pages of the paper.

Graphic emphasis can be given to text, display type, photos and illustrations in the following ways (as well as other variations):

• **Text**—Overprint on color or gray screen but not more than 20 percent so as not to discourage those who wish to read the story; or the text can also be set in a box with or without shadows on two sides.

• **Charts**—Look for statistics in stories; test for possible infographs to complement the linear explanation in the story. Is there a metaphor that could be used effectively to present the information graphically?

• **Display Typography**—Set a mood or theme with novelty type. While the main headline should be in the same face as used in the rest of the paper, Oriental lettering could be used for a story on Asian culture, or Western type for a cowboy story.

• **Illustrations**—Add depth with screens to show flesh tones, clothing or environment color shades.

• **Photos**—Cut away background parts such as telephone poles and other distracting areas that do not contribute to the photo.

These methods can influence a design, but should always be compatible with the publication's Total Page Concept—on each page, and from page to page. When a designer lacks the ability to implement graphic elements consistently, it can lead to a disjointed effect that does nothing to organize the newspaper for the reader. It is also an indication that the editor has not understood the value of bringing all the elements of newspaper design together into a cohesive whole. The reader will not be impressed by an array of spectacular graphic effects that are used for no apparent reason.

According to Les Helsdon, former editor of the *Navy Civil Engineer* in Port Hueneme, Calif.—quoted in *Ragan Report* (1984)—there are two reasons for making illustrative material fit together. Both have the potential of increasing reader interest. Helsdon said that

> First, the art work will make the job of the layout artist more interesting and challenging—consequently, he or she will do a better job. Also, the knowledgeable layout artist will try hard to avoid large, dull areas of gray space. They are deadly to readership. An artist worth his or her salt knows that large areas of text should be broken up with line art or photos, or at least with subheads or blurbs—anything to break up the monotony.

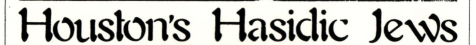

Special art type used in this Houston *Post* story tells readers who recognize the typestyle something about the story even before they read it. Reprinted by permission.

It is sometimes appropriate to use an art type for special effect, such as on a section page like this one in the Syracuse (N.Y.) *Herald-American.* Reprinted by permission.

The second reason is no less important. Next after the use of art work to create interest for the page designer is its psychological appeal to the reader, said Helsdon.

> You must keep readers interested and happy. They become discouraged when they see large areas of gray on a page and usually move on to the next page. If too many pages are "gray," they may stop reading your publication altogether.

For all publications, legibility is the key to appropriate and professional-looking special effects. Placing the emphasis on legibility rather than on cleverness will more frequently render a final design effort that is a harmonious blend of typography and art. Some say that reader attention elements used to sell the news are completely ethical because the reader may delve more deeply into the newspaper as a result of them. Others argue that their use cheapens the newspaper's image as a source of news. Some treatments of art work are effective, while others are not. The best way to understand which treatments have the potential to work is by experimenting.

If the preponderant opinion of the editors is that newsstand sales are essential to the newspaper's marketing scheme, then displaying reader attention graphics is throughout the newspaper is justified as a drawing card. On the other hand, if sales are primarily to home circulation readers, the graphic gimmicks are more suitably used to organize the paper and orient the reader. Helsdon said that, "when used effectively," art work "will illustrate and clarify important points; it will add interest to your pages, and it will attract your audience to read the story."

THE MORTICE

Sometimes a portion is cut out of a picture or text block to make a "mortice," within which is set another picture or text block. For a photo mortice to work as a graphic element, the photo must have an area that lends itself to an inset (interior cut-out area) or notch (cut-out area on the edge). The mortice is a tempting device to use, and it can be effective when it adds to communication/ clarity. Used carelessly, however, the mortice can result in a graphic disaster of photos with holes poked in them by convenience of the designer—with no concern for communication or for the intent of the photographer who made the picture.

Ernest Hines of the *Contra Costa Times* in Walnut Creek, Calif., says,

> We use very few mortices. Usually, when we do them, I don't like them; I think a good tight crop is generally better. The mortice just destroys the integrity of the art work, generally speaking. There will be some exceptions to that, but they are rare.

Hines further explained,

> You can't make hard and fast rules that you never mortice; my experience has been the moment you make a rule, 15 minutes later someone is asking you, "What about this?" And it is a perfectly good reason to make an exception to the rule. I talk about guidelines, not rules.

SCREENS

Gray screens and special screens—such as mezzotint—can be worked into a design for effect, but care must be taken that the screen is not such a heavy percentage of black that it will detract from the text copy. Black against white is the most legible typographic possibility; placing a story under a screen of more than 20 percent or 30 percent gray decreases legibility. If a designer believes it necessary to use a screen, its use should be applied sparingly. The designer must understand that color—including gray displayed thoughtfully—reflects interest, but that screens used poorly and indiscriminately can discourage readership.

Michael Hall, an editorial artist at the Los Angeles *Times,* said that at his paper there is no blanket rule, but [screened copy] is generally frowned upon. It has got to be a very special circumstance, and has caused problems with last-minute editing, changing copy at the last minute on the floor. Editing is all-important here; anything that inhibits that process naturally will be discouraged.

Also referring to the use of screened text, Matt Moody, another artist at the L.A. *Times,* says, "Sports does it occasionally. Every department is different. There is an art director who oversees everything, but there are so many people who oversee the pages, design and layout the pages, that there may be things done out there; the suburban sections are independent, so they may be doing it."

Hines of the *Contra Costa Times* tells a classic story of what not to do to the reader. One day he picked up a paper published by one of the other divisions at the Walnut Creek newspaper plant. "There was a story about summer reservists out on bivouac; all the type was camouflage," Hines said. "The camouflage was picked up from the uniform and a camouflage screen was put all over the page." As he added in jest, "This was a successful job because there was no way that you could read the story. It was a beautiful design, but what did it mean?"

Another example that Hines gives had to do with a special football section— a Super Bowl preview—

where the statistics were done through a screen, the nature of the Super Bowls imposed over agate type, and you could not tell that it supposedly was Candlestick Stadium. It was great design work, but it destroyed the readability. Design's purpose is not to destroy readability. It has to be simple and straightforward. And that's really what we're trying to do. You have to be able to produce it easily and efficiently, and also for the ease of the reader.

Only the most dedicated reader will take the time to read through a color like blue, brown, purple or red, or through a gray screen printed at 50 percent or 100 percent. In fact, a reader who can do the latter is performing a miraculous feat.

Pegie Stark, former graphics editor of the Detroit *News,* explained that gray screens should be run over text only if the screen is 5 percent or 10 percent. She said that, with other colors,

The highest I go over type is 20 [percent] yellow, 10 percent red. And I wouldn't use anything darker. I think screens are overused in newspapers. I think they are unnecessary. It's true that color attracts attention, but it's also true that color over type reduces readability.

If you are going to do it, I wish type could be increased a point or leading could be increased.

In fact, Tony Majeri of the Chicago *Tribune* has elevated Stark's suggestion to the status of a guideline. At the Southern Newspaper Publishers Association Foundation seminar, "Layout, Design and Graphics," Majeri said, "If screening over type, push the type size up a point or two or it won't be readable."

As much as screens may add variety, most designers believe that their overuse can cause the newspaper to have an ashen, dull, unappealing look.

BORDERS

Borders used to box stories are created by applying black-cellophane border tape during the graphic process or with a graphics program on a computer. Like screening, their use must be purposeful to be effective. When newspapers changed from hot to cold type, most of them discontinued the use of hairline (half-point) rules between columns. While these rules may still be not worth the difficulty or expense of placing them between all columns, they are commonly used today for boxed stories.

A system of borders of 1 point for most boxes and 2 point to 4 point occasionally—for special horizontal instances, to give the page a broader appearance—will provide a sense of page continuity and organization. According to Hines, "We do a 2-point rule on all of our art work to hold it together. That gives it a nice, clean, crisp look that you don't get when you are not doing that." Boxes are also useful in the modular page format to assist the reader in quickly ascertaining which photo or illustration goes with which story, or where the story continues.

A delineation between vertical side-by-side stories—or "tombstones"—can be made effective with hairlines or 1-point borders and/or variations of bold and lighter typefaces. It is usually easy enough to read stories that are tombstoned, but the headlines on these stories run up against one another in an uninviting jumble. While it is not a requirement that adjacent stories be placed in boxes, if a story is boxed, it will be most easily read if the type is indented at least 1 pica inside the box to avoid jamming into the border.

SHADOW BOXES

One additional graphic treatment—popular half a century ago and currently being revived—is the shadow box. It can dramatically call attention to—for example—statistical matter, a set of instructions or a list of rules.

Sam Matthews, copublisher of the Tracy (Calif.) *Press,* discussed the recent trend in the use of shadow boxes. Matthews said,

Many newspapers have found that shadow boxes with the "shadow" formed by six-point solid rules—the bottom and right sides appear to be the preferred placement with movement flowing to the bottom right—are most effective when the boxes are screened, usually with gray but also with color.

There is another variation that Matthews mentioned: The "screened shadow box, with two tones and possibly two colors—the tint and black 'shadow' and border—provides an attractive element for a short story, helping to break up the grayness of body type on a page."

Matthews said that the *Press* uses Helios for a body or text type in its screened

Haven new ratings leader

After a little tinkering with the top 10, Pizza Haven returns to the head of the class in the Men's B weekly softball ratings. In Women's Class A standings, Insurance Specialists-Lite Ladies remains at the peak, with Metro Tournament champion Shear Pleasure securely in second.

The big shake-up comes in Class B, with our leader the last few weeks, B.J. Flowers, tumbling to fifth place after four straight losses in the Bill Sigler League.

Pizza Haven, third last week, jumps over Chalet Lounge to the top spot, based on a consistent league-tournament showing. Lums, a Sigler League division winner, gets strong consideration for the top spot. In fact, any of our top six teams could win the ratings war by the end of the season.

In Class A Women's play Shear Pleasure won the Metro Tourney last weekend in a field that didn't include ISI-Lite Ladies. New Era placed second and Bank of Bennington finished third.

Those three teams join host team Lite in the Class A Regionals in Omaha Aug. 21 and 22.

Here's a look at the triumphant ten's:

MEN'S CLASS B	
1. Pizza Haven	44-12
2. Lums	32-8
3. Chalet Lounge	42-12
4. LeRoy's Jag Inn	33-14
5. B.J.'s Flowers	50-12
6. Lodge	52-19
7. O'Flaherty's D.J.	30-11
8. Outlaws	51-18
9. Bursick's Corner	39-20
10. Crown Court	23-10

WOMEN'S CLASS A	
1. ISI-Lite Ladies	45-13
2. Shear Pleasure	53-16
3. New Era	30-17
4. West's Bottles	42-21
5. Coors	25-16
6. Filling Station	36-12
7. B. of Bennington	32-14
8. Offutt Jets	39-29
9. Style Select	31-9
10. Bob Rogers	17-7

A boxed story in the Bellevue (Neb.) *Leader* includes statistics separated by a vertical bar. Reprinted by permission.

U of I device finds Uranus magnetic field

IOWA CITY — A scientific instrument designed and built at the University of Iowa has given scientists the first indication that a magnetic field probably exists on the planet Uranus.

The U of I plasma wave instrument aboard the Voyager 2 spacecraft began detecting radio bursts from Uranus on Monday, according to Donald Gurnett, U of I professor of physics and astronomy at the Jet Propulsion Laboratory in Pasadena, Calif.

He said the implication of the radio bursts, detected in the 30 to 50 kilohertz frequency range, "suggests that the planet probably has a magnetic field. The planets Earth, Jupiter and Saturn — all three — produce radio bursts that are directly related to the magnetic field strengths of the respective planets," he said.

Gurnett said the detection of a magnetic field at Uranus is important to scientists because a magnetic field is necessary for a planet to have a radiation belt and gives a clue as to the interior composition of the planet. He also said the repeating pattern of radio bursts is a way of finding the rotational period of Uranus, which has not previously been detected because of the planet's heavy cloud cover.

Fire destroys huge feed plant at St. Ansgar; $1.5 million damage

By Deb Wiley
Gazette Northeast Iowa Bureau

A massive fire that could be seen 40 miles away caused an estimated $1.5 million in damage and destroyed nine buildings at the NorOats Inc feed processing facility in St. Ansgar Wednesday night.

Cause of the fire, which started about 6:30 p.m. remains under investigation by the State Fire Marshal's Office. The fire was too hot for investigation Thursday.

The wood and metal plant, which processed rolled and pulverized oats for feed for race horses and other livestock, covered the length of a city block in this Mitchell County community in northeast Iowa. The elevator section was 125 feet high.

The entire processing facility was lost, according to owner Jim Mills, but the office and its records remained. Four metal storage bins were also saved.

The building was built as a feed mill in 1959, and Mills purchased the operation 3½ years ago.

St. Ansgar Fire Chief Duane "Snorkie" Mullenbach said fire departments from Osage, Staceyville, Grafton and Carpenter assisted, bringing about 80 firefighters to the scene. The fire was under control

IOWA TODAY

by about 1 a.m. and firefighters kept a watch on the smoldering remains the rest of the day.

Mullenbach said the plant, located in the middle of town, was "one big ball" of fire. A trucker told Mills that he had seen the flames in the sky from Cresco, 40 miles away.

The chief said the fire started in the department where feed was processed for race horses but there was no machinery in operation at the time. Smoke was smelled by two employees working in another part of the plant and that end of the building was engulfed in flames when firefighters arrived.

Water was poured on nearby buildings, including a lumberyard across the street, to keep the fire from spreading. "We're lucky we didn't have a wind," said Mullenbach.

Mills said he employs 19 full time workers and plans to rebuild as soon as possible in St. Ansgar, although probably not at the same location. He said the plant was fully insured.

University presidents, legislators talk money

By Judy Daubenmier
Gazette Des Moines Bureau

DES MOINES — Presidents of Iowa's three state universities met with legislative leaders Thursday to discuss more funds for higher education and ways the institutions can help boost the state's economy.

House Majority Leader Lowell Norland, D-Kensett, called the session a "frank" discussion.

"There was a sharing of concerns by both parties of the need for stable, adequate funding, reliable financing (for higher education)," Norland said.

At the same time, he said, legislators urged the university presidents to use university resources in ways that will help boost the state's economy.

"That has been an ongoing request. How can we tap those university resources?" he said.

Norland said the university presidents reiterated their requests for more money for faculty salaries and $3.7 million in additional funds to replace the tuition used to retire university bonds.

University of Iowa President James Freedman said after the private meeting that he stressed higher faculty salaries are an important component of economic development.

"We want higher salaries, they (legislators) very much want a

greater increase in things that are short-run economic development measures," he said.

"As important as the short run economic development steps are, the long run is equally important."

States such as California, North Carolina and Massachusetts that have built strong economic development efforts have been able to do so because of their universities, he said.

"If this state is going to be successful in economic development, it is going to be because people throughout the country look at Iowa and say we have research universities of the quality of Harvard, Duke and MIT," he said.

Freedman said the state can't afford to short faculty salaries and university research facilities.

Freedman said university officials also cautioned that a House plan to trim $2.5 million from the University of Iowa Hospitals and Clinics appropriation for medical care for indigents could harm the institution.

"That's 10 percent of the state appropriation to University Hospitals," he said.

"Add that to Gramm-Rudman, which is cutting $6 million from the University Hospitals this year, and you're talking about a lot of money. It's going to be very harmful."

Building drive for Iowa Public TV over 75% of goal

DES MOINES — Slightly more than $4.5 million of $6 million has been raised in a capital campaign to fund a new building for Iowa Public Television, the Iowa Public Broadcasting Board was told Thursday.

Dennis Landerbaum, director of community relations and development for IPT, told the board that the remaining $1.5 million will be raised in 1986. He said a low key invitation for participation effort will be mounted in May or June to secure the additional pledges.

The single-level $6 million facility is being constructed in Johnston, a Des Moines suburb, and IPT is expected to move in sometime in October or November.

The building that now houses the station has been for sale since April.

The MARKED-IT-DOWN-AGAIN

The positioning of these stories in the Cedar Rapids (Iowa) *Gazette* is an example of how stories placed side by side can be easily separated by putting one in a box. Reprinted by permission.

If Henning returns, so might Van Note

By Chris Mortensen
Staff Writer

Jeff Van Note, the Atlanta Falcons' center for 17 years, said his decision on whether to retire in January probably will influenced by Dan Henning's future as coach of the team.

If Henning is retained as head coach, Van Note, 39, said Tuesday the chances of returning for an 18th season are "better than 50-50."

"I don't know, if I say I'm coming back if Dan's back, that may hurt his chances," Van Note said with a laugh. "But, seriously, I would say it matters some. Quite a bit, really. Dan knows me; he knows how I'm playing. If other people are brought in, it will mean an entire new program, and I've been through that plenty of times before."

Van Note has started every

game this year, the only Falcons offensive lineman to do so. He has held off former USFL All-Star center Wayne Radloff to the point where his playing time has increased in recent weeks.

"I think Note is amazing," line coach Larry Beightol said. "He's played his best football in the past two weeks. He wasn't given this job, either. It was his when training camp started, but the other guy (Radloff) had a chance to beat him out. They were about at a standstill when the season started, but Note's just gotten better."

Henning agrees, saying, "I think he's played his best center in my three years here."

That's what Van Note wants to hear, if Henning is around to evaluate personnel for the 1986 season.

"In January sometime, I'll sit down and talk to the coach and

JEFF VAN NOTE: Has been Falcons' center for 17 years

see how he feels," said Van Note. "I need to get on with my life, if there's some doubt there. Personally, I'd like to see Dan back because he's given me an opportunity, not a gift. I feel like I've been productive for him, and I like his approach to the game."

Henning gives fired Campbell phone call

By Chris Mortensen
Staff Writer

Atlanta Falcons coach Dan Henning telephoned Marion Campbell shortly after Campbell was fired Monday as coach of the Philadelphia Eagles. Was it a social call, business or both?

Henning declined Tuesday to say whether he discussed the possibility of Campbell joining his staff in 1986 as defensive coordinator, assuming he is retained as the Falcons' head coach.

"It was a courtesy call, just to show some support," said Henning. "I've known Marion a long time. I have a great deal of respect for him as a coach and as a person. I thought he did a heck of a job with the Eagles this year."

Henning had no comment when asked if he wanted Campbell to take over his spotty defense in 1986. But Falcons presi-

dent Rankin Smith Jr. seemed to leave open an invitation for such a possibility.

"He's a good defensive coach, one of the best, but that would be the head coach's decision," said Smith. "I'm sure a lot of teams would be interested in him. His reputation as a defensive coach ranks with the best."

Smith added that, "Marion is a good friend, and I'm sorry to see it happen to him."

Campbell's firing wasn't his first as an NFL coach. The Falcons fired Campbell after five games in the 1976 season. his third year as their head coach. He served Norm Van Brocklin as defensive coordinator and line coach from 1969 through the middle of the '74 season, when he replaced Van Brocklin.

Campbell, an All-SEC tackle at Georgia in 1951, is recognized as one of the game's keen defen-

MARION CAMPBELL: To be Falcons' defensive coach?

sive minds. In his six years as defensive coordinator with Philadelphia, before he was named head coach, the Eagles allowed the fewest points in the NFL, an average of 15.8 per game.

Campbell has two years remaining on his Eagles contract.

These two related stories in the Atlanta *Journal* have been placed in boxes to create separation. Reprinted by permission.

SEC coaches vote Anderson as best blocker

By Thomas O'Toole
Staff Writer

ATHENS — Saying he feels humbled by it all, Georgia center Pete Anderson accepted yet another honor in a season he calls "a dream come true."

The senior from Glen Ridge, N.J., has been named winner of the 1985 Jacobs Blocking Trophy, which honors the outstanding blocker in the SEC.

Already a consensus All-American, Anderson is the seventh Georgia player to win the award, which is voted on by the head coach and line coaches of each team. The last Bulldog to win was Guy McIntyre in 1983.

Sun Bowl

Georgia vs. Arizona

Dec. 28, 3 p.m.

"This year has been a dream come true for me," Anderson said Tuesday. "At the beginning of the season I was hoping to make an all-conference team and maybe get some mention on All-American team. This has been a great

Unhappy S

By Mike Waters
Banner Sports Writer

Mario Soto, the onetime Cincinnati Reds ace, did not want to be in Nashville or a Sounds uniform Friday night.

And for three innings against the Louisville Redbirds at Greer Stadium, Soto looked like a man who wasn't where he wanted to be.

The Redbirds jumped on Soto, who is still battling back from shoulder surgery.

Sounds

Louisville
Rick Buonanthony
(2-2)
at
Nashville
Scott Terry
(10-10)
Tonight, 7:35

Shadow boxes can dramatize a story display or a sidebar, the latter being the case with these Atlanta *Constitution* and Nashville (Tenn.) *Banner* sports-page starting pitchers and game times, and this Tracy (Calif.) *Press* quoteout. Reprinted by permission.

Obviously, there is more freedom out here. It's the next best thing to going home."
— DVI's Lt. Ed Strader

shadow boxes, while other papers use regular text type and some newspapers have also used the screened shadow boxes for quotes pulled from a story. "An unscreened shadow box can add a tone by using benday [halftone-appearing border tape] for the 'shadow' on two sides of a story's 1-point rule box."

All the boxes on a page should have the shadows on the same two sides—following the logic that, if the boxes were actually affected by the sun or some other light source, all the shadows would fall in the same direction.

Hines of the Contra Costa *Times* says, "Shadow boxes are in right now . . . and I guess they serve a purpose. I am not a great advocate, but clearly they are seen as good design elements and I will live with those."

As important as reader attention elements can be in a newspaper's overall design, it is possible—even when they are implemented appropriately—that they might become a source of discontinuity. The reader is interested in the news content. Therefore, there should be not so many nonnews elements arranged in such a way that they take away from text typography, photographs and informational graphics. Certainly, the mortice is OK in its place, screens may be used and shadow boxes are permissible—but these devices must only be used when they guide the reader to the news and through the pages of the TPC newspaper.

13   Color

We have a lot of abuse of color. I am seeing a lot of good news stuff
that's just being buried in a sea of unnecessary color, and we'd better
get a handle on that because if we don't, we're going to lose a lot of
our credibility. This whole thing that color sells and that readers want
to see more color, that's true, but I think it's getting in the way. I've
seen so much stuff that the real news on the page was just overwhelmed
by the gratuitous color. It's terrible.

> John Bodette
> managing editor
> St. Cloud (Minn.) *Times*

The world as we see it is not just in black and white and shades of gray. However,
until recently, most newspaper content was. By contrast, the use of color has
been commonplace for some time in magazines, movies, and television. Color
is not absolutely essential for the Total Page Concept (TPC) newspaper because
readers look to it for information, not for a dazzling display of color. Also,
printing in color is so expensive that many newspapers cannot afford it very
often and some do not have the mechanical capability for more than an occasional
spot of color. However, papers that do have the equipment and finances are
publishing much more color now than ever before.

In the 1985 article written by Tom Goss for *Print,* Rob Covey—while art
director at the Seattle *Times*—said that color has indeed come quickly to the
fore. "There's been a dramatic difference in a decade," Covey said. More color
is on all the pages of most newspapers; it is no longer even limited to feature
pages. Newspapers are publishing with "more color on sports, more color on
page one, color throughout, throughout the country whether on big papers or
on little papers. It's happened on papers that, I think, didn't really want to get

TUESDAY PM
JULY 8, 1986

ST. PAUL
PIONEER PRESS DISPATCH

25¢

MINNESOTA'S FIRST NEWSPAPER

METRO·FINAL

Pipeline blows; inferno kills 2

Fireman hose down an adjoining house to protect it from the wall of flame created by a Williams Pipe Line explosion in Mounds View this morning.   Richard Marshall: Staff Photographer

Hundreds evacuated, flames shoot 50 feet

A woman and child were killed, and hundreds of Mounds View residents were evacuated from their homes early today when gasoline from a ruptured pipeline exploded and burned.

A third victim was hospitalized in serious condition with burns she suffered in the fire.

Witnesses at the scene said parts of the neighborhood resembled a battle zone, with streams of fire rolling down streets.

Flames shot 50 feet into the air and billowing black smoke surrounded the explosion site at Long Lake Road and Woodcrest Drive, a tree-lined residential neighbor-

THE REPORTERS
This report was written by Theresa Monsour, based on reporting by Brian Bonner, Dorothy Lewis, Karl J. Karlson and Jim Ragsdale.

hood.

Lawns were stripped of grass, mail boxes melted, power lines were knocked down, trees were defoliated, roads buckled and cars were set afire in the area surrounding the 4:40 a.m. explosion.

Please see Fire/3A

Evacuation Area
CO. RD. H-4
COUNTY RD. 10

Mounds View
New Brighton

■ Today's explosion the latest episode in a troubled history for Williams Pipe Line Co. in Minnesota. Page 2A.

Blast area residents wake to wall of flame

By Karl J. Karlson,
Brian Bonner
and Dorothy Lewis
Staff Writers

Jim and Judy Sruoc woke up early this morning to the sound of a woman screaming and pounding on their front door.

Her clothing was all singed and she looked burned. We took her into the kitchen where we rinsed her off with water and called 911, said Judy Sruoc of 5190 Long Lake Road.

Their neighbor Donna Workland, 5190 Long Lake Road, said the woman who ran to the Sruocs had been delivering the Minneapolis Star and Tribune.

You could see the tires on her car on fire. Everything around it was burning like crazy, she said. Eventually an ambulance came for the woman and neighbors said the car exploded.

It reminded me of Gone With the Wind — a wall of flames — I didn't know how we would get out of there, said Judy Anderson, 28, who lives in a house directly in front of the main gas explosion at 5084 Long Lake Road.

Please see Scene/3A

Rickover dies

Adm. Hyman Rickover, the salty engineer who goaded the Navy into the nuclear era, died today at age 86 at his suburban Washington home.

Obituary, Page 4D.

Big quake rocks S. California

Associated Press

PALM SPRINGS, Calif. — The strongest earthquake to hit Southern California in seven years shook a wide region early today, triggering rockslides, shattering windows and knocking out power to 100,000 customers.

Several major injuries were reported, and damage estimates were expected to mount as businesses opened and took stock of broken windows, cracked walls and merchandise dumped from the shelves.

The 6:51 a.m. CDT earthquake measured 6.0 on the Richter scale and was centered 12 miles northwest of Palm Springs, said Donna Meredith of the California Institute of Technology, Palm Springs is 110 miles east of downtown Los Angeles.

It's a big one, Meredith said.

In Washington, D.C., U.S. Geological Survey spokesman Don Finley said the epicenter of the quake was about 10 miles east of San Bernardino in mountains near the edge of the Mojave Desert.

Early reports said there was some damage in the epicentral area, he said.

Please see Quake/2A

WEATHER

There's an echo in here, from day to day the same forecast: partly cloudy tonight, possible evening shower or thunderstorm; low 60s. Wednesday, sunny and pleasant, low 80s. Have a sunny and pleasant day. Weather, 8A

INSIDE

Business	6B	Movies	8C
Classified ads	4D	News Briefing	5A
Comics	4C	Obituaries	4D
Crossword	6C	Reviews	8C
Dear Abby	3C	Sports	1B
Editorials	8A	TV, Radio	7C
EXTRA	1C	Weather	8A
Metro	1D		
Mini Briefing	2D		

15 Cubans' 4th threat cools down in Anoka

By Bill Gardner
Staff Writer

Federal authorities were so worried that 15 Cuban prisoners might cause a disturbance during the Fourth of July Statue of Liberty celebration in New York City that they shipped the Cubans to the Anoka County Jail for a week.

The idea was to try to defuse a situation which we thought might flare up over the Fourth of July, said Charlie Tros, head of public affairs for the eastern region of the U.S. Immigration and Naturalization Service. We did not want any kind of riot conflagration — you name it — breaking out. There is a lot of tension at that facility, and moving the 15 out was an attempt to defuse any situation that might

The 15 prisoners were among about 70 Cubans being held at the INS processing center in New York City. Several thousand Cubans are being held in federal and state prisons and county jails across the nation until they can be deported back to Cuba Tros said.

Over the past year there had been escapes, hunger strikes and other unrest at the New York City center. Tros said. Authorities wanted no trouble during the Statue of Liberty festivities which were attended by President Reagan.

There was a high probability of trouble brewing over the Fourth of July weekend. Tros said, although he declined to be more specific.

We felt we had to move 15 of these prisoners, he said.

Please see Cubans/3A

Color—especially red—provides intensity for the story of a fire; it was used for this front-page deadline coverage in the St. Paul (Minn.) *Pioneer Press and Dispatch*, July 8, 1986. According to Bill Cento, associate editor, "The explosion occurred at 4:40 a.m.; the first edition was off the press at 10:48 a.m. that morning. That is 12 minutes before the scheduled start of 11 a.m." Principal editors that day were Phyllis Jacobs, news editor; Pat Sweeney, city editor; and Craig Borck, photo editor. Reprinted by permission.

Table 9
Four-color Usage on Newspaper Front Pages, by Circulation

Circulation	Regularly	Occasionally	Rarely	Never	Chi-square
Less than 50,000	34.1%	34.1%	25.0%	6.8%	—
50,000 +	33.3	21.2	15.2	30.3	8.138*

*Significant at .05 level.

df = 3; tabled chi-square = 7.81.

Source: Sandra H. Utt and Steve Pasternack, "Front Pages of U.S. Daily Newspapers," *Journalism Quarterly* (1984):879–84.

into color." As large and even small newspapers replace their outdated presses they acquire the capability to print full color, Covey reported.

In their 1983 study of front pages, Steve Pasternack and Sandra Utt said,

> Among the larger dailies, 30.3 percent never use 4-color on their front pages; by contrast, 6.8 percent of the smaller circulation newspapers do not use front page 4-color. However, in both circulation categories, about one-third of the newspapers regularly use 4-color on page one [see Table 9].

Further, Pasternack and Utt found that "while a newspaper's circulation was found to be a predictor of its use of 4-color, the presence of a competing newspaper was not." Actually, more papers without competition (85.5 percent) use 4-color than "dailies with direct competition, 77.3 percent," the researchers said.

APPLICATION OF COLOR

A single spot of color is bright and splashy and can be used to enhance a page and to enlighten readers. Line art and photos are even stronger when the 4-color process is used: cyan (light blue), magenta (red plum), yellow and black. Black is a constant color; it is present even if the other three are not. Pegie Stark, formerly of the Detroit *News*, says that black and white can be used to make color by using "all the tonal ranges from black to white; there are hundreds of different tones." She feels that editors ought to explore the 30 percent, 50 percent and 80 percent tones of black, and then push to the extreme on their presses to see how good or bad it prints. "With black and white," Stark said, "you have to really study how tones can create dimension." Thus, color—including black—is another design element whose purpose must be understood if it is to be used effectively as part of the Total Page Concept.

A newspaper is not an advertising circular, a cereal box or a comic book. According to the article by Goss, Covey echoes this idea in the *Seattle Times Design Stylebook,* which reads "Loud, comic book color does not lend credibility to the editorial product. For this reason, we try to use full color with carefully selected screens to produce a subtle palette of distinctive, not raucous, color." Four-color should be used in the paper as a partner in the communication of news.

Robert Lockwood of NewsGraphics expressed some of his reservations:

> Our capacity to reproduce four colors is having an enormous impact. Color or the misuse of color is one of the new things we should be more careful about; we seem to be making the same content and design mistakes, but now we're making them more colorfully.

In other words, 4-color should be used with discretion in measured amounts to facilitate understanding, impact and realism.

Stark wonders if the many layout people using 4-color are trained to use it or have any notion regarding its impact. "My biggest concern right now is that color is in the wrong hands and I wish people would take time to learn—take a color theory class or read Johannes Itten's book, the *Elements of Color*—to understand that there's more to it than just picking your favorite colors." For instance, when blue is placed next to yellow, the yellow changes the blue. "People keep missing the point that we don't see colors by themselves," Stark said. "In reality, we see colors next to each other, and next to each other, colors change. The whole area needs to be explored, and it needs to be explored quickly because it's getting out of hand."

Tony Majeri of the Chicago *Tribune* agrees with Stark regarding the thoughtful use of spot color. "Don't put primary colors next to a 4-color photo or graphic; they compete," Majeri advised at the Southern Newspaper Publishers Association (SNPA) Foundation seminar, "Layout, Graphics and Design." "In fact," he added, "avoid using primary spot color whenever possible. Bright reds, yellows and blues are glaring and often garish. For screens and the like, try blending primary colors for more subdued tones—example, 20 percent red and 30 percent yellow gives a sand tone." When this principle is not well understood, newspapers wind up looking like cheap advertising fliers.

Color display in the three color-wheel shades and black—like choice of type fonts—must abide by effective design principles, and must be integrated into the whole communication package. "Editors," Stark said, "are told they must use color, so people who don't know anything about color use colors, and they don't know anything about complements or contrast." An editor—she insisted—would not go to the art department, hand an artist a story and say, " 'Oh here—by the way, you have to edit this and write a headline.' But we go up to editors and say, 'Oh yeah, while you're laying out the page, choose five colors that go with that page.' People are missing the point that black and white is very colorful and creates dimension if used in the right way."

Just as page designers should avoid the habit of throwing 72-point headlines and rub-on type just anywhere in the newspaper; the same restraints must be assigned to color use. Four-color should never appear on the front or any other page solely because it was available piggyback from a color advertisement printed on an adjacent page. Used with the kind of care that only comes when sufficient time is allowed for planning, color can be inviting to the reader; but a proliferation of color is a blinding turnoff.

At its best, 4-color design can enhance and draw attention to the news and create a style or personality that sets one newspaper apart from another. Covey was quoted in the *Print* article as saying that the Seattle *Times* and the Allentown, Pa. *Morning Call* "tend to lean on illustration" and also that "we [the Seattle *Times]* try to make good use of the illustration talent we have on staff." Goss—who wrote the article—said, "The *Morning Call* tends to use its full color on photographs and to use spot color for its illustrations."

In his 1983 study of graphic illustration in three Washington, D.C., newspapers, Philip Geraci found that, since 1982, *USA Today* has been a great influence on the use of spot color and 4-color display. According to Geraci, *USA Today* began "using color illustrations profusely in marketing a new newspaper concept to the American reader" where "color was a page-one standard, every day."

Also, Geraci found that "the [Washington] *Post* rarely uses illustrations in color" and, "when it does, they are nearly always on the food or travel sections. The [Washington] *Times* mixes color with black and white on its front pages, while *USA Today* uses several full-page color photographs on every cover."

The effect of color on the eye might, Lockwood of NewsGraphics said,

> work either way. It's not only what is done that's important, but also how something is done. I think you can control a reader's eye across a page very effectively with the use of color, if you choose to do that. You can also do it with black, white and gray. I don't question any device, as much as how it's used.

Designers who study their own newspapers and others can observe and compare attention-getting color presentations as well as other special features, and then create a newspaper design policy geared toward the community that they serve. Such research demonstrates when it is appropriate for them to use color in charts and graphs—or two colors, for a "duotone."

Nanette Bisher of the *Orange County Register* in Santa Ana, Calif., reminded the SNPA Foundation seminar audience that color use also relates to emotions.

> Different colors evoke different emotions—red is active, yellow allows the most light to the eye, and blue is most calming. Red and

The Washington *Times* provides its readers with a great array of news and features with color; red, white and blue were used in this case for a logo story about the lottery. Reprinted by permission.

yellow expand on the page; blue contracts. So, for excitement, use red or yellow; for informational graphics, blue is more respectable.

Photography in color is popular, especially for upbeat subjects (such as children, fashion, food, flowers and sports) and also for disasters on a grand scale. Sometimes, though, the color photos tend to resemble something found in a high school or college yearbook rather than a newspaper: sunsets, fall colors or the first snow of the winter.

In *Print* (1985), Goss quoted Maureen Decker of the *Morning Call* in Allentown, Penn., as she recalled the early efforts of the paper in printing color. "We had trouble judging how an ink would look printed on newsprint," Decker said. "At first, our full color was either too muddy or too garish." But now the paper uses a lot of spot color and more pastel colors "not because we're pastel buffs, but because pastels look better on newsprint. They look more refined."

Color is not a very subtle design element. Certain limitations must be respected by the photographer and page designer when working with a 4-color format. And spot color should never look as though a can of ink fell on the page. Even spot color can cause an overload if used haphazardly for headlines or if stories are placed on screens of more than 10 percent or 20 percent color.

In addition to its potential for being offensive, color can sometimes create legibility problems when reproduced on newsprint. On top of that, a color photo is actually seven or eight times more expensive to print than a black-and-white photo.

"Color," says Lockwood of NewsGraphics, "shouldn't be used arbitrarily; it should be used to support the content, to illuminate it rather than just to embellish it." Stark, while at the Detroit *News,* recommended that designers not follow strict rules when they use color. For example, she advised against ever saying, "the only colors you should use on your front page are buff and blue; for every situation, every market, each climate is different."

In all cases, the underlying reason for printing any news publication must be inherent in the content—in the story being told to the reader. The use of either color or black and white should never be the prevailing objective of design or cause a diversion from the reading. With or without 4-color, the basic strategies of page design described in Chapter 3 must be followed.

ASSISTANCE IN REPRODUCTION

Printer's proofs of pages are important, for they provide the editor with a before-publication check for copy errors, they assist in the positioning of headlines and blocks of type, and they help the editor to anticipate possible publication problems. Because of the cost and impact of color, it is even more critical that the proofs of pages on which spot color and 4-color appear be given a careful review. When a newspaper prints in color, its production staff must look for ways to make the color as economical as possible. One method of keeping costs in line with the budget is to use a color chart. Richard C. D'Agostino, design director of the Baltimore *Sun,* said that his paper uses a "customized chart which shows preferred colors—pastels—and amount of dot gain [that] colors will encounter." The color chart is "critical to standardize the 'tone' of the product." While there is no guarantee that all the editor's best efforts will result in the final color reproduction as the page designer envisioned, there is a greater possibility of this occurring if the editor conscientiously looks at every detail of the proofs and gives precise instructions to the printer. These instructions to the printer should be marked on the face of the proof or listed in an accompanying memo.

The vendor that supplies the printing ink should be consulted about the product and about what it can and cannot do. The sales representatives of these companies often know how to achieve the best color reproduction results that are available.

If care is lacking in the performance of these printing and proofing stages, readers will see the negative results. Readers tend to use the full-color 120–150-line screen photos in magazines as their point of comparison. They have no understanding or interest in labored explanations about the 65–85-line screen system of newspapers, but only want to know this: If magazine photos are so clear, then how come newspaper photos are not? Nevertheless, the reason for the difference in print quality from one print medium to another can only be comprehended by looking at the screen indications—the number of halftone grid lines or dots per inch—in a halftone photograph. The most common line screens (or dots per inch) used in the various categories of publication are as follows:

- letterpress newspapers—65 and 85 lines;
- offset newspapers—100, 120 and 133 lines;
- magazines and commercial letterpress—120, 133 and 150 lines;
- offset lithography—133 and 150 lines; and
- offset lithography color reproduction—200 and 300 lines.

If the color is on register—with images in exact alignment—the reader will be satisfied. If, however, the cyan overlaps the magenta or the yellow overlaps the black, the reader will be disappointed in the product.

Color is—after all—only one element in design. If a photo does not render a strong and positive image in black and white, it will not do so in 4-color. In such a situation, it would be better to substitute an illustration or something else in spot color or black and white that does work. Majeri of the Chicago *Tribune* told the SNPA Foundation seminar that "color usage can make or break the way a paper looks" and that "most papers with color capability abuse it."

The probability that readers will be satisfied with the color in their daily or weekly newspaper is directly related to whether its publisher is supportive and willing to spend the money, and to whether it has exhaustively planned for its color usage from camera to pressrun, has access to suitable equipment to do a first-class job, hires a committed quality control staff, and involves the skills and teamwork of everyone at the paper.

At the level of individual stories, these guidelines will enhance the communication potential of color:

Newspapers frequently display color on their inside feature-section page fronts, as in these examples from the Portland *Oregonian,* which used pastel blue to denote the cool of the water, and the Las Cruces (N.M.) *Sun-News*, which printed a sand color for a backdrop. Reprinted by permission.

- Illustrate the colors of opposing sides or relative positions by means of flags, banners, maps, charts, team uniforms or clothing fashions; or show aspects of nature, such as brown hills or autumn shades.

- Denote a festive occasion such as a holiday or sporting event, using color in photographs only so long as faces or other dominant components are distinguishable.

- Tell the news with color when it is more effective in the story than black and white—but only if the colors can be easily separated by the reader. Color should never be a sea of closely related tones— several shades of the same color, say, with none dominant.

The possibilities are many for providing depth to the news with color. In fact, stories to be told in color are limitless for the newspaper that has the money. But the availability of money must never be the sole criterion for deciding to use color in the Total Page Concept.

VI   PUTTING IT
ALL TOGETHER

The TPC publication is expected to continue evolving via computer systems affecting word processing, graphics creation and page design. Many papers' designs have already changed because of and through the computer work of consultants and on-site designers. The results of redesign are then transferred to design style guidelines in order to standardize and encourage the consistent use of the newspaper's Total Page Concept on the part of all its employees. As a side benefit, the student of graphic design can research these stylebooks to discover the steps that the design process follows during the layout of each newspaper page. The final three chapters set forth the modern application and philosophy of the Total Page Concept.

Trade deficit widens

Japan reports a 30 percent increase in its trade surplus with the United States during 1986

E1

Santa Rosa's new garbage cans being delivered
B1

'Onion Field' killer stays behind bars **A3**

THE
Press
DEMOCRAT

Santa Rosa, California, Saturday, January 17, 1987   130th Year. No. 88   • 25¢

AIDS drug approval a step closer

Advisers urge 'extraordinary measure'

New York Times

ROCKVILLE, Md. — In a highly unusual step, a panel of expert medical advisers to the Food and Drug Administration recommended Friday that a promising drug against AIDS be licensed for sale despite what the scientists described as major gaps in knowledge about its effectiveness and safety.

"An extraordinary situation requires extraordinary measures," said one of the panelists, Dr. Stanley M. Lemon of the University of North Carolina. The drug, azidothymidine, or AZT, is the first shown to prolong the lives of AIDS patients.

The recommendation to license the antiviral drug is not binding on the federal agency, which is not expected to decide the issue for weeks. But it sharply improved the prospects for approval of the drug, which is manufactured by the Burroughs Wellcome Co. of Research Triangle Park, N.C.

Through the day of discussions the committee was torn over what several of its members termed an excruciating dilemma. Members noted that knowledge about the drug, known to have serious toxic side effects, was far more limited than what is normally required to approve a drug for marketing. But the panel concluded that an exception should be made for the only drug yet found effective against a spreading killer for which no other treatment exists.

Once a drug is licensed, doctors may prescribe it to any patient they feel it will help. But the panel restricted approval of AZT only after hearing assurances from

See AIDS, Page A8

Demonstrators march in front of Santa Rosa's City Hall Friday protesting effluent outfall options

China's communist chief ousted in shakeup

New York Times

PROFILE OF NEW LEADER PAGE A7

PEKING — Hu Yao-bang, the chief of the world's largest Communist Party, was forced to resign Friday after being accused of major "mistakes" during his tenure.

Hu dismissal followed recent demonstrations for freer expression and democracy in China. Hu, who had sometimes been mentioned as a successor to Deng Xiaoping, China's leader, was formally accused of "mistakes on major issues of political principles," according to a communique issued by an enlarged meeting of the Politburo of the party's Central Committee.

Prime Minister Zhao Ziyang, also mentioned as a possible successor to Deng, was appointed to replace Hu, at least temporarily, as acting general secretary of the party.

But Hu, who delivered a self-criticism of his mistakes, was allowed to retain his position on the Politburo's five-member Standing Committee, which exercises power over the party and state, as well as his membership in the broader Central Committee.

The cause of Hu's downfall remained unclear. The communique did not specify his purported errors. But his resignation culminated nearly six weeks of accelerating political disarray in China brought on by a tide of student protests that demanded more Western-style freedoms.

Hu disappeared from public view on Dec. 29 and was soon rumored to be in serious political trouble as party newspapers unleashed criticisms of educated Chinese sympathetic to "bourgeois liberalism," a disparaging ideological codeword for Western democratic ideas. The press attack halted a modest flourishing of political and

See China, Page A7

Outfall options spark protest

By TONY GALLODES
Staff Writer

Ocean disposal of Santa Rosa's effluent, as well as alternatives that would keep it in the Russian River, took their knocks from about 100 protesters at a noon-hour demonstration in front of City Hall on Friday.

The lively group, the majority from the Russian River area, was led by Tom Lynch of Guerneville, also known by the tongue-in-cheek alias of Measure Max. He said the event was staged to increase public consciousness.

"If you increase public awareness, I think that will increase public pressure against ocean outfall and river discharges," Lynch said.

Lynch said he believes Santa Romans have become more concerned about the disposal of their wastewater since the city's consultants, CH2M Hill, proposed percolation ponds near Windsor as another disposal alternative.

Effluent from the ponds, adjacent to the Russian River, would enter the river indirectly through infiltration. But it would be approach from a major domestic water source.

The Sonoma County Water Agency, which supplies municipalities in Sonoma and Marin counties with drinking water, draws the water through pumps in the river near Wohler Bridge, downstream from Windsor.

The pumps are upstream, however, from where the wastewater now goes into the river from the Laguna de Santa Rosa.

"I'm glad CH2M Hill came up with this idea because now that they're planning to put the discharge pipes above the intake valves for 600,000 people, there's 600,000 people that can appreciate how we feel on the Russian River with the wastewater in our drinking water," Lynch said.

The demonstrators marched with signs

See Protest, Page A8

Ecuador leader freed as kidnap demand met

Associated Press

QUITO, Ecuador — President Leon Febres Cordero, kidnapped Friday by renegade paratroopers during a visit to the Taura air base, was freed more than 10 hours later when the government released the leader of an earlier revolt.

The Taura base is near the port city of Guayaquil, 170 miles southeast of Quito, the capital.

Radio reports said the president, Defense Minister Gen. Medardo Salazar and others seized by the paratroopers left the air base in a caravan of cars and went to the Guayaquil governor's mansion. People were reported gathered along the streets of the caravan's route and applauded as the cars passed.

The broadcasts said the president and his party were freed immediately after Gen. Frank Vargas Pazos, who had been jailed following an attempted revolt last March, arrived at the Taura base aboard a special

See Kidnap, Page A8

'RETIREMENT EDENS'

Elizabeth Judy waters her garden at Santa Rosa's Spring Lake Village

Empire spots rated ideal for seniors

By CAROLYN LUND
Staff Writer

The word's out about our "retirement Edens."

Author Peter A. Dickinson, whose 1976 guide to San Belt retirement havens sold 200,000 copies, now touts the virtues of Sonoma, Santa Rosa and Mendocino in his new book, "Retirement Edens Outside the Sunbelt."

He likes the climate, the natural beauty, the friendliness, the cost of living, the medical and recreational facilities and the senior services.

Santa Rosa it, he said in a telephone interview Friday from his own home in Larchmont, N.Y. "the nicest town of its size within the shortest distance of San Francisco," and "I really like Sonoma, too — for some of the same reasons and its smaller

See Retirement, Page A8

PLEASURES

Night on the town doesn't beat working

Associated Press

DETROIT — Whether you're an assembly-line worker or back vice president, chances are you get more pleasure out of a day on the job than a night on the town, according to a study.

Asked to rank 15 activities in order of preference, about 3,600 men and women in a nationwide survey conducted by the University of Michigan ranked going to work third, behind child care and socializing with friends and relatives.

Work beat such leisure activities as going to the movies, watching television, playing sports, reading, working on a hobby, cooking and shopping, economics professor F. Thomas Juster said Thursday in a telephone interview.

However, it ranked last, he said.

The study found the satisfaction level of any activity depends primarily on the amount of interaction with other people it involves.

"It's odd that the jobs are interesting and fascinating," he said. "It's the interactive nature of the environment."

Why, then, the Monday blues and the thank-God-it's-Friday high?

Juster said a lot of people just like to complain.

UN-HOLIDAY

Much ado about nothing

Associated Press

TAMPA, Fla. — Take off your shoes, put up your feet, sit back and relax. There's no other appropriate way to spend National Nothing Day.

The un-holiday, noted by its fans Friday, was the brainchild of newspaperman Harold Pullman Coffin, who thought Americans needed a day without celebrating, observing or honoring anything.

Since Coffin dreamed up the idea in 1973, people have been doing nothing about it ever since. For instance, take University of South Florida President John Lott Brown, who wouldn't say if or how he would observe the day.

"I have nothing to say about nothing," he said.

WEATHER

Frigid, but warming up

High: 56
Low: 27

Bridge	D2
Classified	E5-26
Editorials	B2
Ann Landers	D2
Obituaries	B2
Television	D4
Theaters	D1
Weather	B4

The Santa Rosa, Calif. *Press Democrat*—with its clean, easy-to-read structure—brings to readers in that Northern California area the news told with a regional perspective. Reprinted by permission.

14 Computer-initiated Text, Graphics and Page Design

Today, through the "paper-hanging" aspects of cold type, intricate layouts are nothing to produce in a composing room of a major newspaper. Today, too, with the proper pagination program for area composition, type can be designed in exotic display with no more effort than keystrokes.

Ron Patel
associate managing editor
Philadelphia *Inquirer*

The computer has become a necessary aspect of the Total Page Concept (TPC) for today's newspapers. Even the smallest weeklies have type set by computers. But photoelectronic typesetting and page composition, and photolithographic printing, are relatively new. Twenty years ago publications were set in type using hot cast metal—thus the term "hot type"—to create galleys of text, and headlines were hand-composed on wooden typesticks for processing into metal. This process—called "letterpress"—is rarely used by commercial newspapers today.

THE EVOLUTION OF TYPE IMPROVEMENTS

Photoelectronic makeup and photolithographic advancements—however significant—are only part of what is arguably the most profound technological revolution in communications. The evolution of movable type ushered in the Renaissance, the Reformation and the 18th-century spate of revolutions. It permitted the spread of literacy beyond the ranks of the clergy, who took up the printed word to spread the Gospel and bred many other users, including politicians who wrote and circulated partisan messages. People in business were next to see the value of printing the news for everyone—as a means of turning a profit.

German-born Johann Gutenberg (1400–68) and Ottmar Mergenthaler (1854–99) are recognized as the pioneers of printing. Gutenberg is linked with devising —in the 1440s—raised movable metal type that could be assembled in a wooden frame, and then inked and impressed onto paper within a winepress kind of device. Mergenthaler invented the Linotype machine in 1884 for setting hot lines of type from a keyboard. In America, Ben Franklin (1707–90) was one of the first to use movable type to produce handouts and other Colonial literature of the 1770s.

Early publishers took the efforts of Gutenberg, Mergenthaler, Franklin and others, and extended them into profitable commercial newspaper enterprises. They included Horace Greeley (1811–72), Joseph Pulitzer (1847–1911), Edward Wyllis Scripps (1854–1926), William Randolph Hearst (1863–1951), William Allen White (1868–1944) and Frank E. Gannett (1876–1957). The manual typewriter was developed by newspaperman Christopher Latham Sholes (1819–90) and manufactured by E. Remington & Sons beginning in 1874.

During the past quarter-century, many men, women, newspapers and corporations have worked separately and together in effecting the changeover to today's offset press publishing. While the result of offset lithography—also called "cold type"—is the same as with letterpress, the process is altogether different. Cold type is set photoelectronically or by some other computer process, printed on photosensitive paper, shot with a camera for printing on a metal plate, and transferred to a blanket cylinder for printing on paper. Although there are more steps to take for offset, in the end the process is quicker, and photos printed from the blanket cylinder are far superior in published print quality to those printed from zinc metal used in conjunction with letterpress.

Where the manual and common electric typewriters left off, the use of an optical character reader (OCR) ball element on the electric typewriter took over. In this process, the OCR element allows stories to be typed on regular 8½ inch by 11 inch typing paper, and then the pages are fed manually into an electronic scanner. The scanner is able to read the text and to perforate a half-inch paper tape as it translates the letters and spaces. A person in the composing department then takes the paper tape, places it in a composing machine, and punches in (that is, keystrokes) the column-width typeface and other requirements assigned by the editor. The composing machine automatically projects the selected typeface from a plastic font strip onto photosensitive paper in a light-tight metal canister. The paper remains in the canister as it is manually placed in a processor for developing, fixing and washing. Drying is done in a heater box adjacent to the processor. After it is dried, the paper is waxed, cut up and put on pasteup boards according to a miniature preliminary layout called a "dummy" page.

OCR was an intermediary step between manual/electric typewriters and computers—but at least copy could be set by an automatic scanning of the typed pages. Cathode ray tube (CRT) technology led to development of the video display terminal (VDT), which uses a 12-, 15-, or 19-inch television screen for viewing and can store type on a floppy disk.

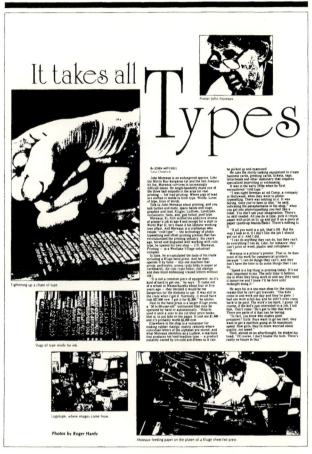

A story about typographical history and how one man in the Thousand Oaks, Calif. area still uses hot type is told with photos and text in the *News Chronicle.* Reprinted by permission.

On some newspapers, the VDT has replaced both the typewriter and the OCR and now provides direct access to the computer that drives the typesetter, onto which reporters file all local copy. Some newspapers made this change quickly, while others are still in the process. For instance, Ken Bruns at the Los Angeles *Times* said,

> We went right from typewriters to VDTs. It was handled very well and professionally, as most things are at this newspaper. Training classes were set up and the editors went to them. They all picked it up very easily. There was some resistance at first, by a few people,

but once they got used to it, they found it much easier and that there were many advantages to it.

Typists use other VDTs for typesetting wire press association copy, syndicated columns, stories that arrive in the mail and letters to the editor. Indeed, computers are quickly becoming the main tool for producing today's newspaper. Publishers—not frequently as news trained as they are business educated—have been especially sympathetic to the upgrade in equipment because, although computer typesetting is new and different and does require a training of personnel, its presence is cost efficient.

Discussing the changes in the newspaper industry attributable to computers, Robert Lockwood of NewsGraphics concluded,

> If we separate the technological changes from the content changes, the biggest changes are in technology with the introduction of computers and now computers for graphics—especially the trend toward smaller computers, with increased speed and power. They might give us front end systems that will help us integrate the various departments into some sort of rational system that can produce better newspapers.

Terry Schwadron, executive news editor/metro of the Los Angeles *Times,* says that the computer "has changed editing." As Schwadron explained,

> It has made the process a lot more cumbersome in some ways. The electronics of editing have changed the demands on copy editors. We used to work with paper. Then changes were made where somebody typed it in. Now what you release is what you get. As far as the graphics side is concerned, we've learned that computers can set black and white rules and white space. We have, to varying degrees, tried to use the computer to try to generate some of those kinds of materials. We can control the information [better, speaking in terms of content].

As a result of the changeover to computer use, rooms with low light levels and design desks are becoming standard work stations for reporters. All of this is done for consistency, speed and cost savings. Because changes are still constantly being made and happening so quickly, by the time new printing equipment has been installed and personnel have been trained to use it, it is no longer the most up-to-date instrument available.

COMPUTER-INITIATED TEXT

A 1985 article in *Editor & Publisher* said that computers were rapidly replacing graphic artists' mechanical tools. The article referred to a Society of Newspaper

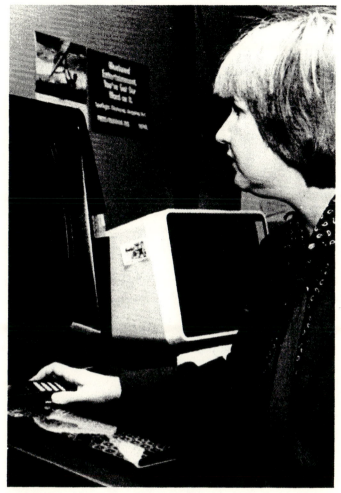

Ann Bailie of the Long Beach, Calif. *Press-Telegram* works at a pagination-system page makeup station. Photo by Troy Maben. Reprinted by permission.

Design survey conducted by David Gray of the Providence, R.I. *Journal-Bulletin*. "The survey found that computers, typesetters and dot matrix printers are rapidly replacing mechanical pencils, compasses and T-squares as a newspaper graphic artist's tools of the trade." Gray's findings were that nearly 40 percent of the 174 newspapers in the survey said they "prepare graphics using their editorial system and typesetter or a stand-alone or micro-computer."

The transformation to computers means that newsroom editors can now be virtually in complete control of reporters and the TPC page design. In addition, at-deadline or late-breaking news can be easily accommodated by the system. The biggest changes to come to the newsroom have to do with extended and multiple deadlines, according to Bill Hodge, a designer with the *Press-Telegram* in Long Beach, Calif. Hodge spoke at the 1987 mid-winter faculty meeting of the Journalism Association of Community Colleges, held in Morro Bay, Calif. "You can chase stories up to deadline, plus these systems can roll back deadlines," Hodge said. Also, editors have "the ability to electronically change a story in 30 seconds—the time it takes to move a file from front end system to pagination system"—and "since you can chase a story like that, you can obviously fix copy errors as well."

The ability to correct errors or otherwise change stories while typesetting the page is quickly becoming commonplace, as is the ability to create detailed copy-fitting and wraparounds for special graphics effects. Schedules can also be altered to increase the time available for more thoroughly editing a particular story.

Hodge predicted that the editing process will have a greater impact as more newspapers become part of the computer age. Some departments within a paper's overall staff "will gather new people and some will lose, but there are lots of changes ahead for the structure of papers."

William Lemmer, the graphics director at United Press International (UPI), believes the impact computers will have on newspaper graphics "can only have a positive effect." Lemmer added,

> The television news industry pioneered the field, and essentially footed the R&D [research and development] bills. Now, newspapers can reap the rewards. A whole new world of image control opens up, and the dynamics of informational graphics evolve to the next higher form. Even mundane locator maps, charts and graphs rise to dimensions previously reserved for editorial feature art. Feature art becomes stunning. And it's all there on a daily basis.

As for conventional graphics people who complain that computers will replace artists, Lemmer said,

> Basically, I'd say they're insecure with their own abilities in mastering the new medium. Rather than replacing staff, the impact in my department has been an increase in staff. Artists who have no working knowledge of digital graphic production fail to realize that these systems are nothing more than electronic drawing boards. You work faster and work better. The systems do nothing by themselves. Also, page composition systems . . . throw people off in their assessments. Production artists are seen being laid off by automatic composition, true. Informational, or editorial graphics, produced on higher-end systems, is another science entirely. The real impact is going to be in the traditional progression from production artist to editorial status. The process will have to be revised.

Hodge thinks that specialization will continue in some areas:

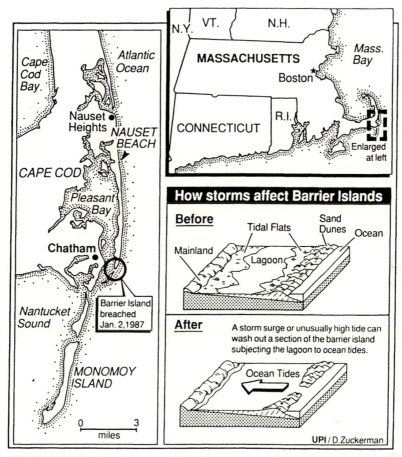

ADVANCE WEEKEND JULY 18-19 OR THEREAFTER WITH "BC-SCI-BREAKTHROUGH"
BY ELIZABETH RICCI
WAP071403-7/18/87-CHATHAM,MASS.: Residents of Cape Cod's most easterly
point, who watched the Atlantic's fury sever a protective finger of land
fear the ocean's ferocious force may also soon savage their homes and
businesses.   UPI   sp/Zuckerman

This UPI map, with its visual reference, gives the reader more information than the story alone provided. Reprinted by permission.

- Copy editors will have more time to check spelling, syntax and facts.
- Design editors will lay out the pages, determining typefaces and column widths; they will make sure that the whole page worth of headlines, pictures and copy is designed for the reader.
- News editors will have more time to follow the wires.

As the typical day's production process evolves, Hodge said, "While I look over the news editor's shoulder, he is looking over mine."

"Bits," "bytes," and "megabytes" (Mbytes) of memory or output are terms that are important to people in business, industry, and newspaper front offices and purchasing departments—as well as to people shopping around for home computers. Most reporters, however, are not especially impressed with these and other words and terms of the computerese vocabulary. For them, the computer is simply a method—word processing—and a machine that can transmit copy from news source to editor and eventually to newspaper page. From the reporters' standpoint, the name of the software disk program may be as unimportant as whether the system includes an option for either hyphenated or nonhyphenated lines, or whether it counts lines for the purposes of story measurement.

The system should not be so complicated that the reporter must be "smarter than the machine" to operate it. Also, the computer must be dependable enough not to "go down" (lose all power) while a story is being "filed" (written) or sent to an editor across the room or across the nation. Reporters and news organizations need a machine that features high resolution viewing, on a monitor that can be tilted to avoid glare. When a reporter must face the pressure of filing stories into a monitor that is hard to look at because of a weak display image, this can quickly lead to eye fatigue, other health problems and eventually job burnout.

Success is sure to follow when a newspaper organization exercises enough sense to purchase machines that have simple commands—in English—so that text copy can be easily entered. Also a sufficient amount of time must be allowed for editors and reporters to learn the meaning and correct execution of terms like "delete," "insert," "replace," "search" and a few other commands. The machine does not have to become the enemy; it can be a friendly extension of the reporter's writing and the editor's production process.

Some newspapers have computers with a traditional typewriter keyboard of approximately 7 inches by 19 inches and a small rectangular cursor location indicator on the VDT's monitor or screen. Other systems have a "mouse"—a hand-held, plastic-covered plotting or drawing instrument (usually 2 inches by 3 inches in size) that is activated electronically. The click of a button on the mouse directs a pointer on the monitor. For both the keyboard/monitor-cursor and the mouse-clicker/pointer methods, it is possible—depending on the system's sophistication—for the reporter or editor to call up, view, edit and position a story, graphic or whole page, as well as to delete parts. It is also possible to pass the story, graphic or page to a hard-copy proof or to the plate from which the newspaper will be published.

In its simplest VDT form, the computer serves as a device for single-item input (entry), but its screen can also serve as the monitor for typesetting or "desktop publishing." Once the reporter or editor has learned how to "boot up" (activate) the manufacturer's formatted disk so it will accept commands, he or she can store advertisements, halftone photos, line art, text and whatever else the user has entered. When needed, the stored materials can be accessed

The mouse is used on a page-makeup-station tablet at the Long Beach, Calif., *Press-Telegram;* each square provides a makeup design function. Photo by Troy Maben. Reprinted by permission.

via the names assigned to these files on the disk directory or "menu." Ease in file management is improved by using an entry method that records a rigid, encyclopedic listing of disk contents.

Hodge at the *Press-Telegram* pointed out that, in the ever-changing world of computer systems, there is a constant search for opportunities to make them more valuable.

> It's exciting trying to make these new systems work, yet very frustrating. When the system crashes, or I can't execute a function and I'm right on deadline, it's hard to remember how fun it is; yet streamlining and improving the system has its joys.
>
> The real challenge is better utilization of computers. The problems they present in the newsroom will be the opportunities for new systems and solutions to our everyday problem. The computer will provide the catalyst for change.

The computer offers its user the opportunity to check story length, either by watching a pica or inch indicator on the monitor or by vertically scrolling through the text. The story may be set as wide as 70 picas and to various pica depths, depending on the system; it may be cross-referenced for quick retrieval by the reporter or editor if it is to run with a graphic element. Another computer aid to publishing is that many text input systems have a compatible dictionary program for checking word meanings and spelling.

After a story has been keyboarded, edited and stored on a text disk by the reporter, the layout or systems editor can retrieve the story for measuring and assigning—that is, placing it on a page. The story may be too long or too short and need a little or a lot of editing; it may have to be merged with another story. The computer makes it easy to transfer the text to the original or another reporter for editing if necessary. The editing process itself is one of transposing copy blocks and letters, words, sentences or paragraphs, or of reformatting in a different column width or a different type family or font. The tasks once done by composing room personnel and now done by desk editors also eliminate one additional step: that of proofreading the hard-copy page.

COMPUTER-INITIATED GRAPHICS AND PAGE DESIGN

In addition to their heavy use as text input devices, computers have also become valuable in graphic design. The monitor's screen is white, and the images generally appear in black. Using a mouse clicker to point to various windows located around the edge of the monitor, the user is able to select digitized graphic elements. These windows contain pictures of objects as well as rule lines and type from 5 points to 144 points (wider ranges than the old 6 points to 84 points) in bold, italic, roman, serif and sans serif—with style characteristics similar to actual hard type.

One graphics editor who sings the virtues of desktop publishing is David L. Riley of the *Kentucky New Era* in Hopkinsville, who spoke at the Southern Newspaper Publishers Association (SNPA) editorial clinic in 1985. Riley said, "Since desktop computers infiltrated the news and composing rooms, few people could argue with the accuracy or the speed with which simple graphs could be produced."

But having the computers available was not enough in itself, Riley added.

> The finesse and sophistication of the finished product was at issue
> and even if one was satisfied with the pie or bar chart produced,
> substantial backshop time often was involved in bordering, screening
> and resetting type in the final illustration so it would blend with the
> rest of the paper's design and style.

Editorial artist Matt Moody reported in the summer of 1987 that the Los Angeles *Times* had "just, in the last few months, actually gotten into computer graphics where the entire chart is done on the computer." Previously, artists at the *Times* plotted everything by hand, or—if someone did manage to work up a chart of information on the computer itself—the computer format would be used along with an artist's plot marks and the newspaper's type.

But we are just now developing and evaluating the different software programs. We have not really decided how to go on this. We've determined there isn't that much difference in time to make the graphic. You could do it on a board with your pen, or you can do it on a machine.

Moody did predict, however, that money could be saved by using the computer for graphics.

The big savings and where this thing will probably work out best is if there are going to have to be any changes made. With the computer, all you have to do is go in and punch the new numbers, and just print it out again. If you are doing it by hand, you have to redraw it, so you are doing it twice. So, as far as doing it, it is a time-saver when you have to make any changes.

Charts, statistical graphics and original illustrations can be created by "drawing" on the screen with the mouse clicker. Riley prefers to develop the graph in as large a size as possible to incorporate greater detail, make it easier to work with and minimize the dot matrix pattern.

Once the graphic is printed, Riley has "it reduced to the desired column width either through a PMT [photomechanical transfer] or a reducing photocopier. However, it is easy enough to have it emerge from the printer in the exact size required."

The mouse clicker can also be used to crop, move, rotate and scale the graphics and type to complement the text length and width on a TPC page. As Riley says,

Spreadsheet or accounting programs—in the right hands—can keep tabs on expenses and department budgets. A number of solid, proven programs can be used for word processing applications that can include spell-checking and an outstanding variety of type fonts, sizes, justification, et cetera. One 3½-inch disk can accommodate as many as 50 typewritten pages.

The ways in which computer-aided text, graphics and design might be integrated to enhance the story and better tell it to the reader are limited only by the reporter's and the editor's imaginations. Riley asked these questions of his SNPA audience:

Do you need sunrises, sunsets, times of tides or moonrises calculated? Do you need Fahrenheit converted to Celsius? What about hectares changed to square miles or quarts converted to milliliters? None of those [computer] applications require exceptional knowledge or experience.

M. Bruce Garrison, in a computer impact study published in *Newspaper Research Journal* (1983), wrote that "Graphics capabilities of a microcomputer help reporters to understand complex statistics and reports."

When Bruns at the Los Angeles *Times* was asked whether he is comfortable with computer-generated graphics, he answered, "No, not really. I don't think that the computer graphics are up to our standards yet. I think they are rather crude for the most part. Also, their typography is not our typography." However, Bruns thinks that there are some advantages to computer graphics. "We can plot charts easily and quickly, and then from that we can redraw it in our own style. I think eventually, perhaps years down the line, it will work well for a lot of things."

Moody agrees with Bruns about computer graphics at their paper. Moody said, "The problem is, we have our own typefaces. The Univers that we use on all of our graphics was drawn by a typographer. We took the standard Univers and gave it to a typographer. He redrew each letter." The computer system at the *Times* does not have a Univers typeface; and even if it did, it would not be the one developed for the paper. "So," Moody said, "in a sense, it's only taken us half way [that is, the computer has]. Right now, this redesign we did when we redid the type sort of backed us into a corner. The *Times* wanted to do this redrawing with the typeface, and it's the way the *Times* works, so they're going to have to do something else to let the computers work for us in graphics."

As a metro editor, Schwadron has seen how the desire to do more graphics because of computers has evolved. Schwadron says, "I think people working at the L.A. *Times,* as well as those who are working at every other paper, are increasingly aware that the world is open to visual representation. The information can be translated to a visual form." The result is a greater visual presentation throughout the industry. "That has nothing to do with computers," Schwadron explains. "What has to do with computers is the question of whether the ease and the efficiency of finding out about those things is any different."

The metro editor then cited a story in which police shootings were being compared.

> The reporter was offering information, or had uncovered information, about police shootings. The question was how to compare them. Do you compare raw numbers, raw shootings? Do you factor them by population or number of police officers or by number of guns registered? How do you factor these kinds; how do you look at them? The question always was, always is and always will be one of content, not one of how you produce this.

Schwadron made this suggestion to solve the problem: "If you don't like looking at the information this way, let's push a button and look at it this [other] way." Computer programs that allow this kind of re-sorting are quite useful, or should become useful to reporters as well as to the people who are actually producing the graphic. It should be part and parcel of the research that they are able to do. They're only able to do it then if they understand the use, the functionality of graphics in that sense.

The virtual limitlessness of a computer's ability in assisting the newspaper to read better and look better were stressed by Riley of the *Kentucky New Era* when he said that, if users develop a

combination of line weight, background pattern, border and title typeface that is particularly attractive and in line with their newspaper's design and format, that configuration can be saved and recalled for any future graph and with only changes in data and axis values, that appearance will be uniform until it is changed.

Don Clement, staff cartographer with the Los Angeles *Times,* said,

A lot of technology isn't even that capable yet. Computer work is okay for some things, but certainly is not the answer in all cases. If you can't do it at your desk, you can't do it on a machine. I think a lot of people forget that. You get computers and say, "Gee, it does graphics, we have a program here or several programs." But it doesn't do graphics if you can't do it at your desk with pen and ink.

Martin Crutsinger, a newsman at the Associated Press (AP) bureau in Washington, D.C., wrote in *AP Log* (1987) that "there's no doubt" graphics can "help sell a story." Discussing how reporters and graphic artists work together, Crutsinger related an experience from his beat at the U.S. Treasury Department. He had "grappled for a way to explain a complicated government report on foreign trade so the reader would know it tracks not only merchandise transactions, but also trade in services and a miscellaneous category that includes foreign aid." In the end, Lynn Occhiuzzo, an AP lasergraphics artist, created a graphic for a story about a government report, breaking out each of the trade opponents so that "readers could tell at-a-glance how the United States is faring under this broadest of trade measures."

According to Crutsinger's account of how this came about, he had been disappointed with the Commerce Department's "Current Account Trade Report," which he described as "an arcane set of numbers" used infrequently by AP-member media. After the graphic was created to accompany the report, 15 member newspapers—checked on a regular basis—were all using the report. "Given such a demonstration, I was already a believer when I visited the newly expanded Graphics department in New York." Crutsinger had expected to see artists working at drawing boards with pen and ink, and instead was surprised

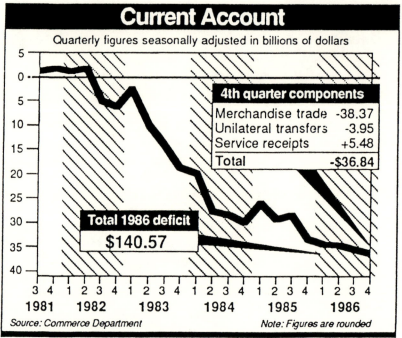

Current Account

Quarterly figures seasonally adjusted in billions of dollars

4th quarter components

Merchandise trade	-38.37
Unilateral transfers	-3.95
Service receipts	+5.48
Total	-$36.84

Total 1986 deficit

$140.57

3 4 | 1 2 3 4 | 1 2 3 4 | 1 2 3 4 | 1 2 3 4 | 1 2 3 4
1981 1982 1983 1984 1985 1986

Source: Commerce Department   *Note: Figures are rounded*

AP/ Lynn Occhiuzzo

How the United States was faring under the broadest of trade measures is illustrated
in this Associated Press fever graph. Lynn Occhiuzzo, "Current Account," *AP Log*
(April 13, 1987):1. Reprinted with permission.

to find informational graphic charts being quickly put together under the supervision of Don DeMaio, the AP director of graphics.

"On that day," Crutsinger wrote, "the artists were completing illustrations
on the efforts to right the capsized ferry Herald of Free Enterprise, the inner
workings of a turtle trap used by Gulf Coast fishermen and locations of ancient
Mayan ruins in Central America." Members of the AP art staff were also busy
preparing the NCAA (National Collegiate Athletic Association) basketball pair-
ings, stock market charts, graphs on personal income and spending figures released by Washington. In all, 14 charts, maps and illustrations were being
completed in addition to regular work.

"All the technological advances mean better graphics," Crutsinger concluded.
"And as a writer, I know that better graphics help make the story make sense."

With the "old" process in which only copy was entered into the computer,
line art was sent to a process camera, and photos were made into halftone dot
patterns on Velox paper at 85-line to 133-line screens for newspapers and 120-
line to 150-line screens for magazine reproduction. However, the new desktop
publishing computers use a direct digital scanning process for both line art and
photos.

According to Hodge of the *Press Telegram* in Long Beach, electronic wizardry now gives to news media "a new opportunity to redefine the backbone of journalism." Furthermore, "With digital manipulation/enhancement, we can literally move mountains, but we must never do it." Hodge was alluding to the ethics of altering photos. "It's an opportunity to look at any manipulation of pictures and judge that manipulation by today's standards, not [Civil War photographer] Matthew Brady's." Hodge explained that, for the past 100 years, photographers have been able to burn in parts of a photo, dodge out other parts and chemically enhance still others without any thought to ethics. "Historically it has been okay to do this," he said. In fact, the two techniques of burning in and dodging out present different ethical considerations. The former brings out what is already there; the latter holds back undesirable content. "Now, we can take a fresh look at manipulating practices with the coming of digital pictures," says Hodge.

In addition to halftones, the special effects such as grid patterns, gray shading—at any percentage of black—and reverse type on black can also be run through the scanning process. The design or systems editor can use the computer to indicate a mortice notch on or an inset within a photo or other piece of art. While computer-aided graphics are indeed expedient and cost efficient, they do have their limitations: Page editors can not enlarge or reduce a photograph once it has been made into a halftone dot pattern without distorting the photo—because the dots will also be enlarged or reduced. Rescanning a photo leaves a double dot pattern, also known as the "screen door effect."

Like the rest of the desktop publishing process, laser printers became state of the art in 1987 when companies began manufacturing machines that would print 300 dots per inch. In addition to printing pages in sizes from 8½ inches by 11 inches to 15 inches by 22 inches, laser printers can also put out reduced-size pages that are suitable for use in evaluating design, and proof sheets for checking page spreads of special standard-broadsheet and tabloid-format sections.

Referring to all the changes in today's newspapers, Ron Patel of the Philadelphia *Inquirer* viewed the evolution from hot metal type to cold paper type as a simple matter of progress. Patel went on:

> It is little wonder, then, that newspapers today look much better than the newspapers of my initial experience. It is little wonder, too, that so much of newspaper design has been turned over to artists, rather than editors, since it is possible now to craft pages as opposed to grinding them out.
>
> At the *Inquirer,* at least, the major editors' role continues to be that of overseer, much as we watched over layout editors in the past. But I have heard of revisionist thinking on that score at smaller papers where artists have overwhelmed editors.

At these newspapers, news judgment—not design—must prevail if what Patel suggests can happen is to be avoided. "The last step in this logical path is one of reconstitution of the Benjamin Franklin form of journalism," Patel said. The changes from full editorial control to printer control and back to editorial control has made printers out of journalists, as was the case 200 years ago.

> Since so much of typography and composition is now within the hands of editors, working through computers, we have truly little difference from Franklin in principle. He wrote the story, set the type and locked up the pages. Someone else pulled the press.
>
> We write the stories, set the type and deliver the pages out of a pagination system. Someone else turns the press. And the best layout editors are those who understand the full process, much as Franklin's worth to his readers was as an accurate typesetter as well as a writer.

Charles Brumback, the president of the Chicago *Tribune*, appreciates the changes that have led to the computer age and—like Patel—sees current uses of the computer as being only on the forefront of technological development. Brumback addressed the issue of pagination when he spoke to the Inland Daily Press Association in 1985. "The technology explosion will continue to accelerate," Brumback said. "Pagination will become a reality within five years. Direct to plate systems will be perfected soon. Computer to press systems will follow."

Underlying the full circle of change that has emerged in printing and graphic control, there must be guidelines governing page design. If the newspaper itself is not to become an art form, its editors must have power over the artists in judging where the most graphic weight should be applied.

PAGINATION

With desktop publishing, all or parts of a page may be set in type, edited and integrated with graphics for processing on a laser printer. This process of computerized typesetting page makeup is called "pagination." Parts are brought together on the monitor screen and printed on 8½-inch by 11-inch sheets of paper. This size works well for a magazine or other publication that fits this format. For other sizes, these parts may be joined together by literally pasting the formatted columns of side-by-side type onto the newspaper makeup page.

The tabloid 11-inch by 14-inch page or standard broadsheet 14-inch by 22-inch page may also be composed with a full pagination computer to plate process. According to the 1983 computer impact study by Garrison,

> A select number of newspapers are experimenting with full-page pagination, including graphics, in addition to AP Knight-Ridder, for example, placed the full pagination system, with graphics, at its Pasadena newspaper. Operators view and compose whole pages of halftones, line art and type.

Debbie Arrington pulls a full-size broadsheet newspaper page from the pagination developing unit at the Pasadena, Calif. *Star-News*. Photo by Troy Maben. Reprinted by permission.

Garrison predicted that more papers would begin adopting the pagination concept after 1983—which would also mark "the year when the traditional composing room begins to disappear."

All selections and positions are made by an editor who is at the "front end" of the process. Maurice J. Buchart Jr., manager of the Courier-Journal & Louisville (Ky.) Times Co., has defined the "front end system" as a "network of computers, video display terminals, hard-copy printers and CRT typesetters." Buchart discussed editorial quality and computer systems in 1985 before the Federation International des Editeurs de Journaux (FIEJ) Management and Market Symposium on Newspapers in Brussels, Belgium.

According to Buchart, the improvements in editorial quality available from new computer systems fall into three categories: content, timeliness and form.

- Referring to **content,** Buchart said, "The quality of content in local news stories is primarily a function of how well the writers and copy editors perform their duties. These duties are made much easier by the use of video display terminals and sophisticated computer systems."

Compilation and organization of notes is easier using a visual display terminal. "That leads to more story outlining, which improves the structure of the story; story structure is also improved because it's much easier for the writer or editor to reorganize the contents."

Another aspect of content, Buchart said, is accuracy. "We no longer create errors by re-keyboarding the story in the composing room." Stories are also checked with a computer program for spelling—against a stored dictionary of 80,000 words.

- According to Buchart, the next point of vital consideration is **timeliness.** This "in a newspaper is a function of how rapidly you can collect information, massage it and produce it. I think it's fair to say that front-end systems have led to significant improvements in each of those areas."

Timeliness has had its largest impact on wire news service stories. "By the use of special codes that precede each story, they are automatically routed into subject-related queues in the computer. That makes it much easier for the wire editor to sort through incoming material."

- Last in order of importance is **form,** Buchart said. "We have tripled or quadrupled the editor's selection of typefaces, compared to the old days of lead type. And we offer an almost infinite range of type sizes. In fact, we now have such tremendous typographic flexibility that we are in danger of overusing it."

Another advocate of electronic pagination is William L. Winter, director of the American Press Institute in Reston, Va., and former executive editor of the *Star-News* in Pasadena, Calif. Winter puts it this way:

In many newspapers, and particularly the smaller ones, two reactions will characterize the moment when the decision is made to seriously investigate page pagination:

- The production director will experience orgasmic joy at the prospect not only of having a remarkable new toy to manipulate, but also of having the opportunity to permanently endear himself to the publisher by saying, "we're going to eliminate *all* these jobs in the backshop."
- The publisher will rollick in orgasmic delight at the positive impact this diminution of the payroll will have on the bottom line.

While these are not "unnatural reactions," it is not likely that they will bode well for the staff in the newsroom. Winter said,

The editor who's observing all this has two choices:

The Pasadena, Calif. *Star-News* is an example of a pioneer into the fully paginated newspaper; this issue is more dramatic than some because it chronicles the annual Rose Bowl Parade. Reprinted by permission.

- Sit quietly, not daring to diminish the glee of the aforesaid production director and publisher.
- Make a strong case for the notion that you can't eliminate *all* the backshop positions, but rather that some of those slots must move to the newsroom if editorial pagination is to be a boon rather than a burden (emphasis in original).

On balance, "The editor's job is to make it understood that what's happening here is not the elimination of work functions, but rather the mere *shifting* of duties" (emphasis in original).

Editor-driven decisions steer the "back end" production system. The layout or systems editor designs the pages on the computer monitor, then the full pages are sent to a laser printer to produce a photo negative for the final plate. Winter points out that, with pagination, pasteup will continue, but a page makeup station will assume this function—rather than page materials being sent to a backshop table. "You'll still be doing trims, making fixes, sending out chases, but on a tube, not on the table," Winter said.

> The news editor who now dummies a page in 10 minutes and whips it out to the backshop, then turns to the editing of copy, suddenly finds himself or herself locked to a page makeup station for the hour it will take to construct and polish the page. That process can be a joy, given the right number of people. Absent that number, the production function takes over and the word-editing function is minimized.

Whether only a partial page or the whole tabloid or broadsheet page is being produced on the pagination equipment, the page appears electronically on the monitor in the form of a template with an embedded grid of lines representing the columns. The grid will not become part of the final page when it is "shot" (photographed). Also available for the page are nameplates or flags for page one, page-top headings along with boxes or standing heads used on those pages, and formats for quoteouts, readouts, bylines, continued lines and cutlines.

The stories and art, rule lines, photos and other graphic elements are chosen from directories or menus. Comic strips, stock reports and television program listings are easily changed daily: The old element is quickly deleted and the new one is dropped into the appropriate columns. Using electronics instead of pencils, reporters write and file stories; and page editors edit them, write headlines and assign stories and art—when art is to accompany a story—to their respective pages. Artistic illustrations, photographs and informational graphics are also assigned to the appropriate newsroom people and then later sent electronically to layout editors for dummying onto pages in the various sections.

Buchart at the *Courier-Journal* & Louisville (Ky.) *Times* claims that newspapers produced through the pagination system have the potential to look better. "A good pagination system will offer much more latitude for creativity," Buchart said. "It will be easy for an editor to move items around on a page, and to experiment with different designs." The editor can review and edit groups of pages and see what is on them and how the design looks. "With full-page output from the typesetter, we should see an end to composing room pasteup mistakes, such as slanted columns of type, overlapping elements, misplaced headlines, et cetera."

Page text and graphics can be accessed by the systems editor from the files of the story-input and makeup terminals, and moved to the page columns on the monitor display screen. How the text and graphics mesh is instantly visible to the editor: If a story is too long, then part of it can be cut or jumped to another page; if the art is too small or too large, then it can be altered to fit (except in the case of halftones, which—because of the dot pattern—can only be cropped to smaller depths or columns widths, but not enlarged since the dots would also be enlarged).

When indicated, reverse typography or a surprint can be included through a merging process either when the text or graphics are being filed or when they are on the makeup terminal. And with the computer-to-plate pagination system, prescreened photos are put into place on the page just like any other graphic or text element. Editors can be in control throughout the process and are able to make insertions along the way—still proofing the whole page on deadline: but with a minimum of the usual pressure when changes are needed.

Some editors feel "ambushed" by pagination, according to 1986–87 study results published in *presstime*, the journal of the American Newspaper Publishers Association (ANPA). Preliminary findings in 1986 from the study of 32 U.S. newspapers where pagination equipment was in operation included these observations:

- Editors spend an average of 4½ hours a day on pagination terminals.
- There was less confusion when one person in the newsroom had overall responsibility for the system.
- The introduction of pagination systems has meant that some jobs once considered within the province of the production department are now handled in the newsroom.

After reviewing the 1986 survey during ANPA/TEC (Technical Exposition and Conference) '87 at Las Vegas, *presstime* reported that the pagination system's moving of some tasks from the production department to the news department "has led to tension between workers in the two departments." This point was made at the convention's workshop called "Coping with Pagination and New Technology."

In 1983, Garrison's study predicted that experimentation in pagination would continue to focus on digitization of graphics. "As more newspapers computerize their newsrooms, they will continue to consider means by which the news, as well as reporters' notes, memos and other nonpublished materials in electronic form can be preserved indefinitely for later reference," Garrison said.

Communication systems must keep pace with electronic advancements. For instance, reporters must be able to access the materials that they place in the computer terminals; editors and management people need to become comfortable with the proliferation of new machines; and composing room personnel need to be brought into the mainstream of the newspaper plant's operation.

Laura Schwed, assistant managing editor/graphics at Westchester Rockland Newspapers in White Plains, spoke to the ANPA/TEC '87 audience on the topic of enhanced communication. Paraphrasing her speech the *presstime* article on pagination said: "In order for pagination technology to function properly, editorial people must become more technically oriented, and production personnel must learn more about how the newsroom operates."

MECHANICAL COMPATIBILITY

As the use of computers increases and includes pagination software throughout the newspaper industry, mechanical compatibility becomes ever more important. When a newspaper is operating the best hardware at the most favorable price it has made a successful match in the "computer game." Computers must be intercommunicative so that the editor can merge the story-input/editing terminal's files with the page-composition terminal's files. Communication between computers—or compatible networking—is achieved through an interface process. By transferring the formatting commands through filters or interrogators in the machines, an automatic response is set off between them; and an electronic bridge or converter then transfers text and graphics from one system to another, or within the same system.

The advent of the computer in the newsroom has also meant that the one-time-peripheral telephone modems are now as important as the computer disk drive and the laser printer. With the modem, story and photo assignments can be sent to bureaus in outlying areas, and stories and photos then sent back to the newsroom in the city of publication.

An abundant array of hardware and an even greater array of software exist from which the computer user may select. Buchart at the *Courier-Journal & Louisville (Ky.) Times* —referring to the recent changes and availability of equipment—concluded, "So, just as we were in the early 1970s, we are on the threshold of massive change in the technology used to produce our newspapers." There are other similarities to that time period, said Buchart:

> The technology will be very costly and difficult to implement. There will be resistance to this change, and a steep learning curve for the users. But in the final analysis, we cannot ignore the benefits to be gained: a better product at a lower cost.

C. Morgan Brassell, project development manager at the Los Angeles *Times,* has expressed his concern over the personal computer's performance and proliferation, according to *presstime*'s review of the ANPA/TEC '87 convention. "The established newspaper system vendors are under siege," Brassell said. "They must broaden their vision. They cannot continue to ignore new developments in the PC world. Technology and competition from PC developments will force them to provide us better systems."

For the computer to be an effective and creative tool of communication, it must be simple to learn and easy to operate. It must increase the speed of production to the point that there is more time available for ideas and the enhancement of the newspaper, and less emphasis on mechanical procedures and routine tasks. Roger Fidler, director of graphics at Knight-Ridder Newspapers, called for more human considerations when he spoke during the ANPA/ TEC '87 convention. According to *presstime,* Fidler said, "We must not forget that computers, no matter how powerful, are only as creative and skilled as the people who use them."

For all their good reasons to be part of the newspaper industry, computers must be cost effective, saving time and energy without impairing the accuracy and credibility of the publication, and without jamming up schedules for the trucks that deliver the paper to carrier and newsstand locations. In newspaper plants where the new procedures can be successfully implemented, computers will facilitate a positive end product of the TPC design effort, with rewards felt by all who earn their livelihood at the publication.

15   Redesign

Constant evolution is better than revolution. Constantly evaluate how
your paper looks and make small changes to improve its readability.
This is easier on staff and readers than a major redesign every so
often.

Tony Majeri
creative director
Chicago *Tribune*
(Quoted from a report of the Feb. 3–6, 1985
SNPA Foundation seminar)

A newspaper need not be in a state of financial disaster for the publication to
be redesigned. In fact, the success of redesign is likely to be greater if the paper
is in good financial health. The goal of any redesign process must be to create
a better vehicle of communication for the paper's readers. When done with care,
the redesign process and the final product can also rejuvenate the advertising
and news departments as they see how their work might be better displayed.
Additionally, the change can bring a general good feeling to all the other departments as the community responds positively to the striking new look of its
Total Page Concept (TPC) newspaper.

REDESIGN AS CHANGE

A newspaper's readers are accustomed to periodic and even seasonal changes
in magazines, movies and television, and in nonpublication areas such as automobiles, buildings and fashion—where designs are in a constant state of change.
Because of this, redesign will not overwhelm the newspaper's recipients; they
have come to expect change. To keep up with the world, the design of newspapers
as a vehicle of communication has got to change now and then.

While appraising a publication for redesign, the designer should have access to professional market research to understand what the paper is trying to do and for whom it is being published. This involves comprehending the function of each design element and reviewing the news/graphics staff's attitudes, job assignments and skills as well as the potential of all the plant's personnel—including those in support roles—to carry out the redesign process. Accompanying this should be a thorough evaluation of the equipment that produces all aspects of the news product and a study of readership demographics/psychographics. The equipment appraisal is necessary because of the constant changes in technology, if for no other reason.

REDESIGN CONSULTANTS

While it is possible for a newspaper to do its own redesign, an experienced outside consultant can often be a valuable source of information on redesign and readership. When looking for an outside group to assist in the redesign, several questions must be dealt with, including how to find the best consultant at an affordable price and how much time that consultant will spend evaluating the newspaper product and the sociological makeup and expectations of the community. Most good consultants are known to the state newspaper-publishers association. However, a name, an address and a fancy brochure do not make a good consultant. Editors should call around to other newspapers that have dealt with the consultant's organization.

Some groups that work on redesign are owned and operated by one or two individuals, who do all the research and work with the client newspapers. Others are larger and have several consultants working for the group. Management personnel at the newspaper considering the redesign should know whether they are getting the chief consultant or someone hired by the consultant organization. Also important is the personality, experience and working relationship that the consultant has had with past clients. When the redesign has been completed—and the consultant paid in full—the newspaper editors must be able to take over the design process and know what they are doing.

Whether the redesign is done with a consultant's help or by the newspaper's editors, among the matters at issue must be the community's needs and the newspaper structure, including which will implement the new design and the process of change itself.

APPRAISAL OF THE COMMUNITY

A review of community needs will provide direction to the editors as they establish page or section subject areas—such as agriculture, business, living or lifestyle, people, potpourri, sports, travel, weather and others. Readership interest—based on surveys before and/or after a redesign—should determine which subject headings to use and the depth of coverage to provide in these areas.

There is a possessive quality that undergirds most newspapers. Some readers have a love affair—or a love/hate relationship—with "their newspaper." A reader's relationship with the paper is almost a brand identity for those who have grown up in the city or town, and is part of the identity formation of those who have lived there long enough to call it home. If the paper is now called the *"Star Gazette"* but at one time the papers were separate as the *"Star"* and the *"Gazette"* and—before that—the *"Star"* bought out the *"Herald,"* then some readers who have lived through all of these changes might still refer to the area's newspaper as the *"Herald"* even though that publication has not been around for 30 or 40 years.

Editors must listen to the paper's readership and know the community's needs if redesign is to be seen by readers as something more than a mere rearrangement of news and feature columns. Lisa Vanco served as a redesign consultant at the *News Chronicle* in Thousand Oaks, Calif., during the mid–1980s. (Ken Croley was the paper's news liaison with Vanco during the reorganization phase.) When Vanco first asked editor Marvin Sosna what he was expecting of the redesign, Sosna told her that he wanted it to look like Westlake Village, a middle/upper class portion of the circulation area. "If only it could be that simple for every newspaper," Vanco said. "Every community has a personality of its own, the way it looks, the ways it is organized, the way the people are. People have chosen that place to live because they fit in."

Westlake Village was used as the model for the *News Chronicle* because of its distinct style, Vanco explained. "It is a planned community; it is very well organized and the architecture must follow very strict guidelines. And that's the way the paper hopefully comes across as well; well-structured, well-organized and consistent."

Gerald Grotta of Texas Christian University complemented Vanco's philosophy when he spoke to the Southern Newspaper Publishers Association (SNPA) Foundation seminar, "Layout, Design and Graphics." Grotta said,

> The foundation of all layout, design and graphics should be to make it easier for readers to use the newspaper. Newspapers are fairly inexpensive, so readers' biggest expenditures in reading them are time and effort. Anything that can be done to make the paper easier to read will pay off in the long run.

Which groups are being served by circulation of the publication beyond home delivery? Are there groups being left out of the circulation strategy? Are the young and the old as well as those in between—and the social, political and economic needs of the community—being served with information, listings, columns, stories and page sections? Redesigners should look in the phone book, in business directories and at lists of organizations available from the city and county chambers of commerce to discover interest groups that are perhaps being neglected.

Old and new design of the Thousand Oaks, Calif. *News Chronicle* in the mid-1980s shows headline type changed from Bodoni to Oracle. Reprinted by permission.

THE REDESIGNER–PERSONNEL RELATIONSHIP

When Sheila Levrant de Bretteville reviewed the Los Angeles *Times* for possible design modifications in the early 1980s, she began by looking at the design currently in use. Some might call her work on the project "redesign"—but not Ken Bruns, the design director at the *Times* who worked with de Bretteville under the direction of deputy managing editor, John Foley. Bruns said that the term "'refining' is probably the more appropriate word" because "we moved the section headings and stabilized them at the top of the page, and we changed our typography. We didn't change the design of the front page or the basic layout of the paper. We refined the newspaper." Terry Schwadron, the *Times* executive news editor/metro, says that "clearly some aspects of the paper are different; the front page looks different than, say, the sports page. There may be a unity in typeface."

Editorial artist Matt Moody explained that "The *Times* wanted to stay the same, but it wanted to change. It just wanted to make its presentation better, contemporary but not trendy—make it better than it was, but not make it 1980s, because the 1980s are going to pass." Those parts of the paper that needed attention got it, Moody said. But the project did not culminate with a total new look. "They didn't want to throw out everything and start over," he said. "There were too many good things being done already, and there are so many readers [that] it was felt best to just refine what was being done and still have a traditional newspaper look with a contemporary feel to it."

Dugald Stermer interviewed de Bretteville for a *Communication Arts* article

The Los Angeles *Times* redesign style is refined and contemporary, with easy-to-find (and read) contents and changes in headline type/design continuity between the sections and pages. Reprinted by permission.

that appeared in 1982 after the task of appraising headline styles and making suggestions for changes in design had been completed. According to Stermer, de Bretteville said that she "did a needs assessment, meaning that I didn't do anything until I heard from them what it was they wanted. What I heard were such contradictory messages that it became clear to me they weren't sure they wanted anything at all; and that made me proceed very gently. On my own, I researched the history of newspapers, and looked at many of them from all over the world."

As Vanco says,

> As a consultant, you have to realize that each person has his or her own opinion on design. Your client, who will be ultimately executing your design, may have a different sense of aesthetics than you do. Design can, to a certain extent, be subjective. Design can also be objective; it is objective when it is being used to fulfill a specific purpose.

In his story on de Bretteville, Stermer wrote that she was "on her way to designing her 'ideal newspaper.' But she soon stopped, because 'I saw that my idea of a newspaper didn't have a chance of ever getting printed, and I didn't want to get involved in that kind of academic exercise. For the people who were going to actually have to enact that newspaper, it would have been an inappropriate solution.'" De Bretteville also had to confront one other challenge. As Stermer put it: "Nobody's 'ideal newspaper' is going to average 70 percent advertising to 30 percent editorial; that is the highest proportion of advertising to editorial matter in the nation."

The newspaper is an institution with a collection of employees. Therein lies a dilemma faced by the design consultant. Design—especially for the TPC newspaper—is not a slick packaging of stories and large photos, special kinds of typefaces, a certain amount of color and in general an array of things that are beautiful. The newspaper is a vehicle for communicating the news to the community that it serves. Design involves total content, and it is the foundation of the structure that persuades lookers to become readers. It should be nothing more.

James H. Stevenson, assistant managing editor of the *Idaho Statesman* in Boise, was quoted by George Tuck in the *APME News* (1985). Concerning quality content and presentation, Stevenson said, "This argument—of content vs. design—which begins to wear on anyone involved in a newspaper design, is specious. Quality design will not camouflage biased, insipid or incompetent content. Nor is it intended to." Stevenson then added, "There should be no question of 'balancing' content and design," and asked, "Would we weigh good spelling as opposed to good grammar? Do we want our papers to include good reporting or good writing? In all cases, we want and strive for both."

The Boise *Idaho Statesman* provides a clean example of good content and design. Reprinted by permission.

While some of the newspaper's personnel may be initially reluctant to redesign, the barriers are usually broken down if both the planning and execution stages include management and various staff personnel (including designers, editors, photographers and reporters) who will have to live with the changes. For instance, these personnel are the ones to say how the redesign should be introduced—gradually, or all in one issue of the paper.

THE REDESIGN PROCESS

As management sets out to create a new design for its product, it must ask a series of questions. While by no means limited to the following, the list might appropriately include:

- How is the present paper tailored to the local market?
- How is this local market different from any other?
- As to the background experience of the consultant, what has he or she done for what kinds of markets, and what kinds of success can be measured from that work?

USA Today could not have been so influential—given its early quite mixed reviews—if the whole country had not been ready for some changes in its direction. Change is acceptable—and accepted—for most newspapers as long as readers still feel a sense of ownership of the paper that prints the news about them and their special interests.

Design change has a better chance for success if it is accompanied by a review of community needs. Without a community review, the editors redesign without direction. Speaking about the *News Chronicle,* Vanco said that the research aspect of redesign is "the first and most important thing to do." She made two suggestions: "Research readability and research the community that the newspaper will serve." For the *News Chronicle,* Vanco's focus was on "readability and making the look of the paper appealing enough to catch the viewer's eye." In other words, her review looked at the individual reader's interests and those of the community.

Robert Lockwood, the president of NewsGraphics and former art director at the Allentown, Pa. *Morning Call,* agrees that any change in design should be directed at publishing a newspaper that mirrors the needs of the community. Lockwood led the redesign project at the *Morning Call* during the late 1970s; he said that thought was given to "design that would be more appropriate not only for the content, but for the area so that the tone and the look of the paper would accurately reflect the character of the place." The community's population was "rich in diversity" and included farmlands, intercity problems, a large middle class and suburbs. As Lockwood says,

> Also, it was not a formal city, it was a casual place, with a casual pace. Because of that, we used ragged right for the text, which was more informal; it was more accessible and it allowed for other things such as integrating white space neatly into the paper; it had a better setting—you did not get awkward jumps and hyphens where you didn't want them and legibility was improved. Finally, it gave us that freer look we were after.

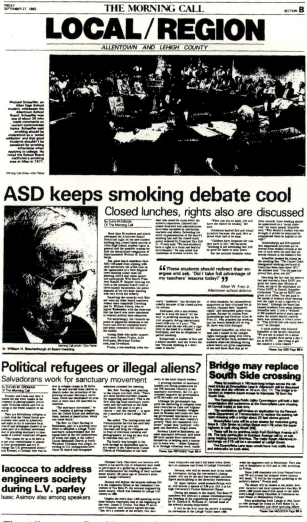

The Allentown, Pa. *Morning Call* is casual in design, and its stories and all other typography are set ragged right. Reprinted by permission of Call-Chronicle Newspapers, Inc.

For Vanco, the next step was to apply what she had learned through readability research to the *News Chronicle* redesign. She believes that newspapers should "emulate the community they serve." During the time of her redesign project, Vanco was living in the circulation area of the newspaper. In addition to her own familiarity as a resident, she interviewed each of the section editors to get a feel for their readers. "The newspaper staff [members] knew their community very well," she said. "Most of them are out talking to people on a day-to-day basis; and, of course, [editor] Marvin Sosna had a clear idea of the types of changes he wanted to see in the newspaper."

In another instance of design change, the *Press Democrat* in Santa Rosa, Calif.—owned by the New York Times Co.—was redesigned in the mid–1980s, bringing a major revision to the look of the newspaper. Guiding the redesign was Louis Silverstein, the former New York *Times* assistant managing editor and corporate director and presently consultant to the Times Co. Handling the on-site redesign work in Santa Rosa were George Delmerico and Randy Wright. Silverstein says that "the redesign started with, and included examination, improvement and additions in virtually every area of content."

Other than a different appearance, the redesign provides the *Press Democrat* reader—Silverstein said—with "many more features, more news coverage—by specific design, not in any vague way—a much greater variety in how news is treated—greater editorial focus—more coverage in specific 'themed' sections, more business coverage, a more predictable, structured and easy-to-use configuration." All of this comes "in addition to the general pleasure readers in the community expressed in having 'their' newspaper a contemporary, vital organ."

Delmerico—now creative director at the Santa Barbara (Calif.) *Independent*—said that one of the highlights of his career as a newspaper designer was his participation in Silverstein's redesign of the *Press Democrat* during 1985–86. Delmerico says that he "certainly learned—or is it relearned?—a great deal. Lou Silverstein is America's premier newspaper designer, and the godfather, as it were, of us all."

Silverstein "reached into his arsenal of graphic ideas and came up with a beautiful, yet functional array of typestyles," according to Delmerico. It was "an innovative approach to the front page, and countless other devices that expand on the section-front idea he pioneered and developed for the New York *Times*."

The return to verticality was one of the most important approaches to the *Press Democrat*'s redesign. According to Delmerico, as a general rule Silverstein

> felt that daily newspapers across the country—most of them willing hostages by now to the benign restrictions of top-flight art directors— had gone overboard in their "horizontality," or the sweep of stories across the page [with their] bands of stories five and six columns wide, but not very deep.
>
> [Silverstein] was searching to renew the vertical axis of a page in a way that avoided the classic dangers of "tombstoning" headlines and increasing the page's density. And in this, I think, he succeeded— the *Press Democrat* is "balanced " in ways most newspapers can't achieve.

Speaking about Silverstein the man, Delmerico said,

> Lou works mysteriously—it's as if his eyes are on what's going to happen *after* you cross the finish line, and he's sending back reports. Randy Wright, the paper's brilliant graphics editor and computer expert, and I were constantly confounded on the details we were assigned to polish: Did Lou want 6 points or 24? Why was this log reversed out, but not this other one? Were we allowed to actually decide these things for ourselves, or did it mean another coast-to-coast call? (emphasis in original)

However, Delmerico recalled that he' and Wright were never disappointed. Silverstein had a steady hand on the project.

> Lou knew exactly where he was going, and like all great artists, he was flexible and open until the end. He knew exactly what his most important priorities were, and when to worry about details. He had a complete understanding of the scope of the project, from the design of the weather map to the layout of the ads to the design of the freshly-painted trucks. And on press day it was all complete.

Delmerico will never forget the confidence that Silverstein had in his own

> artistic intuition and how it perfectly complemented his common sense; he had a healthy respect for "business reasons" too.
>   Yet, I think one more factor for the success—and beauty—of the *Press Democrat*'s design must be mentioned, and that is the total support we had from every department in the paper, from the publisher on down. Everyone was positive and encouraging, and open to innovation. This is doubly rare at a paper owned by a company 3,000 miles away, but it was real and apparent at the *Press Democrat,* and it paid off.

Referring to the importance of the design–content relationship that must prevail for a newspaper to be successful in its particular circulation community, Delmerico claimed that the *Press Democrat* "was a new paper, enriched not only by its new look, but new content—much of it inspired by Lou's design—as well."

Many newspapers—responding to the presence of *USA Today*—have completely created a new design for their paper, while others have only concentrated on a heavy use of informational graphics for page one. Steve Pasternack and Sandra Utt found this to be true when they reviewed the results from their 1983 study of the front pages of the nation's daily newspapers.

However, neither a total redesign nor the introduction of infographics will be so successful if the basis of change is not first tailored to strategies for the particular market. Any dramatic change of a newspaper should be enacted according to these three steps:

• **Evaluation of Market**—Pegie Stark, formerly of the Detroit *News,* has also worked in design for the Detroit *Free Press* and the St. Petersburg (Fla.) *Times.* The redesign that she created for the St. Petersburg *Times*—Stark said—she would not have repeated in Detroit. "When we were redesigning the *Times,* we eliminated all the above-the-nameplate teasers and the only color we had around the nameplate was a thin, green rule underline." In Detroit, the *News* and the *Free Press* are next to one another on the newsstands; and so, both papers include color and teasers above the nameplate. "In either place," Stark maintained, "I can't say that one is good design and one is not good design. But for those specific situations, each approach seems to fit." Vanco, speaking about the *News Chronicle,* underscored the point that "it is important that purpose-oriented design be based on research" because "people of differing taste can then accept the design as fulfilling a goal, as opposed to just being able to admit that it looks nice."

• **Review of Artistic Principles**—These include readability and good design. In Stermer's *Communication Arts* article, he quotes de Bretteville as saying that her plan for the Los Angeles *Times* "was consistent with the idea that if you design a storefront, it is not necessary that you do something that cries out at you, that makes you say, 'Wow. Who did *that*?' Instead, you do something that upgrades how it relates to its neighbors, how people feel when they enter the story, how it enhances their experience of the place" (emphasis in original). Vanco dealt with similar challenges at the *News Chronicle.* One of these had to do with typography for the suburban newspaper. "Typefaces have to be chosen not by their readability, but by the mood that they relate, as well. I chose a flag typeface and a headline typeface that suit the *News Chronicle* community."

• **Establishing Standards**—Newspapers that hope to see the fruits of their labor create a design stylebook. Lockwood of NewsGraphics—who is a force in redesign and the ongoing evaluation of the nation's newspapers—recommends that every publication have a stylebook. Most newspapers, "if they worry about style, usually have a stylebook—an editing stylebook and a design stylebook." When a design change is made, updates are entered in the old book or a new book of guidelines is printed. "I think, since most newspapers don't have a point of view about design, they probably don't have a stylebook," says Lockwood. "They design from a habit of having done things a certain way. The stylebook is usually, 'We've always done it that way.'" Throughout the redesign process at the *News Chronicle,* a style guide was being created—all of it coming from Vanco's notes on readability, she said, "plus snippets of the original design that we had agreed on for each individual element."

Therefore, the new flexible but consistent design standards should be contained in a stylebook and used by the staff. This design book should include a clear explanation of the design strategy so the staff can publish the newspaper without facing problems even if there is no resident designer.

Although this is a tall order—especially when much of the newspaper is put together at deadline—adequate time for new pages to be laid out attractively should be built into the new design schedule. This should be done in conjunction with the use of modern and stylized but legible typefaces, modular packaging, copy breaks, readable text, consistent widths, style consistency for logos, and— when available—a discriminating placement of color. When a review of the redesign is made, the style guide should restrict the use of cutouts, mortices, the tilting of photos, gray screen blocks and other graphic elements that become gimmicks if overused.

Vanco said that her needs assessment for the *News Chronicle* included—in addition to one-on-one interviews—three other steps:

- I developed a detailed questionnaire that asked section editors what they believed needed to be changed, based on the design problems they faced while turning out the pages on a daily basis.

- Then I met with the production department to find out whether the changes we wanted to make were actually feasible, and if they could execute the design on a day-to-day deadline basis. At that point, I became the link between all of the different departments of the newspaper—not much of a relationship had existed before that time.

- Once you have determined the requirements of redesign, the next step is to use the information that you have gathered to come up with a design that is going to fulfill those requirements.

When a newspaper's management and staff seek to redesign the product, the effort should not be a copycat design that simply replicates others in the community or across the nation, nor should it be a cosmetic quick-fix. Redesign most frequently occurs for the suburban paper, or for the second paper in a medium-to-large–size city.

Bruns at the Los Angeles *Times* says that, in many cases, suburban papers "are trying to find a way to increase circulation. We weren't faced with that problem. It has been my experience that when papers change radically, they do so because they are having a hard time making it and are looking for a way to change it around."

The major dailies usually make minor changes—cutline style, number of columns, a cleaner version of the same headline type, a front-page listing of section names, reference packages—but no dramatic substantive redesign. Whether a redesign is done to improve an already good product or to create a whole new look depends on the long-term philosophy of the newspaper's management.

The St. Cloud (Minn.) *Times* was redesigned by Mario Garcia, associate director of the Poynter Institute for Media Studies in St. Petersburg, Fla. John Bodette, the paper's managing editor, says that the style guidelines established

The Los Angeles *Daily News* made a design change during the late 1980s; these examples of its old and new look indicate a headline typeface change and easier access to the pages—with a left-hand column of briefings and a cleaner design with additional white space. Reprinted by permission.

by Garcia have been passed down to all who have worked there since. Uppermost in these guidelines is the importance of training "the hands and eyes of the people who are going to work with that design everyday."

What this means, says Bodette, is that

> when you come on as a copy editor at our paper, whether you've been doing papering for 10 years or for 10 days, we train you in design, and I think that's important. It's not so much the framework and typography, although that's extremely important—and you have to get that straight—but once you do, it then becomes that you have to make the guts of the page come alive every day.

Another Garcia-redesigned newspaper is the *Forum* in Fargo, N.D. Joseph Dill, editor, maintains that out of the experience with Garcia came three points:

- Only good, solid, accurate, responsible, interesting content will sell the paper. A pretty design will not mask poor content.

- I select[ed] people from the newsroom to work with him throughout the redesign project, so they could carry on his work after he departed.

- A graphics editor [must] be appointed to ramrod the design rules and policies with the entire news staff.

Dill asked for volunteers to work with Garcia before the project began; and a photographer, copy editor and entertainment writer were chosen. "I told them that one of the three would be selected as graphics editor before the project ended," Dill said. "This gave me ample time to observe them and their work. I selected the copy editor to become graphics editor, to carry out the design with everybody from the editor to a clerk."

The guidelines on organization of content that are printed in the stylebook

The Bryan-College Station, Texas *Eagle* has the Gannett influence in its redesign of the late 1980s, with more boxes and a change from six to five columns. Reprinted by permission.

The St. Cloud (Minn.) *Times* changed for a day from its usual page one to a special design when the Minnesota Twins won the World Series. On the outside was a page one and section on the series; an additional page one and the usual newspaper were tucked inside. Reprinted by permission.

should show how to package the straight news and feature content according to local, regional, state, national and world areas of interest. The impact of this will always be positive since it serves the reader better than publishing governmental meeting notices on one page for one issue and elsewhere for the next issue, and stories on various social, business and professional groups wherever they fit.

As seen in the preceding chapters, among several guidelines for the new design of a TPC newspaper, the following rank highly:

- Pages should contain a story count small enough that one story and its headline will dominate the others.
- Photos should be tightly cropped with one picture large enough to provide a graphic focus.
- Two pieces of art the same size should not be placed on the same page, unless they are head shots.

- Editors should keep story continuations to a minimum, and when stories are jumped inside, all should go to the same page—preferably the back page of the section in which the article begins.

The newspaper that will effectively serve its community will have a staff that listens attentively and considers the appropriateness of what is published under any number of topic section headings. This system of subject headings eliminates clutter and encourages consistency.

Speaking from her experience at the *News Chronicle,* Vanco believes it is most important that the paper be changed to "make it look consistent; make

The Fargo, N.D. *Forum* uses content—not design alone—to present the news to its readers. Reprinted by permission.

each page look like it belongs to the same paper." She also provided the following "elements that will attract the reader":

- The "gray" body copy is not going to attract the reader; other elements will.
- Although it is most important that body copy be readable, other elements will mean more in the overall redesign. Those elements are the flag, the headline typeface, standing signature heads, and photographs.
- Probably the thing that will matter the most is choosing strong photographs and displaying those photographs to their best advantage.

When the change in the paper's look has been completed—Grotta told those attending the SNPA Foundation seminar, "Layout, Design and Graphics"—a review of the project should be made. "After design changes," Grotta said, "research should be done immediately and then again about a year later. These results should be compared with circulation figures to see how they relate." Readership interest, based on surveys taken before and after a redesign, should determine which subject headings to use and the depth of coverage desired on these topics.

By evaluating the redesign with some imagination and a thorough understanding of the Total Page Concept, the designer for the computer age can bring together all the elements necessary for a truly superb newspaper. The TPC publication can be a complete chronicle of history in a world that—at the same time—is being changed by newspapers, the very vehicle by which news and history are disseminated.

16 The TPC Design Stylebook

The stylebook provides an overall guide and direction to the manufacture of your product. It's the foundation on which the building can be built every day and provides a stated formula by which styles and formats can be created in the computer system.

Richard C. D'Agostino
design director
Baltimore *Sun*

Within the Total Page Concept (TPC) design elements, readers expect consistency in a newspaper—from headlines to stories to photographic and caption presentations. Each page and section should look like it belongs in the same newspaper with every other page and section.

While no one approach is necessarily better than another—beauty being in the eyes of the beholder—one goal rings true: consistency. An attractive and inviting publication serves the readers better because it is cleaner and more readable and does not visually overwhelm them as they turn from page to page.

DESIGN GUIDE FORMULATION

The formulation of a design style guide belongs in the hands of the news department because content is the main purpose of a newspaper. But the art department—if its personnel are knowledgeable of and sympathetic to news and are committed to solid design principles, not just flashy displays—should play a key role in the creation of design style standards.

Four of the nation's many newspapers that have developed and printed specifics for designing their publications are the Baltimore *Sun*, the Orlando *Sentinel* in Florida, the Philadelphia *Inquirer*, and two newspapers produced under the same ownership: the *Virginian-Pilot* and the *Ledger-Star*, both in Norfolk. While each newspaper serves a different reading community, the various personnel are committed to excellence and their paper's mechanical capabilities, and all are in concert on this thought: Both organization of the production process and design of the publication's pages must serve to produce the best product possible. To implement this dual precept takes a strong journalistic philosophy—one that is easily sensed by the potential reader deciding whether to read this publication that sells for less than 50 cents on weekdays and Saturdays and maybe $1 on Sundays.

This chapter cites examples from design stylebooks at the four papers mentioned above, chosen because of their different audiences and different geographical areas. Throughout the chapter, some generic principles at the heart of TPC newspaper design will be delineated or reemphasized.

PHILOSOPHICAL FOUNDATION

A newspaper's philosophy regarding organization of the production process commences with the introduction of the design book. For instance, the *Baltimore Sun Typographic Design Stylebook* begins:

> The purpose of this stylebook is to minimize confusion without stifling creativity. It sets forth guidelines for consistency in the appearance of the newspaper, but it is not intended to be a typographical strait-jacket.
>
> This book does not pretend to address all the situations you may encounter in putting together the newspaper. Unusual problems will call for innovative solutions—occasionally ones that violate the guidelines set forth here.
>
> Nevertheless, the guidelines set forth here should be regarded as the norm. Deviations from these guidelines should have a clearly defined purpose and should be compatible with the overall design philosophy of the paper. They should not arise out of whim, a simple desire for variety or a preference for the old ways. Typographical devices that run counter to the norm should not be adopted as standard tools without consulting the design director.

The introduction to the *Orlando Sentinel Design Guide* speaks to the specifics of design—calling it the "servant of content" and adding that "the two march hand in hand in today's world more than ever." Further, the introduction states:

> If a newspaper is to properly serve its readers, it must deliver impact and orderliness as well as quality in content. It must have a clear and comfortable identity that is forged not only by content, but by design. The most powerful story in the world packs no punch if no one reads it, or if no one can find it.

All four of the design manuals under discussion provide ample guidance for typography, layout and the use of graphic elements. Although the newspaper appears to the reader as a whole product, its typography, layout, and graphic elements must be studied as single entities before the staff can bring them together for use in a design style guide.

Typography

Taking the principles of design in order, typography standards are established first. The Baltimore *Sun*, which uses Bookman for its headline type, establishes typographical guidelines in its *Stylebook* in this way:

> Typography is both a set of aesthetic standards and a system for the logical organization and presentation of information. It has its complexities, but it is also very simple. The validity of any solution to a typographical problem can be tested by asking two simple questions:
>
> • Will it make sense to the reader?
>
> • Does it look good?
>
> If the answer to either is no, it's time to look for another approach. It may take a little more work, and you may have to ask for technical assistance, but it will pay off in the appearance of the paper.

The designer applies typography to the page as an artist would paint a seascape. In the dominant interest area of the canvas, the artist's brush strokes may be wide to grab the viewer's attention; in areas of less importance, a contrast is created by lighter, more delicate strokes. On a TPC newspaper page, the key news area is immediately caught by the reader because of the typographical mass of the headlines. The size of the headlines signals the relative importance of a page's story. Afterward, the reader sees the text or body type of the stories, captions and any other typographical elements. Size alone makes headlines initially more important than text type. It is for this reason that their use should never be taken for granted.

Headlines

The seriousness of headline use is underscored in the *Virginian-Pilot and Ledger-Star Design Stylebook*, which says, "Headlines are not merely graphic devices to break up body type. The size and position of the headline indicates to the reader the relative importance of the story." The *Pilot* mainly uses Times Medium for its headlines, while the *Ledger* uses Helvetica Medium as its primary headline face. Italic headlines are not used by either newspaper. Both papers use boldface heads as an accent headline for news briefs and in hammer, "label" and signature headlines.

Guidelines for headline use should always be provided in a stylebook, including the paper's philosophy and specifications for main headlines as well as drop, "label" and signature headlines—with typesetting directions peculiar to that newspaper.

The *Philadelphia Inquirer Typographical Manual* has rules for using Century Bold, roman or italic, for its news sections and Century Light, roman or italic, for feature sections. The *Inquirer's* stylebook—like the others—covers capitalization, noting that headlines are to be in down style with only the first word and proper nouns capitalized. The major exception is for a Page 1-A streamer in which all words are capitalized except articles, prepositions of fewer than four letters, conjunctions and the word "to" in an infinitive.

The *Typographical Manual's* guidelines for headlines include directions for letter and word spacing and for dummying headlines, along with a statement that says, "Most headlines are set flush left." The only exceptions to this are:

- combination headlines;
- hammer headlines;
- headlines below labels; and
- decks of one-column headlines.

Photo examples are placed with statement paragraphs in the stylebook, providing a graphic reference point for its users.

In the "Writing to Space" headline section of the *Typographical Manual,* writers of headlines are admonished to write to fit the column width:

In general, a headline more than three-quarters of a column short is unacceptable. Exceptions:

- The bottom lines of combination headlines, which should be roughly a column short of full measure.
- The decks of one-column headlines, which are indented a pica from the left and should be written as short as possible.

The *Virginian-Pilot and Ledger-Star Design Stylebook* says that drop heads—headlines placed below the main head—should be set no smaller than 18 point and no larger than 36 point in 6-point increments: 18, 24, 30 and 36. If the headline is 48 points, the drop line would be half of 48 (24 points) plus 6, or a total of 30 points. When the arithmetic yields an in-between size, the guidelines advise setting the drop head in the next-higher standard point size.

"Label" headlines are used for identification to remind the reader of a continuing feature or series. The *Design Guide* for the Orlando (Fla.) *Sentinel* states that the label is used mostly on page one. At the *Sentinel,* when this element is used for news it is called a "news label"; it might be used for a series title, but never for an entire newspaper page of material. The *Sentinel* also uses column

Hammers

A hammer headline consists of a short, dramatic line in large type and a longer line of smaller type, indented from the left. (Two-column hammers have two lines of smaller type.) Hammers work well to highlight stories of strong reader appeal, but they should be employed sparingly; they lose their punch when too many are used.

It is preferable to use hammers in three- and four-column widths; wider ones create too much white space. The top line should consist of no more than three words.

1-PT RULE

REQUIRED INDENTIONS FOR LOWER LINE OR LINES, ACCORDING TO HEADLINE WIDTH:
2 COLUMNS: 2 PICAS
3 COLUMNS: 4 PICAS
4, 5 or 6 COLUMNS: 6 PICAS

6 POINTS SPACE

Combination headlines

A combination headline consists of a top line in large type, written as fully as possible, and a second line in smaller type, written short and centered. One is roman and the other italic.

Combination headlines can be useful in displaying feature stories, but they should be used sparingly. The two fonts and two sizes of type involved can make a layout seem cluttery if there are many other typographical elements on the page.

For this reason, combination headlines are never used on stories that require labels.

One-column headlines with decks

Such a headline consists of three lines of large type followed by two lines of smaller type, indented one pica from the left. One-column headlines with decks may be employed only for lead stories on non-feature section fronts and on open pages inside news sections.

The deck should be written as short as possible.

Writing to space

In general, a headline more than three-quarters of a column short is unacceptable. Exceptions:
• The bottom lines of combination headlines, which should be roughly a column short of full measure.
• The decks of one-column headlines, which are indented a pica from the left and should be written as short as possible.

IN COMBINATION HEADS, THE BOTTOM LINE IS WRITTEN TWO-THIRDS (⅔) OF A COLUMN SHORT

This page from the *Philadelphia Inquirer Typographical Manual* explains several forms of headlines used at that newspaper. Reprinted by permission.

Design guide

Column sigs /42

This page from the *Design Guide* used at the Orlando (Fla.) *Sentinel* sets the standard for signature headlines on columns. Reprinted by permission.

labels instead of standing signature heads for regularly featured material that does not carry a picture of the writer.

Column labels might be used for movie reviews, obituaries or a police beat story at the *Sentinel*. However, the paper's *Design Guide* cautions that the column label "should not be used as a condiment to pepper every page. Use this label only when a good headline still requires some support."

The other kind of standing headline is the signature column—or sig—headline. The *Philadelphia Inquirer Typographical Manual* spells out a style for the paper's sigs as follows:

- A sig is a graphic device, identifying a regular feature, that contains a linear-definition portrait of the writer. All sigs must be approved by the managing editor.
- A sig is one column wide and comes in two versions: 1⅜ or 2 inches deep.
- The 2-inch version is used when the story appears either in the leftmost column of a page or in a ribbon display (sig head in left-hand column, text of column all to right of sig head) at the bottom.
- The smaller sig is used within body type in the same manner as a label; at least 12 lines of type must appear below it.
- It is preferable that a sig be kept separate from other kinds of art.

Headline typography has many other uses, which should all be included in the newspaper's manual of design style. The *Orlando Sentinel Design Guide* details the use of headline type for promotional headlines, for instance, referring to these headlines as "the whip" or "daily promo" and "the Sunday promo." The headline type for a daily promotional reference line is standardized as one deck and must be set to cover the length of the page. The promotional material for Sunday is set in two boxes. Both promos are set above the nameplate.

The *Baltimore Sun Typographic Design Stylebook* exhibits a difference from the other three style guides in the way headlines and all aspects of its design are placed on the page, on account of the *Sun's* grid-based system of layout. Its grid is based on the depth of one line of body type: 9.5 points. According to the grid system, one inch equals 7 units; two inches equal 15 units; and three inches equal 23 units. Therefore, the *Stylebook* notes that "grid units do not divide evenly into inches: there are roughly 7½ grid units, or lines of body type, to the inch." The half-unit difference is to allow for a gutter of white space between columns of type.

The reasoning behind going to the grid system is stated this way in the *Sun's Stylebook:*

The purpose of the grid system is to help standardize the typographical practices of the newspaper, so that we may present readers with a consistent "look" that does not vary from day to day according to the preferences of individual editors or printers.

Used effectively, the grid system will give editors greater control over the appearance of the newspaper. [There is some loss of "fudging" room, but the editors think the tradeoff is acceptable.] Under this system, paragraph spacing should be employed only when absolutely necessary, and extra-leading should be avoided entirely.

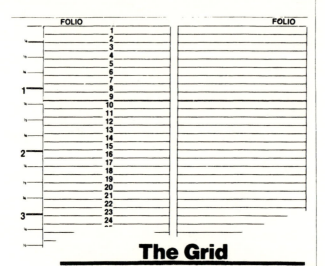

The Grid

As part of the new design scheme, The Sun is adopting a grid-based system of page layout.

The purpose of the grid system is to help standardize the typographical practices of the newspaper, so that we may present readers with a consistent "look" that does not vary from day to day according to the preferences of individual editors or printers.

Used effectively, the grid system will give editors greater control over the appearance of the newspaper. There is some loss of "fudging" room, but we feel the tradeoff is acceptable. Under this system, paragraph spacing should be employed only when absolutely necessary, and extra-leading should be avoided entirely.

The grid is based on the size of one slug of body type: 9.5 points. All page makeup boards and dummy sheets will be marked off in grid units, and these units will become the standard vertical measure for typographical devices.

In other words, depths that were formerly measured in inches or picas will now be measured in grid units. It will take some getting used to, but the size of headlines will be reckoned in grid units rather than points. The new headline formats have been written to conform to the grid, and do not necessarily coincide with the old standard point sizes (18, 24, 30, etc.).

As much as possible, we will avoid dealing in fractions of grid units. Photographs, for instance, should be placed on a page with the top resting on one grid line and the bottom on another. One grid unit of space will be allowed between photo and cutline.

Using the grid, it will be possible for layout editors to determine exactly how much space they have for each element on a page. There will still be some inconsistencies in the composing room, but the grid will help keep them to a minimum.

Grid units do not divide evenly into inches: there are roughly 7½ grid units, or lines of body type, to the inch. However, the following scale should help you convert story lengths into grid units:

1 inch	7 units	8 inches	60 units	15 inches	114 units
2 inches	15 units	9 inches	68 units	16 inches	121 units
3 inches	23 units	10 inches	75 units	17 inches	129 units
4 inches	30 units	11 inches	83 units	18 inches	136 units
5 inches	38 units	12 inches	91 units	19 inches	144 units
6 inches	45 units	13 inches	98 units	20 inches	151 units
7 inches	53 units	14 inches	106 units	21 inches	159 units

3

THE BALTIMORE SUN

Its unique application of the grid in layout is explained on this page in the *Baltimore Sun Typographic Design Stylebook*. Reprinted by permission.

Text Type

As for text typography, news matter is set in 9-point or 10-point type, and usually from a family different than headline type elements. How text type should complement the 14-point to 72-point type used for headlines is discussed in each of the example design guides.

Text typography itself is usually set in serif type, in a measure that amounts to half the point size of the pica width (for example: 10-point type with maximum of 20 picas). For editorials and occasional special features, the type may be set in wider measure, such as a 24-pica width and a corresponding 12-point type.

Most newspapers indent the type at least one pica if the text is placed inside a box: For example, the type would be set 11 picas for a 12-pica column width. Also, the majority of papers set all text justified on the left- and right-hand sides, but some set ragged right for feature or special articles. A few newspapers set all text ragged right.

The four example stylebooks also give instructions for such things as how a block of text should complement a photo display.

Other Type Elements

Each of the design stylebooks under discussion has established typographical guidelines for the relationship between text and captions, the use of large initial caps and the handling of other text complements. Suggestions applicable to the TPC newspaper include:

- Captions placed below or adjacent to photos, or to describe illustrations, are usually set in a heavier face than text type.
- The kind of type used for the headlines is sometimes also used for an initial cap or monogram that is actually part of the text. The larger letter is embedded in the story at the beginning of a paragraph.

Guidelines are given for setting type used for the following additional text complements:

- bylines at the top of a story, signature lines at the bottom of a story, and credit lines with photographic or illustrative art;
- briefs that provide a roundup of items including international/national/local news, sports and entertainment;
- copyright lines;
- datelines;
- editorials and letters;
- folios for page number and the newspaper name on inside pages;
- indexes for page one and section fronts;
- jump lines for stories that continue on another page;

- "precedes"—the editor's notes or quotes that precede a story;
- question/answer displays;
- reference lines to alert readers about a related story elsewhere in the paper; and
- series lines for articles published two or more days and linked by a common theme.

The *Orlando Sentinel Design Guide* makes a specific point about the best use of text type: that "it should never be set narrower than 6 picas" and that "anything set narrower than 9 picas should travel a very short distance," such as around an inset or label. Also, the *Design Guide* says, "Body type should never be set wider than 25p4 [25 picas, 4 points], and anything set this wide likewise should travel a very short distance," as in brief sidebar or a wrap.

In sum, all typography should be legible and consistent in the TPC newspaper. All headlines and text should look like they are in the same paper if the type is to lure readers into the stories and encourage them to read the photo captions and various other typographical elements.

Layout

Guidelines for layout begin with specifications concerning page format. Measurements are in picas or inches for depth and picas and points for width. For instance, the *Orlando Sentinel* has a guideline for page depth of 126 picas or 21 inches including the folio line (page number, date, and newspaper name), and column widths of 12p2 (12 picas, 2 points) on a six-column page of 78p6 (78 picas, 6 points). The Philadelphia *Inquirer* page is 133.5 picas or 22.25 inches deep including the folio line, and has column widths of 12p3 on a six-column page of 78p6. The general rule for gutters (white space) between the columns for these two newspapers—and most others—is one pica. Most papers are set in six columns, but some use a five-column or four-column page format with one- to two-pica gutters.

Page One

Guidelines for inside page formats at all newspapers are governed by the advertising. However, on page one always—and on section fronts usually—the designer lays out an open page containing no advertising. The page-one layout is ever a challenge because, as both the editor and the reader know, page one is the front page of the newspaper. It is the picture window. The lines of continuity begin on this page. The *Orlando Sentinel Design Guide* states that

> the front page is the face of the newspaper. Just as it reflects the news of the day, it reflects the character, the personality of the entire product. The design elements on the page form the framework for presenting the news, and they make a statement of their own—cre-

ating familiarity with the paper for the readers, and establishing a style that is carried through the rest of the pages.

Further, the *Sentinel* guide says:

> The front page is designed to be eye-catching in the [news] rack. The best offerings of the day should be visible above the fold.
>
> Of course not every page is going to make the reader do backflips. The news just doesn't work that way.
>
> But on the days when the news doesn't provide drama, the layout editor can deliver variety—three or four choices above the fold. Variety, in fact, is the rule. The occasions when one story dominates the top half of the page are the exceptions.
>
> Beginning with the front page, the layout must guide the reader from headline to story, and photo to caption and page to page and section to section.

For the TPC newspaper, it is helpful for the designer to pretend that readers are taking a trip, and then make the elements act like a map to guide them from point to point.

Section Fronts

After the front page and first section, the section fronts announce the importance of the specialized news that they contain, carrying forward certain design variations established on the paper's front page. The *Philadelphia Inquirer Typographical Manual* states that "every section front should include a dominant element that can be seen above the fold; this may be a large picture, a large headline, or a prepack [packaged story and photo or illustration]." These guidelines also say that the ideal number of stories on a front page or section front is six.

One method to move the reader through the newspaper is to use a horizontal (or modular) layout on as many pages as possible. This can occur through the harmonious arrangement of horizontal elements combined with vertical elements positioned adjacent to one another. The *Inquirer's Typographical Manual* states that, with the exception of a tabloid newspaper's page front, every section front page should contain a vertical element and a dominant photo or a packaged news story/photo presentation. If this design pattern is implemented, then "on the rest of the page, horizontal makeup plays off these elements."

Continuity of Elements

With the goal of all pages having "an active, yet uncluttered appearance," the *Philadelphia Inquirer Typographical Manual* promotes page designs that are generally simple and functional and that group related stories together on a page, or within a section. Further, the *Typographical Manual* says:

- Every page with space for it should have a strong piece of art.
- Every page should have a dominant headline [at least one size larger than the others on the page].
- Every alley [vertical gutter] should be crossed at least once [between the top and bottom of the page].
- Type must wrap directly from one column to another; it may not skip across pictures or advertisements. The path from the bottom of one leg [column] to the top of another should be as short and direct as possible.
- There may be no more than two depths of type in one story, except when the ad layout dictates otherwise.
- Long stories generally should wrap to the outside of the page. [This helps avoid a concentration of text type in the center.]
- News editors should dummy every page as completely and precisely as possible. Dummies should indicate the width and depth of each picture or graphic, and should specify whether or not a credit is required.

The reader views the page from left to right. Therefore, the "read" direction should be from left to right. The "flush left principle" is explained in the *Orlando Sentinel Design Guide* by the statement: "Most type elements are designed to be flushed left. Headlines, bylines, cutlines, readouts, quoteouts, logos all line up along the left-hand margin."

Packaging of stories and art must be done thoughtfully, especially when the designer is dealing with multielement packages that include the headline, drop head, photograph, informational chart, and text. There must be a smooth integration of all the parts. The *Virginian-Pilot and Ledger-Star Design Stylebook* notes, "In almost all cases, the package constitutes only one of several stories on a news page," and "along with being well-organized, the package should be in harmony with other stories on the page." The problem—the *Design Stylebook* states—is that, "in most instances, the juxtaposition of two large elements of comparable size creates tension and makes the page seem static." The solution given is to "vary sizes and shapes when possible to make the page more interesting."

The *Design Stylebook* makes these other points:

- Consider the makeup of the entire page to avoid conflicts and bumped heads.
- Use body type to separate competing elements within a package.
- Use 1-point boxes to contain multielement packages.
- Place columns along the bottom or left edge of the page.
- Combine mug shots with liftouts or quoteblocks to produce better graphic elements.

Most type elements are designed to be flushed left. Headlines, bylines, cutlines, readouts, quote-outs, logos all line
up along the left-hand margin.

THE ORLANDO SENTINEL / 1982

The Orlando (Fla.) *Sentinel* "flush left principle" is explained on this page of its *Design Guide.* Reprinted by permission.

A layout design that includes two stories on a single subject is a "twinout." The *Philadelphia Inquirer Typographical Manual* states, "On rare occasions, a twinout display may be employed. This involves two stories that read out of a single headline, with or without their own decks."

On inside pages, it is not unusual to have a "single subject page" in which several stories pertain to the same material. When the design is done well, the reader is not likely to realize immediately that the entire page deals with only one subject. Guidelines that design editors might use for this kind of a page are listed in the *Virginian-Pilot and Ledger-Star Design Stylebook:*

- Use labels to show when all stories on a page are related.
- Size and place headlines relative to their importance.
- Place graphics under the appropriate headlines to show their relationship.
- Give similar kinds of information similar kinds of packaging.

The reader is more likely to see the page as a whole if all columns of text type in the story are headlined. This means that, if the story is four columns across the page, the headline should be four columns wide. The *Philadelphia Inquirer Typographical Manual* makes exceptions for feature layouts: Where the headline can be placed beside a photo, the headline and photo together must span all of the story's columns. Also, the *Typographical Manual* allows for headlines to be placed alongside the text type when it is below a photo, but the photo must then cover all columns of the story.

Photos

Under photos that are more than two columns wide, some newspapers position the caption in two or three columns. Others place the caption not in columns, but wide enough to extend under the entire photo. The *Baltimore Sun Typographic Design Stylebook* states that captions "will not be set in legs [columns], no matter what width," and those "wider than 44 picas [approximately 7⅓ inches] must be held to one line deep."

The reader is more easily led to the importance of a picture if he or she does not have to grapple with why some pictures have captions and some do not, and which caption explains which picture. Regarding the importance of a common sense layout of captions, the *Orlando Sentinel Design Guide* says to "write a cutline for every picture" and "do try to put the cutline beneath the picture—not over it, beside it and most especially, not in it." The photo should be left whole. As the *Design Guide* states, "Don't amputate corners of pictures to have a spot for a cutline. Photos should be rectangular, not L-shaped."

Some editors will make an exception to this rule if an area of the photo is totally devoid of any body parts of the person in the picture, and if a caption inset can then be set cleanly into the photo, or a notch cut off to fit the layout.

Multielement packages

One of the most difficult design problems is combining several elements — a headline, drop head, photograph, graphic and text — into one package.

These elements may not be graphically compatible, yet they need to be smoothly integrated.

In almost all cases, the package constitutes only one of several stories on a news page. Along with being well-organized, the package should be in harmony with other stories on the page.

The Ford plant package on the original page, right, contains all the elements mentioned above. The remade page uses the same elements in a more pleasing configuration.

In most instances, the juxtaposition of two large elements of comparable size creates tension and makes the page seem static. Vary sizes and shapes when possible to make the page more interesting.

Body type can separate potentially competing elements. On the original page, the graphic and photo shared a common margin.

On the remade page, the text is used to keep them apart. A 1-point box on the remade page binds together the elements in the lead-story package and separates them from other stories.

- Consider the makeup of the entire page to avoid conflicts and bumped heads.
- Use body type to separate competing elements within a package.
- Use 1-point boxes to contain multielement packages.
- Place columns along the bottom or left edge of the page.
- Combine mug shots with liftouts or quoteblocks to produce better graphic elements.

A page with several typographic and art elements and its more successful remake are shown here in the Norfolk *Virginian-Pilot and Ledger-Star Design Stylebook.* Reprinted by permission.

Section fronts

Every section front should include a dominant element that can be seen above the fold. This may be a large picture, a large headline or a prepack.

The ideal number of stories on Page 1-A or the Metropolitan section front is six.

APPROXIMATELY 2 INCHES OF BODY
TYPE IN A STRIP

On rare occasions, a twinout display may be employed. This involves two stories that read out of a single headline, with or without their own decks.

2 OR MORE STORIES MAY READ OUT
OF A SINGLE HEADLINE IN A TWINOUT

Section fronts for the Philadelphia *Inquirer* are designed according to the newspaper's *Typographical Manual*. Reprinted by permission.

Refer lines

APPLICATIONS:
■ Used with articles on section-front pages to refer to related articles inside. Replaces the sandwich device formerly used.

TYPE:
■ The refer lines are set in Geneva Regular (Face 41), 9.5 on 9.5 point, kern 2. The page numbers are boldface, kern 2. One-line per listing is preferred, and the refer can be written as a label.

RULES:
■ Hairline rules top and bottom.

PLACEMENT:
■ Can be put directly under the headline at the top of the second column, or at the very end of the article, after the jumpline, if any.

Cutlines

REGULAR:
■ Face 59, 9.6 on 9.5 point, condense 6, kern 2.
■ Flush left.
■ Capitals & lower case.
■ Should be kept to minimum number of lines.

NAMELINES:
■ Face 60, 9.6 on 9.5 point, condense 3, kern 2.
■ All caps, flush left.

IDENT & EXPO
■ Name is set Face 60, 9.6 on 9.5 point, condense 3, kern 2.
■ All caps, flush left.
■ Expo set Face 57, 9.6 on 9.5 point, condense 6, kern 2.
■ Flush left, no ellipsis.

SPACING:
■ Allow one unit between art and cutline. Credit line, if any, should fall within that unit, 2 points below the art.

LEGS:
■ Cutlines will not be set in legs, no matter what width. Cutlines wider than 44 picas must be held to one line deep.

It's a breeze of a project

based on the size of the area you want to cool. In general, a fan that is 52 inches in diameter (blade span) will service areas such as living rooms that are up to 400 square feet. If your room is 225 square feet or less, you'll only need a 38-inch blade, though many people still prefer the 52-inch size. Spaces that are larger than 400 square feet, such as a long and narrow ... require two

... above the floor, ... that no one is struck by the moving blades. The same applies to lighting fixtures on the fan. If your ceiling is low, you should only buy special low profile lighting accessories made specifically for lower ceilings.

See **ALTOBELLI**, A2, Col. 2 ◄1 unit
◄1 unit

Democratic field narrows	A2

Democratic field narrows	A2
Reagan assails his rivals	A3
Iowa results please Hart	A2

◄1 unit

As many a household handyman and weekend construction engineer can tell you, home improvement projects that look quick and easy have a t... ...rat-

SPACING:
■ The refer line device always takes up 1 more unit than the number of lines of type in it.
■ If run in the second column, square off the top with the type and allow 1 full unit space underneath.
■ If run at the end of the story, allow 1 unit of space between refer lines and jumpline (or last line of type).

1 unit
THE SUN/JED KIRSCHBAUM
KONSTANTIN CHERNENKO
Brezhnev ally gets top spot

1 unit ►
Included in 1 unit space
2 points
THE SUN/JED KIRSCHBAUM
Eskimo-style craft proves appropriate on a cold river.

NOTE
Photographs should be trimmed to begin on a grid line and end on a grid line. To provide a margin of error, editors should size cuts to leave approximately ⅛-inch trimmable extra depth.

18

THE BALTIMORE SUN

This page in the *Typographic Design Stylebook* of the Baltimore *Sun* shows how the newspaper's reference lines and captions are placed. Reprinted by permission.

But such acts of morticing should be kept to a minimum, and for feature layouts only. Photos on news pages must never be run with a mortice cutout because of the integrity that readers expect of straight news.

Tabloid Format

A display format that should incorporate the important tenets of layout is the tabloid front page. The *Virginian-Pilot and Ledger-Star Design Stylebook* says that "like the front page of the mainsheet, tabloid covers must display their most important content as well as provide a sense of the entire issue. In most cases, a promo should be used." The *Design Stylebook* says that clutter should be avoided and that "no more than three significant elements, such as a promo, headline and textblock or photo, should appear on the cover." The tab cover sometimes will use a news story as the dominant design element; sometimes it is a feature, but—the guidelines say—"When it's news, we should avoid making it look like a feature."

In sum, if applied competently, layout techniques will take the reader through the paper; if done poorly, they discourage reading. In the TPC newspaper, good layout should provide guidance for the reader so news and special topics can be easily found.

Graphic Elements

Newspaper readers are being constantly bombarded by graphic messages from magazines, expensive and sophisticated brochures, and the mailings of advertising and public relations practitioners. However, these promotional pieces are not vehicles for the communication of straight news; they are written and designed with the bias of the producer. The dollars poured into this material that originates in advertising and public relations departments can be matched in newspapers only by maintaining high standards in well written and edited stories, clean typography, organized layouts and strong graphic elements via photographs, illustrations, informational boxes and charts.

Rules and Borders

Rules and borders are almost always used for all forms of graphics. When they accompany photos, some newspapers put borders only around feature pictures; others use them for all pictures. Rule lines are commonly made to box information, thereby highlighting it or pulling together related elements.

With reference to the effective use of rules and borders, the *Orlando Sentinel Design Guide* says:

• Rules are one of the most misunderstood devices in newspaper design. Not that that stops anyone from using them—underusing, overusing, misusing.

- The thing is, rules used improperly can make pages downright un-ruly—creating as much confusion as they're designed to eliminate.

- Their purpose is to provide definition and/or weight. Layout editors should be able to articulate the purpose of any rule they apply to a page.

- Do use rules to highlight, to group, to separate, to eliminate confusion.

- Do not use rules just because they're there. Every story package, every page does not need a collection of lines criss-crossing here, there and everywhere.

- Because so many of our formats—such as bylines—come equipped with rules, additional lines should be applied sparingly, and they should not bump. Avoid, for instance, putting a refer [reference] line at the top of the column adjoining the byline.

The point size of rules permissible at the *Sentinel* are 0.5, 1, 2, 4, 6, 8 and 12. Guidelines are listed for the use of each, along with this statement: "They should be applied constantly, but not constantly applied."

Photos

Photos themselves are a graphic element. The assignment, the selection from a roll of exposures, and the printing, cropping and positioning of pictures can assist or detract from how they are received by the reader. Newspaper designers are especially interested in cropping and page positioning. These relate to the layout function, but are important to the graphic element as well. What the reader sees—the cropped product, its size and placement—serves to enhance the photo itself just as much or as little as it does the page.

Illustrations

Illustrations must be treated with as much importance as photos if they are to enhance the TPC-designed pages. When an assignment is made, the illustrator must collect sufficient knowledge about the story by reading it and/or conversing with the writer, if possible. If the art is to be dominant, it should be black enough to stand by itself. If it is to be complementary to text and photos, it can be lighter, but not so soft that the reader does not immediately distinguish its purpose.

Charts

The *Baltimore Sun Typographic Design Stylebook* encourages the use of the bar chart, suggesting that three-dimensional bars provide graphic depth:

The aesthetic value of a bar graphic can be enhanced by giving each bar a three-dimensional appearance through the use of a gray-toned shadow. This can be done by placing a centered vanishing point 4 picas below the baseline of the grid.

However, this extra design element is an option that should be used only where appropriate. If you have multiple bars on your chart, this extra feature might be more confusing than attractive. Therefore, you should limit the use of this device to charts of 12 or fewer bars. The maximum width of the drop shadow on the bars is 8 points.

Charts are the newest graphic technique being used in newspapers. They appear as bar, fever, line and pie chart formats to enhance the informational value of the newspaper, whether by supporting a news story or as a stand-alone piece of informational art.

Infographics

Various forms of informational graphics can be employed, depending on the best approach to extending the story's meaning and on the time and personnel available to create the infograph. Informational graphics may combine photographs, illustrations, charts or other elements. The most effective informational graphics are the result of a clear line of communication between the news and art departments. One example of how the two departments might work together to make a successful informational graphic is the creation of a "fast-facts box."

The Norfolk *Virginian-Pilot* and the *Ledger-Star*—like the other three newspapers examined in this chapter—use fast-facts boxes to catch the readers' attention. The papers' *Design Stylebook* says that they display this kind of box because "we'd like everyone to read the paper thoroughly, so we try to make it inviting. But the reader shouldn't have to wade through a long story just to get the few facts that may be important to him." The established style for the fast-facts box at these papers calls for boxes to be placed at the top of the second column of the text in multicolumn stories, though sometimes it is necessary to deviate from that rule if the box happens to compete with another piece of art.

Color

In addition to informational graphics, the use of color has rushed into newsprint in the last decade, making it possible for most newspapers to have a display of color in at least a limited way—if only with spot color on boxes and special headlines and to provide an overall dressed-up look to the publication. Color as a graphic element can be either a plus or a minus. Color should enhance the page. As stated in the *Virginian-Pilot and Ledger-Star Design Stylebook,* the challenge is "to use color dramatically, but appropriately."

In sum, graphic elements provide interest in the TPC newspaper. However, they must be chosen carefully. Graphic elements should never be dropped in just to fill a hole, or just to attract the reader to a story. Space is a precious commodity and should never be wasted on a piece of bad art or an unnecessary display of facts.

INSIDE

FOOD

Strange tails from the deep
Virginia has some exotic fish that make extraordinary fare to please your palate/**FOOD**

SPORTS

Boris Becker is the one to watch
German tennis sensation Boris Becker has been wowing them at Wimbledon with his amazing skill/**C1**

Baseball could be a peacemaker
Baseball's record shows it has the ability to bring people together/**C3**

The fast-facts format of the Norfolk *Virginian-Pilot* and the *Ledger-Star* are detailed in this example. Reprinted by permission.

EVALUATING THE DESIGN PRODUCT

Page and story enhancement is the reason behind using any of the tools available to the designer of a TPC publication. Brian Steffens of the Los Angeles *Times* Orange County Edition is a firm believer in the value of a written style guide. He feels, however, that a book of guidelines is not sufficient in and of itself to keep the newspaper design staff aware of how it is doing.

"Papers of all sizes," Steffens said, "don't take enough advantage of Monday morning quarterbacking. I mean that in a positive sense." The content and graphics editors, the photographers, and any other staff members who are making contributions to the paper's look should meet and read through the paper. Their discussion should be centered on the question "Where did we miss opportunities?" And none of the issues that arise should be lodged as challenging threats, insisted Steffens.

> Don't take it as an opportunity to say, "You screwballs goofed up and didn't make this assignment." It's easy to do that, but it's better to say, "We can make this package better the next time if we learn from this experience." If you don't review the glitches in last night's problems, you are very likely to repeat them.

In sum, appraisal of the design project should include all aspects of the end product. But also, for a TPC publication, the review should include an evaluation of the whole community's purpose in reading the paper, of the working relationships among the paper's personnel and of methods for making continuous improvements. However, too many changes—forever making refinements to the design—can lead to a feeling of chaos for readers and newspaper staff alike. The staff might then sarcastically ask, "How are we doing it this week?" In order to maintain consistency in the Total Page Concept, any and all change must be purposeful.

COMPOSITE SUMMARY

This chapter has examined four design guidelines from example newspapers. But no chapter in any textbook—and, in fact, no whole design stylebook of guidelines—could cover every aspect of or instance for the implementation of graphic journalism. This chapter serves as a model for the student of design, who is encouraged to form his or her own working style guide. Any parts that can be incorporated because they fit the specifics of a particular newspaper should be adopted. The others are best excluded.

Many elements explained in this textbook are common to all forms of printed communication: to advertising circulars, brochures, newsletters and newspapers. Using the explanations here as a base, more detailed style guides can be developed. Publications enlarge upon their own stylebooks in fitting the general principles to the particular situation. Every publication has its purpose, satisfied in terms of a particular audience. Details must flex widely to accomplish a specific purpose for a particular audience; and therefore, much is added to the general principles as time goes on. Nevertheless, the stylebook standards are a basis for handling all specific instances.

Whatever the print medium, its guidelines should be placed in a loose-leaf binder. In that format, adjustments can be made as the staff grows in its ability to apply the principles of the Total Page Concept, which—as we have seen—is the organized relationship of all the parts or elements needed to create any page in a publication that is designed with the reader in mind.

References

"AP Lasergraphics a Phone Call Away." *California/Nevada AP Report* (February–March 1986).

Bain, Chic, and David H. Weaver. "Readers' Reactions to Newspaper Design." *Newspaper Research Journal* 1:1 (November 1979): 48–59.

Batten, James K. "What Do We Do Next in the Newspaper Business?" Address before the Southern Newspaper Publishers Association Annual Convention, Boca Raton, Fla., November 13–16, 1983.

Bisher, Nanette. "Show Windows of the Newspaper: Page One and Section Fronts." Presentation on Layout, Design and Graphics, University of Oklahoma, Norman. *SNPA Foundation Seminar Report,* edited by Lisa Purser. Southern Newspaper Publishers Association, February 3–6, 1985, pps. 2–4.

Bodette, John. St. Cloud (Minn.) *Times.* Personal interview. Santa Ana, Calif., June 7, 1987.

Brumback, Charles T. "The Future of American Newspapers." Panel discussion before the Inland Daily Press Association Annual Convention, Chicago, October 22, 1985.

Bruns, Ken. Los Angeles *Times.* Personal interview. Los Angeles, August 24, 1987.

Buchart, Maurice J., Jr. "Editorial Quality and Computer Systems: The Best Is Yet to Come." Address before the FIEJ Management and Market Symposium on Newspapers: Prospects for Growth, Brussels, Belgium, October 24–25, 1985.

Clement, Don. Los Angeles *Times.* Personal interview. Los Angeles, August 24, 1987.

"Computers Rapidly Replacing Graphic Artists' Mechanical Tools." *Editor & Publisher* 118, 45 (November 9, 1985): 19 and 36.

Covey, Rob. Seattle *Times.* Personal interview. Santa Ana, Calif., June 6, 1987.

Crutsinger, Martin. "Reporter and Graphic Artist Working Together." *AP Log* (April 13, 1987): 1–2.

D'Agostino, Richard C. Baltimore *Sun.* Correspondence interview. August 14, 1986.

D'Agostino, Richard C., and Michael Dresser. *Baltimore Sun Typographic Design Stylebook.* N.d.

Delmerico, George. Santa Barbara (Calif.) *Independent.* Correspondence interview. October 13, 1987.

Dill, Joseph. *Forum,* Fargo, N.D. Correspondence interview. September 3, 1986.

Ferguson, John. *News Chronicle,* Thousand Oaks, Calif. Personal interview. Thousand Oaks, Calif., October 8, 1987.

Finberg, Howard. "The Vitality of Visuals." Presentation on Layout, Design and Graphics, University of Oklahoma, Norman. *SNPA Foundation Seminar Report,* edited by Lisa Purser. Southern Newspaper Publishers Association, February 3–6, 1985, pps. 4–5.

Fitzgerald, Mark. "Freelance Graphics." *Editor & Publisher* 118,45 (November 9, 1985): 18.

———. "Front Page Still Off-limits to Art Departments." *Editor & Publisher* 118, 45 (November 9, 1985): 19.

Fosdick, Sam. York (Pa). *Daily Record.* Correspondence interview. August 7, 1986.

Garrison, M. Bruce. "Impact of Computers on the Total Newspaper." *Newspaper Research Journal* 4, 3 (Spring 1983): 41–54.

Geraci, Philip C. "Comparison of Graphic Design and Illustration in Three Washington, D.C., Newspapers." *Newspaper Research Journal* 5, 2 (Winter 1983): 29–39.

Gordon, Michael. *Herald Examiner,* Los Angeles. Correspondence interview. October 13, 1987.

Goss, Tom. "Designing the News." *Print* (May/June 1985): 57–69 and 130.

Gray, David B. Presentations during Informational Graphics Session and Spotting Graphic Potential Sessions, Ninth College Press Convention of College Media Advisers and Columbia Scholastic Press Association, New York, March 11–14, 1987.

Grotta, Gerald L. "Layout, Design and Graphics: Do Readers Really Care?" Presentation on Layout, Design and Graphics, University of Oklahoma, Norman. *SNPA Foundation Seminar Report,* edited by Lisa Purser. Southern Newspaper Publishers Association, February 3–6, 1985, pp. 1–2.

Haley, Allan. "fy(t)i: Legibility and Readability (Part 2)." *U&lc* 13,3 (November 1986): 56–58.

Hall, Michael. Los Angeles *Times.* Personal interview. Los Angeles. August 24, 1987.

Hardin, Tom. *Courier-Journal* & Louisville (Ky.) *Times.* Personal interview. Santa Ana, Calif., June 6, 1987.

Harrington, Craig. *InterMountain News,* Burney, Calif. Correspondence interview. September 26, 1987.

Helsdon, Les. "On Visuals: Articles Sell Faster with Artwork/I." *Ragan Report* (April 16, 1984).

Hicks, Donna E. "Unity: Key to Perfect Picture Page Layouts." *Editors' Forum* 8,2 (February 1987): 6–7.

Hines, Ernest E. *Contra Costa Times,* Walnut Creek, Calif. Personal interview. Walnut Creek, Calif., August 20, 1987.

Hodge, Bill. "Technology: New Opportunities, New Ethics and Later Deadlines." Address before the Mid-winter Faculty Meeting of the Journalism Association of Community Colleges, Morro Bay, Calif., February 20–22, 1987.

Holmes, Nigel. *Time,* New York. Personal interview. Santa Ana, Calif., June 7, 1987.

Hunter, Bill. "Corporate Publication Design: *USA Today's* Format Shows Up in Corporate Publications." *Communication World* (December 1983): 22 and 24–26.

Jacobs, Harvey C. Indianapolis *News*. Correspondence interview. August 12, 1986.

Jacobson, Alan. *Virginian-Pilot and Ledger-Star Design Stylebook*. Norfolk, Va., n.d.

Lehmenkuler, Robert. "Type Awareness." Compugraphic Corporation. Cited in "Bonus Item: How to Use Type More Effectively—Part 2." *Communication Briefings* 4, 11 (September 1985): 8a–8b.

Lemmer, William W. United Press International, Washington, D.C. Correspondence interview. September 22, 1987.

Lockwood, Robert. NewsGraphics, New Tripoli, Pa. Personal interview. Santa Ana, Calif., June 7, 1987.

Lynch, Patrick. Los Angeles *Times*. Personal interview. Los Angeles, Calif., August 24, 1987.

Majeri, Tony. "How Are We Doing?" Presentation on Layout, Design and Graphics, University of Oklahoma, Norman. *SNPA Foundation Seminar Report,* edited by Lisa Purser. Southern Newspaper Publishers Association Foundation, February 3–6, 1985, pp. 5–6.

Marshall, Jonathan. "Some Answers That Are Interesting, Fascinating, Compelling." *APME News* 147 (April 1984): 10.

Matthews, Sam. Tracy Calif., *Press*. Correspondence interview. August 29, 1986.

Mattson, Walter E. "What Do We Do Next in the Newspaper Business?" Address before the Southern Newspaper Publishers Association Annual Convention, Boca Raton, Fla., November 13–16, 1983.

Maurer, Tom. Bakersfield *Californian*. Correspondence interview. September 23, 1987.

Miller, Susan. "The Associated Press Is Joining the Graphics Revolution." *APME News* 155 (August 1985): 3.

Moody, Matt. Los Angeles *Times*. Personal interview. Los Angeles, August 24, 1987.

Morison, Stanley. Cited by Dugald Stermer in "Sheila Levrant de Bretteville." *Communication Arts* 24,2 (May/June 1982): 38–42.

"Newspapers Are Benefiting from the Power of PCs." Report from the American Newspaper Publishers Association Technical Exposition, Las Vegas, Nev., 1987. *presstime* 9,7 (July 1987): 31.

Oliver, Merrill. Cincinnati *Post*. Correspondence interview. September 26, 1987.

Pasternack, Steve, and Sandra H. Utt. "A Study of America's Front Pages: How They Look." Paper presented at the Association for Education in Journalism and Mass Communication Annual Convention, Corvallis, Ore., August 1983. Reprinted in abbreviated form by Sandra H. Utt and Steve Pasternack. "Front Pages of U.S. Daily Newspapers." *Journalism Quarterly* (1984): 879–84.

———. "Subject Perception of Newspaper Characteristics Based on Front Page Design." *Newspaper Research Journal* 8, 1 (Fall 1986): 29–35.

Patel, Ron. Philadelphia *Inquirer*. Correspondence interview. August 19, 1986.

———. *Philadelphia Inquirer Typographical Manual*. N.d.

Phillips, Darell. Manteca (Calif.) *Bulletin*. Correspondence interview. November 9, 1987.

Poppenhagen, Ron. Green Bay (Wis). *News Chronicle*. Correspondence interview. September 20, 1987.

Quinn, John C. "They Call Us McPaper, but Why Are They Stealing Our McNuggets?" Address before the Arkansas Press Association Awards Banquet, Hot Springs, February 13, 1987.

Riley, David L. "Computer Graphics on a Shoestring." Address before the Southern Newspaper Publishers Association Editorial Clinic, Atlanta, Ga., March 26, 1985.

Rorick, George. "Ten Quick Tips to Help You Out." *Design* 20 (1985):9.

Rumbach, Jack. *Herald,* Jasper, Ind. Correspondence interview. October 5, 1987.

Sams, Reid. St. Helena (Calif.) *Star.* Correspondence interview. August 22, 1986.

Schermer, Lloyd G. "The Future of American Newspapers." Panel discussion before the Inland Daily Press Association Annual Convention, Chicago, October 22, 1985.

Schwadron, Terry. Los Angeles *Times.* Personal interview. Los Angeles, Calif., August 24, 1987.

Schweitzer, John C. "Newspaper Front Pages Revisited: Reader Reactions." *Newspaper Research Journal* 2, 1 (October 1980): 12–17.

Sevrens, Don. San Diego *Union.* Personal interview. San Diego, Calif., August 15, 1987.

Silverstein, Louis. New York *Times.* Correspondence interview. February 23, 1987.

"Some Editors Feel 'Abused' by Pagination." A report from the American Newspaper Publishers Association Technical Exposition, Las Vegas, Nev., 1987. *presstime* 9:7 (July 1987): 32.

Sosna, Marvin. *News Chronicle,* Thousand Oaks, Calif. Personal interview. Thousand Oaks, Calif., September 30, 1987.

Stano, Randy. Miami *Herald.* Personal interview. Santa Ana, Calif., June 6, 1987.

Stark, Pegie. Detroit *Free Press.* Personal interview. Santa Ana, Calif., June 6, 1987.

Steffens, Brian. Los Angeles *Times* Orange County Edition. Personal interview. San Clemente, Calif., August 14, 1987.

Stermer, Dugald. "Sheila Levrant de Bretteville." *Communication Arts.* 24, 2 (May/June 1982): 38–42.

Stevenson, James H. Quoted by George Tuck in "Quality Content and Quality Presentation Are Not at Odds." *APME News* 155 (August 1985): 4–5.

Stone, Gerald C., Schweitzer, John C., and David H. Weaver. "Adoption of Modern Newspaper Design." *Journalism Quarterly* 55, 4 (Winter 1987): 761–71.

Tobin, Nancy. "Understanding Changes in the Growth and Shape of Newspaper Art Departments." Results of a survey prepared for the Society of Newspaper Design, October 1985.

Trapnell, Tom. Los Angeles *Times.* Personal Interview. Los Angeles, August 24, 1987.

Tuck, George. "Quality Content and Quality Presentation Are Not at Odds." *APME News,* 155 (August 1985): 4–5.

van Benthuysen, Daniel. *Newsday,* Melville, N.Y. Correspondence interview. September 29, 1987.

Vanco, Lisa. Westlake Village, Calif. Personal interview. Thousand Oaks, Calif., August 7, 1987.

Walker, Joel H. "The Future of American Newspapers." Panel discussion before the Inland Daily Press Association Annual Convention, Chicago, October 22, 1985.

Weiler, Joseph A. "72 Great Thoughts and Ideas from Your APME Reports." *APME News* 152 (January/February 1985): 17–20.

Welch, Wayne. *Advance-Register,* Tulare, Calif. Correspondence interview. September 22, 1987.

Williams, Mark A. *Design Guide: Design and Layout Rules for the Orlando Sentinel.* Orlando, Fla., n.d.

Wilson, Robert L. *Commercial Appeal,* Memphis, Tenn. Correspondence interview. October 21, 1986.

Winter, William L. *Star-News,* Pasadena, Calif. Correspondence interview. February 12, 1987.

Wolf, Rita, and Gerald L. Grotta. "Images: A Question of Readership." *Newspaper Research Journal* 6,2 (Winter 1985): 30–36.

Index

About the Author

STEVEN E. AMES is the director of student publications and teaches journalism at Pepperdine University in Malibu, Calif. Between 1971 and 1978 he was a journalism instructor/adviser at Merced College in California.

Publications produced by his students have received collegiate journalism's highest honors—including the national Pacemaker Award from the American Newspaper Publishers Association and the American Society of Magazine Editors; the national Mark of Excellence from the Society of Professional Journalists; All American critical ratings from the Associated Collegiate Press; and General Excellence awards from the California Newspaper Publishers Association and the California Intercollegiate Press Association.

Dr. Ames was named four-year-college national Distinguished Newspaper Adviser by the College Media Advisers in 1985, received a graphic design seminar fellowship for four-year-college professors to attend the Poynter Institute for Media Studies in St. Petersburg, Fla. in 1986, and was selected Outstanding Journalism Teacher at the four-year-college level by the California Newspaper Publishers Association in 1987.

He holds a B.A. in journalism and an M.S. in mass communications from San Jose State University in California and an Ed.D. in higher education from Nova University in Fort Lauderdale, Fla.